3rd Australian Edition

DIY Super

FOR

DUMMIES®

A Wiley Brand

by Trish Power

FOR

DUMMIES®

A Wiley Brand

DIY Super For Dummies®

3rd Australian Edition Published by
Wiley Publishing Australia Pty Ltd
42 McDougall Street
Milton, Qld 4064
www.dummies.com

Copyright © 2015 Wiley Publishing Australia Pty Ltd

The moral rights of the author have been asserted.

National Library of Australia
Cataloguing-in-Publication data:

Author:	Power, Trish, author.
Title:	DIY Super For Dummies / Trish Power.
Edition:	3rd Australian edition.
ISBN:	9780730315346 (pbk.)
	9780730315353 (ebook)
Series:	For Dummies.
Notes:	Includes index.
Subjects:	Pensions — Australia.
	Retirement income — Australia.
	Retirement — Planning.
	Finance, Personal — Australia.
	Investments — Australia.
Dewey Number:	331.2520994

Cover image: © iStock.com/pamspix

Typeset by diacriTech, Chennai, India

Printed in Singapore
M WEP330026 041224

Contents at a Glance

Table of Contents

Introduction

*T*he past few years have been extraordinary in terms of economic downturns, volatile investment markets, and the ensuing bumpy ride endured by investors, including DIY super fund trustees.

Throughout this time, hundreds of thousands of DIY super fund trustees have been investing super money in these volatile markets, and continuing to look after the needs of fund members.

In June 2014, when I began work on *DIY Super For Dummies*, 3rd Australian Edition, the investment markets were rebounding from a torrid few years, although by the time I finished writing this book several months later, the investment markets were again a little bumpy.

More seriously, in mid-2007, when I first met my publisher to discuss writing the first edition of *DIY Super For Dummies*, the world's investment markets were booming and Australia was enjoying an extended wave of economic growth. The super laws had just been changed to deliver tax-free super for over-60s and, as a result, the future was looking very bright indeed for Australia's retirees.

In October 2008, less than 18 months later, when I actually started writing the first edition of *DIY Super For Dummies*, the world's investment markets had imploded, and the international community was facing what has become known in Australia as the Global Financial Crisis — GFC (I explain what happened during the GFC in Chapter 14).

While in June 2011, when I began work on the second edition of *DIY Super For Dummies*, the world's investment markets had still not fully recovered from the 2008 and 2009 GFC. Throughout 2010 and 2011, the international markets remained jittery about the precarious debt levels of Greece and other countries in Europe and the massive debt levels maintained by the United States.

Fortunately, the investment markets recovered during 2012 and 2013, and for most of 2014, although the investment ride became volatile again in late 2014.

Even when investment markets stagger and fall, or even stall for a couple of years, you still have to save for retirement and invest somewhere and in something.

You can do this outside the superannuation system, if you wish; although due to the tax advantages available within super, the more likely scenario is that you're saving for your retirement via one of the large super funds or via a DIY super fund.

Despite the recent volatile markets (or, perhaps, because of these markets), Australians continue to embrace DIY super funds in significant numbers — more than 32,000 DIY super funds were set up during the 2013–14 year. The number of DIY super funds in operation exceeds half a million, and the number of Australians running DIY super funds has already hit the 1 million mark.

About This Book

DIY Super For Dummies, 3rd Australian Edition, is a plain-English and practical resource for anyone running their own super fund, or considering running their own super fund.

Running your own fund can be an exhilarating ride but the twists and turns that you encounter along the way — for example, the GFC, and the investment markets generally — can sometimes be a challenge. Fortunately, you've come to the right place to find out how to face the challenge with confidence by getting the resources you need to be a successful DIY super fund trustee.

Written specifically for DIY super fund trustees, or prospective trustees, you'll find that *DIY Super For Dummies,* 3rd Australian Edition, covers the most important super rules and tips you need to know about running your own fund.

DIY super is a specialist area within the super sector because it is a microcosm of the entire sector — involving fund administration, compliance, investment management, tax management and retirement planning.

DIY Super for Dummies, 3rd Australian Edition, is a product of the most common questions and answers that I have been asked about DIY super, reinforced by a plain-English explanation of the super rules applying to DIY super funds.

You can delve into and read the sections that interest you. This book can help you run your DIY super fund, or help you decide whether a DIY super fund is suitable for you, including working out the costs of running a DIY super fund. And if a DIY super fund is right for you, this book then takes you through the steps you need to take to set up a DIY super fund, shows you how to run a DIY super fund, what you need to do to pay a super pension from your fund, and where to go for help. Investing your super monies and retirement planning are big deals, too.

To make delving into the world of DIY superannuation easier for you, this book follows certain conventions:

- ✔ New terms and important phrases appear in *italics*, followed by a brief definition of their meaning. ***Note:*** You can also turn to the handy glossary for a quick reminder. Check out www.dummies.com/go/diysuperaufd where you can download the glossary for free.

- ✔ The term 'DIY super' is really a nickname — the official term for a DIY super fund is a 'self-managed super fund (SMSF)' but because the term 'DIY super fund' is so popular, I use 'SMSF' and 'DIY super fund' interchangeably throughout this book.

- ✔ The Australian Taxation Office, which is the SMSF regulator, is more commonly known as the ATO so I use 'ATO' in most instances throughout the book.

- ✔ My free website SuperGuide (www.superguide.com.au) is mentioned throughout the book as an up-to-date reference on the DIY super rules, and as a second resource for those who wish to delve into a general super topic in more detail, such as working out how much money you need for retirement, or insurance, or the effect of your super benefits on your Age Pension entitlements (although I cover this topic in this book too).

Foolish Assumptions

If you're reading this book, I assume that you run your own super fund, or you're considering running your own fund. I also assume that a few financial advisers and accountants may be flicking through the pages of this book, and even the occasional regulator or politician. Hope you enjoy the read!

You no doubt want a book that provides a warts-and-all look at DIY super, and that gives you the simple facts on the subject in an easy-to-read format. It's also likely that you don't want to get bogged down with terminology but you may need to get on top of some super terms, which are clearly explained throughout this book and in the glossary as well. (Jump online to www.dummies.com/go/diysuperaufd to download this book's glossary for free.)

My final and most important assumption involves the issue of independence. It's a strong probability that you want an independent view on DIY super, from someone who knows a lot about super but doesn't make a living from setting up DIY super funds and, significantly, runs her own super fund, which is what this book gives you.

Icons Used in This Book

Everything in this book is worthwhile reading, but some paragraphs jump out at you as an important piece of information to remember or a handy tip to help you with your super.

In the margins of the book, you can find the following icons marking certain paragraphs containing that kind of special information.

Here's what they mean:

Beware! Watch your step! An ATO Alert icon flags compliance pitfalls or serious legal issues that you need to be aware of when making DIY super decisions. In many cases, the ATO has issued a specific warning or reminder to DIY super trustees on an issue flagged with an ATO Alert.

The internet is a great mate for DIY super trustees. I use this icon when I refer to a website that can give more information on a subject, or has a handy tool that you can use, or can help when you want the latest figures available.

You may be surprised by the number of forms involved in running your own super fund. When you see this icon, you may be given the details of any necessary forms that your super fund needs to complete. Want more information? This icon can also point you in the right direction for more information on a superannuation-related form, or a topic.

The Remember icon prompts you to store important information in your DIY super memory. You may want to circle this information as a memory prompt.

This icon highlights gems of information that can help save you money, time or worry. Sometimes this icon simply notes information that makes you smarter about DIY super.

Interesting DIY super information that puts a few more brain cells to work. You can read and enjoy, or skip and continue on with the chapter. 'Technical Stuff' isn't mandatory reading, but these paragraphs can provide you with a more complete picture.

Beyond the Book

I hope you enjoy *DIY Super For Dummies*, 3rd Australian Edition, and find it useful when running your self-managed super fund, or considering setting up a SMSF.

This book is a solid base for your DIY super education, and in addition this book comes with some web-based resources that you can access at any time. Check out our free Cheat Sheet at `www.dummies.com/cheatsheet/diysuperau` where you can refer to handy checklists helping you with retirement planning, superannuation terminology, making super contributions and other information sources.

For complimentary companion articles to this book, you can visit `www.dummies.com/extras/diysuperau`. And `www.dummies.com/go/diysuperaufd` to download the glossary for free.

If you're seeking the latest super thresholds or updated information on changes to the super laws since this book was published, you can access this information by visiting my free website, SuperGuide (`www.superguide.com.au`).

Where to Go from Here

You're ready to use *DIY Super For Dummies*, 3rd Australian Edition. Find what you're looking for in the Contents at a Glance — a list of all the chapters in the book — or head directly to the Table of Contents, which breaks down the structure of each chapter.

Make *DIY Super For Dummies*, 3rd Australian Edition work for you. You can open any page and easily find your way around the book. If you're just beginning your DIY super education, Chapter 1 is an excellent starting point, and read straight through if you like. Alternatively, as a warm-up you can begin with Chapter 3, and discover how much money you need to live a comfortable life in retirement.

If you already run your own super fund, you may be one of the many readers who want to head straight to Part IV, to check that you're making the most of your fund's investment opportunities.

And if you're close to retirement, then Part V can take you through the issues you need to consider when paying a super benefit from your DIY super fund (and if you're under 60, what you need to do to ensure that your super benefit is tax-free).

The decision is up to you. No matter how you go about reading the information provided here, I hope you enjoy, and also profit by, what you find in this book.

Part I
Taking Control of Your Super

getting started
with

DIY super

In this part ...

- ✔ Understand why super exists, and why the super fund you choose is so important.

- ✔ Decide whether a DIY super fund is for you, and explore whether you're up for the compliance and investment challenges.

- ✔ Explore the most popular question in super — how much money is enough to deliver you a comfortable lifestyle in retirement?

- ✔ Learn about the two types of super contributions, and determine when, and how much, to contribute to your DIY super fund.

- ✔ Appreciate the different experts available to help you with your DIY super fund.

Chapter 1

Is DIY Super Right for You?

*T*aking control has never been so popular. One of the most talked-about trends in superannuation is the spectacular growth in the number of DIY super funds — 534,000-plus funds and counting.

Although each *DIY super fund* (officially known as a self-managed super fund) can have no more than four members, these humble structures now control nearly a third of all superannuation wealth in Australia — roughly one in every three super dollars is held in a DIY super fund! Even more remarkable, industry researchers DEXX&R report that DIY super funds control around two-thirds of all super money financing retirement pensions. (A *pension* is an income stream payable from a superannuation fund.)

Survey after survey confirms that the number one reason motivating an individual to set up a DIY super fund is the desire for control. Of course, other reasons for starting a DIY super fund stand out as well, such as cost considerations and dissatisfaction with the investment performance of an individual's existing large super fund. Typically, a DIY super trustee wants to take control of their super savings and run their own pension in retirement. As a trustee, you're responsible for looking after your retirement savings and ensuring your DIY super fund complies with the super and tax rules, and the investment rules.

This chapter gives you a panoramic view of the world of DIY super, including where DIY super fits into the government's retirement policies.

I set you my 'DIY Super 6C Challenge', which enables you to stress-test your decision to run your own super fund. I explain the two types of DIY super funds, and I outline the main tasks that you take on as a DIY super trustee. As a special finale to the chapter, I present you with your own retirement super star — a guide to the exciting tax-free super world that you enter in retirement.

The official term for the most popular DIY super fund (a super fund with four or fewer members) is a *self-managed super fund* (SMSF) and the terms 'DIY super' and 'SMSF' are used interchangeably in this book. I explain this terminology in more detail in the section 'What Does a DIY Super Fund Look Like?', later in this chapter.

Taking Control is a RIPper Plan

Taking an interest in your super savings is always a good thing. Stepping into the role of superannuation trustee, however, is lifting your interest to a whole new level. Taking total control of your superannuation benefits isn't necessarily a difficult task, but it does require a different way of thinking; after all, the buck stops with you — every time — as a DIY super trustee.

In the good ol' days (think right up to the 1970s), Australians generally worked from the age of 15 until the age of 65 (unless you were a married woman and then you may not have been allowed to work at all). Your employer paid you a wage that hopefully enabled you to buy a house and feed the kids, and that helped you prepare your children for a life at least as good as, and hopefully better, than your own.

If you were still alive at age 65, you were entitled to receive the Age Pension (at age 60 if you were a woman) — most retired Australians relied mainly on the Age Pension. If you were one of the very lucky, and loyal, employees of a large company or a government department or authority, then you were likely to receive a guaranteed superannuation pension for the rest of your life. After you died, and if you were fortunate, your wife — until relatively recently, only men were entitled to join these types of company or public-sector pension schemes — would continue to receive a reduced pension from the company or public sector fund.

Today, some lucky Australians still receive a lifetime pension from a public-sector fund or corporate fund. Everyone else has to fend for themselves. The federal government has made it clear that saving for your retirement is your responsibility, although it has thrown in a few tax incentives to make that task a lot easier (for info on these incentives, see Chapter 13).

The government's grand plan — Australia's *Retirement Income Policy* (*RIP*) — has four limbs that the federal government is banking on to raise the standard of living of Australians in retirement:

- ✔ **Age Pension:** The federal government provides a basic Age Pension, which is a safety net for those who are unable to fully provide for themselves in retirement, although the majority of retirees receive some Age Pension payment (I explain how your super affects your Age Pension entitlements in Chapter 20, and on my SuperGuide website at www.superguide.com.au).

- ✔ **Superannuation Guarantee (SG):** *Superannuation Guarantee* is the official term for compulsory super contributions made by employers on behalf of their employees. Australian employers have contributed the compulsory 9 per cent SG contribution from 1 July 2002 until 30 June 2013 (and contributed a lower rate from July 1992 until June 2002). The SG rate then increased to 9.25 per cent for the 2013–14 year and increased again to 9.5 per cent for each year from 1 July 2014 until 30 June 2021. The SG rate will gradually increase to 12 per cent by July 2025 (see Chapter 4 for more info on SG and how your SG entitlements are calculated).

- ✔ **Tax concessions for voluntary super contributions:** The government provides tax incentives to encourage you to make voluntary super contributions, and to take an income stream (super pension) in retirement (see Chapters 4, 13, and 18).

- ✔ **Co-contribution scheme:** The government puts extra money in your super account, known as a co-contribution, if you make after-tax super contributions and your income is below a certain threshold (see Chapter 4).

You can take advantage of the government's RIP without having to run your own super fund (and Chapter 2 takes you through some of the super basics), but if you're reading this book, you're probably already asking yourself: Are my superannuation and retirement needs being looked after in my existing super fund? If the answer is 'no', you have some decisions to make.

Joining the DIY Super Club

If you're reviewing your superannuation arrangements, you may be asking yourself: 'Should I set up a DIY super fund, or perhaps move to another large super fund, or is remaining with my existing super fund the best option?'

Changing super funds, including setting up a DIY super fund, is not necessarily the secret to a comfortable life in retirement, but changing super funds may be necessary to achieve your retirement goals.

If your existing super fund doesn't meet your retirement planning needs, then you can decide to set up a DIY super fund, or you can choose between one of the managed super fund options (see Chapter 2).

You don't have to be an expert in super or a guru in investing (although experienced investors survive much better in the investment jungle) or be particularly fond of paperwork to run your own super fund. What you do need to possess is the motivation to build your super savings and to take responsibility for running your super fund according to the super, tax and investment rules.

Setting up a DIY super fund is a relatively straightforward process (which I step you through in Chapter 7), but you need to get it right from the start. Many advisers and some financial services organisations can set up your DIY super fund for you, for a fee. Other licensed advisers are likely to suggest alternatives to DIY super, such as choosing a 'super wrap'. For an additional fee, a *super wrap* is designed to give you the investment flexibility of a DIY super fund without the legal responsibility of being a trustee. Using a super wrap is one option (see Chapter 2), but this alternative can be expensive, and most wraps limit the types of investments that you can invest in with your super money.

If leaving your super in someone else's hands isn't your idea of looking after your retirement savings, you can set up a DIY super fund. The decision to run your own super fund depends on

- ✔ How important it is for you to control your retirement savings (see Parts III and V in this book) and control how your super is invested (see Part IV).

- ✔ Whether you have particular tax planning needs (see Chapters 13, 18, 19, and 24).

- ✔ How much time you have available to devote to your super fund (see Parts III and IV).

- ✔ How willing you are to get on top of the superannuation laws (see Chapters 9, 11 and 15).

- ✔ How much your fund costs you to run (see Chapter 6).

All funds, irrespective of type, must comply with the *Superannuation Industry (Supervision) Act 1993* (SIS Act), including accepting contributions, investing the money on members' behalf, paying contribution and investment taxes, lodging annual returns and sending out member statements.

Doing a number on SMSF trustees

Every trustee of a DIY super fund (self-managed super fund — SMSF) is unique but, if you're over 55 and live in New South Wales or Victoria, you're more likely than other Australians to run a SMSF, according to ATO statistics. Nearly two-thirds (62.9 per cent) of all SMSFs are based in Victoria and New South Wales, and more than half (57.8 per cent) of all SMSF members are aged 55 or over.

If you're under the age of 25 and live in Tasmania or the Northern Territory, then you're the least likely to run a SMSF, with a mere 1.3 per cent of SMSF members falling into the under-25 category and only 1.4 per cent (around 7,478) of SMSFs being based in Tasmania, and 0.2 per cent (1,068) in Northern Territory, according to the ATO.

Queenslanders, however, control a healthy 16.4 per cent (around 88,605) of all SMSFs,

and Western Australians run just over 10 per cent (around 55,020) of the 534,176 SMSFs in Australia as at June 2014. South Australia isn't far behind, with 7.0 per cent of all SMSFs (around 37,392) being based in South Australia.

Just under 82 per cent of SMSF trustees (that is, more than 827,000 people) are at least 45 years old, with a quarter of SMSF trustees aged 65 or over.

For those curious about the gender balance within SMSFs, females are only slightly outnumbered by men — 52.8 per cent of SMSF trustees are men, and 47.2 per cent are women, which generally reflects that many couples start a SMSF together.

Source: Extract from article 'Do you fit the profile of a "typical" SMSF trustee?', originally published on my website, www.superguide.com.au. *Copyright Trish Power. Reproduced with permission.*

You can take my DIY Super 6C Challenge (see the next section in this chapter) to help you decide if a DIY super fund is right for you.

Taking the '6C Challenge' — Your DIY Super Roadworthy

Confidence and trust in your own abilities, particularly with financial matters, isn't something you necessarily learn at school, and luck decides whether you learnt these qualities as a young person at home.

For most Australians, confidence in money matters is a lifelong journey that can begin as early as when you start getting pocket money (if any), or when you start your first job, or apply for your first credit card. Perhaps your real lessons with money started when you first lived independently and paid rent, or when you took on a mortgage, or started paying school fees.

Regardless of when you began your financial literacy journey, considering taking full control of your retirement savings is a mature and impressive approach that can potentially catapult you to the top of the class in financial literacy.

Before I congratulate you on reaching such a level of financial acumen, I must warn you: Just because you can, doesn't mean you should. The key question you need to ask yourself is:

> Am I suited to running my own super fund?

I have created a checklist, what I call my *DIY Super 6C Challenge*, to help you decide whether a DIY super fund (or SMSF) is the 'right fit' for you, and for your retirement planning needs. In simple terms, I believe six factors all starting with the letter **C**, determine whether you have the opportunity, means, skills and inclination to drive your own super future:

- ✔ Can you?
- ✔ Control
- ✔ Cost
- ✔ Competence
- ✔ Compliance
- ✔ Commitment

Are you ready for the DIY Super 6C Challenge? If you already have a DIY super fund, the question I ask remains basically the same: Are you ready to find out whether you're up to the DIY Super 6C Challenge?

Can you?

What a silly question; you may be thinking: 'Anyone can set up a self-managed super fund (SMSF), can't they?'

Strictly speaking, yes, anyone can set up a SMSF. If you're self-employed, or not employed, you can choose any super fund that you like, including a SMSF.

If you're an employee, and you have *fund choice* — that is, you have the right to choose the super fund where your employer pays your

Superannuation Guarantee (SG) contributions (see Chapter 4 for information on SG) — you can choose between having your SG paid into a super fund that's managed for you, or running your own super fund. I explain how to arrange your employer's SG contributions to be paid into your SMSF in Chapter 7.

And, if you don't have fund choice — that is, you don't have the right to choose your own super fund for SG contributions — you can still set up a SMSF, though you can arrange for only your own super contributions to be paid into your SMSF. You may also have the opportunity to transfer existing super benefits to your SMSF (also in Chapter 7).

A quick way to find out whether you have fund choice is to ask your employer. Alternatively, you can check out information about 'choosing a super fund' under the Super tab of the Australian Taxation Office (ATO) website (www.ato.gov.au/super). I also explain fund choice in Chapter 2, and on my website, SuperGuide (www.superguide.com.au).

If you're considered a disqualified person (see the sidebar 'Your history may close the door to SMSF' later in the chapter), you can't become a superannuation trustee, which then precludes you from running a SMSF. In Chapter 8, I explain who can and can't become a SMSF trustee.

Control, control, control

Think carefully about why you want to run your own super fund. For most SMSF trustees, the desire for greater control over super savings is reason enough. Some typical and valid 'control' reasons why individuals set up SMSFs are

- ✔ Control over your fund's investment strategy and a greater choice in what you can invest in, including direct property and collectibles, such as works of art. I take you through your SMSF investment responsibilities in Part IV of this book.

- ✔ A belief you can do a better job investing your super money than your existing fund's trustees, and at a lower cost. I explain how much a SMSF costs in Chapter 6.

- ✔ The ability to take advantage of tax benefits linked with super (see Chapters 13 and 18).

- ✔ Flexibility in when and how you fund your retirement, including starting a superannuation pension (see Part V).

✔ Opportunities to purchase business property, such as an office, within the SMSF, and to use the property in your business (see Chapter 17).

✔ Opportunities to make 'in specie' contributions — that is, transfer assets into the SMSF rather than contribute money, subject to contributions caps (see Chapter 4).

✔ For the purposes of estate planning. Any death benefits paid from your fund to your dependants (under the tax laws) are tax-free, and your fund can provide for future generations in a flexible way. I discuss death benefits in Chapter 24.

Cost-effective, or not?

Each year, tens of thousands of Australians set up SMSFs, joining more than half a million Australians who already run a SMSF. Each individual SMSF member brings an average of around $537,000 into the sector, or just over $1 million ($1.02 million) per SMSF (based on each SMSF having an average of 1.9 members), according to ATO statistics.

A curious statistic is that even though just over half of all SMSFs have fund assets exceeding the value of $500,000, the other half or so (46.9 per cent) hold assets worth less than $500,000: One-quarter (22.3 per cent) of all SMSFs hold less than $200,000 in fund assets, and the other quarter (24.7 per cent) of SMSFs holding between $200,000 and $500,000 in assets, based on the ATO's SMSF June 2014 quarterly statistics released in September 2014.

In 2013, the financial regulator, the Australian Securities & Investments Commission (ASIC), commissioned research on the cost of SMSFs, including seeking an answer to the question: What is a cost-effective balance for a SMSF? The report, produced by Rice Warner on behalf of ASIC, found that $200,000 to $250,000 was a cost-effective balance for a SMSF, and was comparable to, or cheaper than, the costs charged by large super funds if the SMSF trustees were willing to do some of the fund administration themselves. Clearly, cost isn't the only driver for setting up your own fund if at least one-quarter of all SMSFs aren't supposedly 'cost-effective'.

The general rule is that you need a superannuation balance of between $200,000 and $250,000, either on your own or among the other members who are to be in the fund, for it to be cost-effective. If you don't have $200,000 in super, opting for a DIY super fund may still be cost-effective if you make substantial contributions in the first few years. I discuss the costs involved in setting up, and running, a SMSF in Chapter 6.

Competence counts

Do you have sufficient knowledge of super, and the skills to run a super fund? For most people, the answer is 'no'. Admitting that you need assistance with your super fund isn't ordinarily a problem because plenty of advisers and service providers are willing to help.

Next question then: Do you have access to an adviser with DIY super expertise? You're most likely going to need an accountant and/or a licensed financial adviser. You may need a lawyer to draft the trust deed (the document or rule book for your super fund) and to assist with any estate planning needs. Depending on your circumstances, you may want to chat to an insurance expert, or appoint a stockbroker to buy and sell shares on your behalf. You may even decide to appoint a fund administrator to assist with the operation of your super fund. I explain the roles that these experts perform in Chapters 5 and 10.

As trustee of your SMSF, you must draft an investment strategy, follow special investment rules, and choose investments that can deliver you a retirement benefit when you finish work. If you know nothing about investing, I don't believe a DIY super fund is the place to begin your investment classes. I take you through what you need to consider when investing your DIY super monies in Part IV of this book.

Compliance calls

Complying with the super rules may not be as sexy as investing your super assets, but if you get the compliance side right, everything else is likely to fall into place. Make sure you understand the rules relating to setting up and administering your SMSF. You can expect fairly onerous administration, reporting and tax requirements — what I call your 'DIY Super CART' (**C**ompliance, **A**dministration, **R**eporting, **T**ax management). Are you up to it? You can find out what CART involves in Part III of this book.

You must sign a SMSF trustee declaration stating that you're responsible for ensuring your super fund complies with the super laws (see Chapter 9). If the ATO 'hits' you with the naughty stick, you can't point the finger at your accountant, your investment adviser, your administration service provider or your fellow trustees. You may have a right to take action against your advisers if you believe the advice you relied on was dodgy, but don't expect the ATO to let you off the hook for your SMSF trustee responsibility.

Commitment issues

Are you attracted to DIY super by your love of responsibility, and the honour of taking control of your super savings? Unlike professional trustees, you're not permitted to receive payment for your task. Running your own SMSF is a long-term commitment — at least until you retire . . . and longer if your fund is going to provide you with a pension, or your children with superannuation benefits. Are you that committed?

Many DIY super trustees have a confidence about them that's related to success in some part of their life, usually in financial matters. From my experience, DIY super trustees are independent-minded individuals who have achieved success in work, or in investments, which reinforces that running their own super fund is the right fit.

The fact that you're thinking of taking control of your super savings is a very good sign for your retirement plans, even if you don't end up running a SMSF.

What Does a DIY Super Fund Look Like?

When investment markets fall dramatically, Australian investors often take a greater interest in the DIY super structure. Some individuals believe they can achieve better investment returns on their super money than

Your history may close the door to SMSF

Have you ever been convicted of an offence involving dishonesty? I'm not playing truth or dare: This question is important if you're considering running your own super fund.

Your character and your financial acumen are important considerations when deciding if you're a suitable person to be a self-managed super fund trustee.

An individual can't be a SMSF trustee if he is a 'disqualified person': For example, an individual with a conviction involving dishonesty, or an individual who is an 'undischarged bankrupt'. If you've been declared bankrupt, you're not permitted to be a super fund trustee until your bankruptcy is discharged.

If you've ever been convicted of an offence involving dishonesty, then forget about becoming a trustee of a SMSF.

The types of dishonesty offences that would deem individuals as 'disqualified persons' are fraud-related, such as attempting to gain financial benefit by deception from the government, which may include something as simple as giving false information on your tax return, although offences that involve time in prison are most likely to exclude you from running a SMSF.

I explain who can, and can't, become a trustee of a SMSF in Chapter 8.

the professionals, or can do it more cheaply, or perhaps they believe: 'If someone is going to be losing my money I'd rather it be me!'

Markets may go up, or down, but when you run your own super fund you're never off duty when keeping your DIY super fund on the right side of the super laws.

A DIY super fund is subject to many of the same rules as other super funds, such as those relating to

- ✔ Contributions, including salary sacrificing (see Chapter 4).
- ✔ Taxation (see Chapters 13, 18 and 19).
- ✔ Investments (see Part IV).
- ✔ Benefit payments (see Part V).

Take your pick — the ATO or APRA

Very few people realise you can actually choose from two types of DIY super fund:

- ✔ **Self-managed superannuation fund (SMSF):** The ATO regulates this type of DIY super fund. A SMSF is run by the fund members in their role as trustees. Your fund must satisfy basic conditions to be considered a SMSF (see 'Satisfying the SMSF definition', later in this chapter).

- ✔ **Small APRA fund:** The *Australian Prudential Regulation Authority* (*APRA*) regulates this type of DIY super fund. APRA oversees the soundness of financial institutions and super funds (with the exception of SMSFs, which are regulated by the ATO). A small APRA fund is run by a trustee that holds an RSE licence — that is, a professional trustee approved by APRA. All super trustees of non-SMSFs must hold such a licence. *RSE* stands for registrable superannuation entity.

Apart from references to small APRA funds in this chapter, and in Chapter 2, and one reference in Chapter 8, I devote the rest of the book to SMSFs.

One of the main reasons APRA regulates small APRA funds is to protect those members who may find themselves in a small fund due to being an employee of the business owners, but not a relative of the owners of the business. A small APRA fund may also be suitable where an individual is disqualified from being a SMSF trustee (check out the sidebar 'Your history may close the door to SMSF' earlier in this chapter, and Chapter 8).

Leading the charge with SMSFs

SMSFs are by far the most popular type of DIY super fund, with 534,000-plus SMSFs in operation compared to just over 2,700 small APRA funds, as at June 2014 (figures released in September 2014).

SMSFs have enjoyed stellar growth in the past decade or so. In 1998, SMSF trustees controlled just over 10 per cent of Australia's super wealth, according to APRA and ATO statistics. Five years later, in 2003, SMSFs held 20 per cent of Australia's superannuation money. Fast forward to late 2014, and the SMSF is now the leading category of super fund in Australia, with the 534,000 or so SMSFs in existence controlling around a third of the country's super wealth.

As at June 2014, SMSFs controlled $557 billion of the $1.85 trillion or so held in super assets in Australia, according to statistics released by the ATO in September 2014. (In contrast, small APRA funds controlled a mere $2 billion of all super money.) Remarkably, this massive amount of money held in SMSFs is controlled by just over 4 per cent of Australia's population; that is, just over 1 million DIY super trustees.

The one common feature of both types of DIY super fund is that each fund can have no more than four members. The key differences between the two types of DIY super fund, besides having separate regulators, is that the professional trustees of small APRA funds can charge (and do!) for their services, and such funds are subject to more onerous member disclosure obligations. Small APRA funds have similar member reporting requirements to larger funds, and members of small APRA funds have access to a complaints process if they have any issues with the fund.

Satisfying the SMSF definition

A super fund must meet basic conditions to be considered a SMSF. If a DIY super fund doesn't meet the basic requirements for a SMSF, it may be deemed to be a small APRA fund, which means it needs to have a professional trustee that holds an RSE licence (refer to 'Take your pick — the ATO or APRA' earlier in this chapter).

The basic requirements of a SMSF include the following:

✔ Each member of a SMSF must also be a trustee of the fund, and all trustees must be members.

✔ No member of the fund can be an employee of another member unless they're relatives, and a relative can include immediate family and extended family. A *relative* of a fund member includes a spouse, parent, grandparent, brother, sister, uncle, aunt, nephew, niece, lineal descendant or adopted child. A relative also includes a spouse, including same-sex spouse, of any of these individuals defined earlier as a 'relative'. For example, if you run a business and your brother is one of your employees, he can be a member of the fund. For more information on the meaning of relatives, see Chapter 8.

✔ None of the SMSF trustees can receive payment for performing the role of trustee.

If a super fund doesn't meet these conditions, the ATO usually works with the trustees of the DIY super fund to help them meet the requirements of a SMSF. Alternatively, the ATO gives the trustees time to wind up the fund, or the opportunity to use a licensed trustee and move to APRA regulation. For more info on the rules applying to SMSF trustees, see Chapters 8 and 9.

If trustees fail to notify the ATO of the change in status of the SMSF, they could be penalised personally with a fine of up to $3,400. I explain SMSF administration and compliance penalties in Chapters 9 and 11.

Banking On Yourself, and Your CART

Becoming a DIY super trustee is all about steering your own super CART; that is, C-A-R-T — looking after your fund's Compliance, Administration, Reporting and Tax management responsibilities.

CART is a term that I coined to help you, as a DIY super trustee, grasp the less glamorous aspects of running your own fund, namely:

✔ **Creating a compliance culture:** Get it right from the start. The superannuation rules create enormous opportunities without the need to put your retirement savings at risk by breaking those rules. I explain how you can set up a DIY super fund the right way in the chapters in Part II of this book, while in Chapter 11, I take you through the main areas of super compliance, including what I call the ATO's seven deadly sins of DIY super.

✔ **Getting active on administration:** The biggest decision you need to make in terms of administration is whether you do it yourself or you delegate this task (but not the responsibility) to a professional administrator. In Chapter 10, I take you through what you need to consider when making such a decision, as well as what tasks are involved when administering a DIY super fund.

✔ **Rigorous reporting reaps rewards:** Are you punctual and particular with details? You need to possess both these traits as a DIY super trustee. Alternatively, you can appoint a service provider who can perform the reporting role for you. In Chapter 12, I explain the accounting records you need to keep, and what returns and forms you must lodge with the ATO. I also explain the important role performed by your fund's auditor.

✔ **Entering a tax-friendly world:** Without doubt, the headline in super is 'tax-free super for over-60s', but that benefit isn't the only good news on the tax front. I explain tax-friendly super contributions in Chapter 4, investing and super tax in Chapter 18, and super's tax goodies in Chapter 13.

If you set up your fund properly (see Part II) and if you steer your CART in the right direction (see Part III), you can really enjoy your DIY super fund. You can then focus your attention on your fund's investments (see Part IV).

It's Your Super Money — Invest Wisely

Although investing your super monies can be very exciting and empowering, you must remember that you're investing on behalf of someone else — yourself! Confused? Fully understandable, because, in a DIY super fund, you're both the DIY super (SMSF) trustee and a SMSF member. In effect, you're wearing two hats, which means you must be very careful to separate your responsibilities as trustee, from your entitlements as a fund member.

As trustee, you must set your fund's investment strategy, and choose investments subject to special investment rules (see Chapter 15). In Chapter 14, I explain the importance of understanding risk and return when investing against the backdrop of the relatively recent Global Financial Crisis. I also explain the restrictions on borrowing money to invest (Chapter 16), and the rules applicable to property investing (Chapter 17).

Super funds enjoy some nifty tax concessions when investing and accumulating assets. I explain the main tax benefits, and concerns, when super investing in Chapter 18.

Your Retirement Super Star

If you're aged 60 or over and retired (or satisfy another condition of release on or after the age of 60 — see Chapter 19), you can access tax-free superannuation benefits from your DIY super fund. If you choose to retire before the age of 60, you may pay some tax on your super benefits. If you're aged 65 or over, you don't even have to retire to access your tax-free super benefits.

The Retirement Super Star in Figure 1-1, essentially a summary of Part V of this book, is a great starting point for kicking off your SMSF retirement plans. You also find the answers to the second, and third, most popular questions in retirement planning:

- ✔ What if I don't have enough super to last for my expected lifetime (see Chapters 19, 20, 21 and 22)?
- ✔ What happens to my super savings, and my super fund, after I die (see Chapter 24)?

I know what's on your mind: If these are the second, and third, most popular questions, what then is the number one question asked by Australians when planning for one's retirement?

That's easy. The most popular question asked by prospective retirees is: 'How much money is enough?' I consider the answer at length in Chapter 3, and cover the topic in even more detail on my website, SuperGuide (www.superguide.com.au).

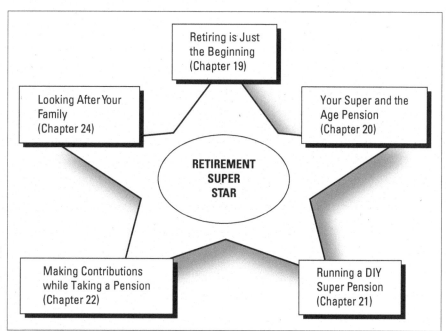

Figure 1-1:
Your
Retirement
Super Star.

- Retiring is Just the Beginning (Chapter 19)
- Looking After Your Family (Chapter 24)
- Your Super and the Age Pension (Chapter 20)
- RETIREMENT SUPER STAR
- Making Contributions while Taking a Pension (Chapter 22)
- Running a DIY Super Pension (Chapter 21)

Chapter 2

Understanding How Super Works

*U*nless you own a goose that lays golden eggs, you need to create your own nest egg for your retirement. Like most Australians, you probably hope you're going to have a good-sized egg, because you want your later years to be free from financial worries.

Your challenge, as a future retiree, is to create the most comfortable retirement that you can afford. The dilemma, however, when thinking about saving for retirement is whether to rely on the Age Pension, or to accumulate superannuation or private savings, or a combination of all of them. For the record, the Age Pension is around $427 a week — paid fortnightly — for a single person, or $644 a week as a couple (as at September 2014, applicable until March 2015, and increased in March and September each year).

In this chapter, I give you four reasons why your only true option is to take superannuation seriously, and explain why living solely on the Age Pension is no longer a lifestyle option. I take you through the key decisions that help you grow your super balance and list the important information you need to know about your super benefits. By reading this chapter, you find out what super fund options are available (including a self-managed super fund), and whether you're in a position to change super funds. I also supply you with lots of interesting statistics that you can quote at dinner parties or use when pontificating at the pub.

Australians are living longer and, as a population, getting older. The federal government has made it clear that the Age Pension isn't going to be as widely available by the time you retire (see Chapter 20 for an explanation of how the Age Pension interacts with your super benefits). Have you seriously considered this possibility?

Australia's standard of living is one of the highest in the world, with one of the world's most advanced health systems, using the latest, expensive technology. Because older people use the healthcare system more than any other age group, and the increasing number of older Australians is putting pressure on Age Pension expenditure, the decision makers in Canberra have peered into the country's cookie jar and realised that the Anzac biscuits are running out. Fewer people are 'making the biscuits' as the numbers of workers entering retirement increases. The federal government is likely to ration the bikkies or break them up to ensure everyone gets their fair share. But workers have grown up expecting that they're going to get a full serve.

What's the solution? BYO — bake your own! Superannuation is Australia's preferred recipe when it comes to ensuring that both you and I, and everyone else, save for retirement.

Facing Four Facts about Your Super Future

The world has changed dramatically since the Australian government first introduced the Age Pension in 1909. In those days, a man's life expectancy was a mere 55 years, and women were expected to live to the age of 59. The expense of supporting the country's small number of older citizens was very do-able. Australia had 16 workers for every retired person, which spread the load very nicely. The government budgeted for a small financial commitment because the numbers of retirement-age and older persons were small and, at that time, few Australians lived beyond a pensionable age.

Aussies are now living longer and the percentage of Australians working is shrinking. Today, around half of federal government spending is directed towards social security payments, health and aged care — with spending on health and aged care expected to escalate during the next 40 or so years.

Government funds are limited and the financial demands of an ageing population is only going to increase. So you shouldn't expect the government to let you join the Age Pension retirement party when you finish your working life without passing a few wealth tests.

Living longer — ageing in comfort

Have you heard the Beatles song, 'When I'm 64 …'? The song from the 1960s is about a man asking a woman whether she'll still love him when he's old and crooked at the grand old age of 64. Nowadays, you need to add another 10 or 15 years to the scenario to make it realistic. Today, a healthy man in his sixties can expect his life to still pack a bit of a punch, just as former widower Paul McCartney has proven by remarrying (and divorcing) and remarrying in his sixties. Imagine …

Australia is certainly the lucky country when it comes to life expectancies, and has one of the highest life expectancy rates in the world. *Life expectancy* means how many years you're expected to live. Statisticians can measure life expectancy at birth or during a person's life.

If you're a woman and retire today at the age of 65, you can expect to live, on average, until you're 87 (another 22 years). If you're a man and retire today at the age of 65, you can expect to live on average until you're 83.5 years (18.5 more years).

Life expectancy figures show that you may experience retirement for nearly as long as you were working, particularly if you stop work well before the age of 65. Are you ready to age in comfort? Have you planned for your long life in retirement? I explain your average life expectancy in more detail in Chapter 3 where I discuss how much super you may need in retirement.

An important exception to the longevity of Australians is the contrasting life expectancies for Indigenous Australians: It's up to 11 years shorter than non-Indigenous Australians, although this rate is improving over time. If you're an Aboriginal or Torres Strait Islander, please note that life expectancies are averages and you may well live as long as, or even longer than, non-Indigenous Australians.

Straining the government Age Pension

I feel sorry for the federal government — seriously. The main source of funding for the government is money that comes from the pockets of Australians in taxes, and it is trying to solve the biggest funding dilemma that the country has ever faced. In 35 years' time the number of Australians of working age compared to Australians of retirement age will be nearly half of what it is today. In 2010, five workers supported each Australian aged 65 or over, and by 2050, only 2.7 working Australians are going to be supporting each retired person, although the federal government increasing the Age Pension age to 70 years by 2035 (subject to legislation, see Chapter 20) will help offset this worker/retiree imbalance.

Understandably, the Australian government is fretting that there isn't going to be enough money in the kitty to pay an Age Pension to all the baby boomers stampeding into retirement and supposedly spending all their money along the way. The really scary prospect for the country's decision makers is that multiple generations could be vying for the right to claim the Age Pension. Imagine — assuming the Age Pension still exists in its current form in the future — you may be able to claim the Age Pension at the same time as your parents or children (see the related sidebar 'Living into your eighties and nineties').

Superannuation is starting to look like a very interesting solution, isn't it?

Staying healthy costs more

Hopefully your twilight years, and mine, are going to be healthy and wealthy. But old age is going to happen and everyone has to deal with it. Realistically, you can expect to take a few more pills than you used to and undertake more medical tests than a younger person.

Australia's hospital system and prescription scheme is bursting at the seams as medical technology removes cataracts from eyes, transplants vital organs and opens up hardened arteries. In the past, conditions that would have killed people, or severely disabled them, in their fifties and sixties, are now cured or successfully managed using common medical procedures. These developments are fantastic and have opened the door to a greater quality of life for older Australians, but this technology also costs money — lots of it.

Due to the ageing population and the understandable demands for reasonable health, the number of prescription drugs subsidised under the *Pharmaceutical Benefits Scheme* (or *PBS*) has risen rapidly, triggering a funding crisis for the Australian government. The PBS subsidises selected pharmaceuticals for Australians and provides concessional prices on medication for those holding a concession or a health care card.

The demand for nursing homes, nursing care and home help inevitably rises as illnesses associated with ageing increase, mirroring the ageing population. These services cost a lot of money and the government subsidises many of them, but are these funding practices sustainable when Australia has multiple generations enjoying retirement at the same time?

Who's going to pay for it all? You, if you're still a taxpayer.

Expecting a reasonable lifestyle

You probably know already that not working costs less. You don't buy lunches as often and you don't have as many transport costs because you're not travelling to work. If you previously worked in an office, you're now going to spend a lot less per year on clothes as well.

For many people, by the time they stop working they've paid off or nearly paid off their mortgage, educated their kids and cleared most of their debts.

So, retirement is supposed to be a breeze on the Age Pension. The Age Pension is around $22,200 a year for a single person or just under $33,500 for a couple (until March 2015, with increases twice yearly after that time). Hmm ... realistic? Your response to this question probably depends on your lifestyle expectations. Will your desired retirement lifestyle cost more than what the Age Pension can deliver? If so, now is the time to start planning for your retirement. For more information on how much super is enough, see Chapter 3. For the latest Age Pension payment rates, check out my SuperGuide website (www.superguide.com.au) or go to the Department of Human Services website via this link: www.humanservices .gov.au/customer/enablers/centrelink/age-pension/ payment-rates-for-age-pension.

The general thinking is that Australians are likely to require between 60 and 80 per cent of their pre-retirement income to lead the active life they're expecting in retirement. For the purposes of exploring the difference between expectation and reality and an example that may help you kick-start the planning process, consider Fred's scenario outlined in the following points:

✔ Fred earns $70,000 a year. For retirement, the optimistic Australian will be expecting Fred to have enough super and other savings to support an income of between $42,000 and $56,000 a year in today's dollars. (Expressing amounts in today's dollars allows you to compare a benefit expected to be received at some time in the future with what you could buy with that money today. See Chapter 3 for more information on today's dollars.)

- Fred is aged 35 and currently has no super since he was previously studying and then self-employed and didn't make any super contributions. He will receive 35 years of Superannuation Guarantee (SG) — that is, compulsory superannuation contributions paid by his employer — and can assume his current income of $70,000 a year increases over time. SG contributions represent the equivalent of 9.5 per cent of an employee's salary (each year from 1 July 2014 until 30 June 2021, then SG gradually increases until it reaches 12 per cent from July 2025). If Fred makes no additional super contributions, then he's going to end up with around $500,000 in today's dollars when he retires at age 70 (the Age Pension age for anyone born after December 1965 is age 70, subject to legislation). For the calculation I have assumed 7 per cent return after taxes, less $100 a year for a life insurance premium, and 3 per cent inflation. The final figure may vary by a few thousand dollars depending on the investment returns that his fund actually delivers, and the fees that his fund charges.

- If Fred retires with a $500,000 super benefit (refer to the preceding point) in today's dollars that would deliver Fred a retirement income of around $50,000 a year (indexed), including his potential Age Pension entitlement. But his super money will run out by the time Fred is 90 years of age, and then he must rely solely on the Age Pension.

- If Fred wants his super to last until he is 100, then he should expect a retirement income of just over $43,000 a year (indexed), which would include his Age Pension entitlement, and work out to be just over 60 per cent of his working income. It is unlikely Fred will have to pay tax on his retirement income (for more information on how taxation affects super benefits, see Chapter 19).

- If Fred doesn't plan to receive 35 years of SG employer contributions representing at least 9.5 per cent (and Australians retiring within the next three decades will not), or he doesn't plan to wait until age 70 to retire, or he believes 60 per cent of his before-tax working salary is not enough to live on in a retirement that may span 30 years, then he needs to starting thinking about super-boosting strategies (such as making voluntary super contributions, as I explain in Chapters 4 and 22).

Unless Australians start thinking about how they're going to fund the lifestyle they want in retirement, Fred won't be the only disappointed retiree. I explore how much super is enough, and what Australians can consider a 'comfortable' retirement lifestyle, in Chapter 3.

Living into your eighties and nineties

The number of Aussies over the age of 85 is projected to quadruple by 2050, and the number of people aged 65 to 84 years is expected to double by 2050, according to the Australian government's 2010 Intergenerational Report.

The report, published every five years or so, basically identifies the issues that Australia will face with an ageing population. According to projections in the 2010 report, men born in 2050 will have a life expectancy at birth, on average, of 87.7 years, while women can expect to live to the age of 90.5

years. Men and women aged 60 in 2050 will have a life expectancy (89.2 and 91.4 years respectively) roughly five years longer than men and women aged 60 in 2010 (83.4 and 86.6 years respectively).

Some experts say that of females born today, one in two women are expected to reach the magnificent age of 100, which to be honest I find difficult to believe. But if it's true, the Queen (or King) is going to be very busy sending out birthday greetings to so many centenarians.

Appreciating a Super Fund's DNA

Trying to describe what makes up a superannuation fund is a bit like describing the body of a human being: I know one when I see one. What you do need to understand is that a super fund has key elements that make it very different from a bank account, or a managed fund, where the money of many investors is pooled into one investment vehicle (for more information about managed funds, see Chapter 14).

A superannuation fund is very similar to the human body — really. Without being risque, picture the human body for a moment. Your mental image of the body may have dark skin, and a head with brown hair and blue eyes. Or, the body may be very tall with a head that has no hair. Or perhaps an image of a Hollywood actor, such as Cate Blanchett, Hugh Jackman or Nicole Kidman, pops into your head?

Irrespective of what type of body you pictured, under all the clothes, your human body is the same as everyone else's. Each body normally has a head, two arms, two eyes and a torso. The shape and size may differ, but you know what a human body looks like and what identifying features allow you to know it is a body.

Just like the human body, your superannuation fund also has key distinguishing features that identify it as a super fund.

Here are six traits that, if present, are a certain giveaway that you're looking at a super fund:

- **An obvious name:** The word 'superannuation' or 'super' appears in the fund's name.

- **Trustee:** A 'trustee' or 'trustee board' runs the fund (I explain the role of the trustee in Chapters 7, 8 and 9). The only superannuation vehicle that doesn't have a trustee is a Retirement Savings Account (RSA). For more information about this type of account, see the section 'Discovering seven fund types on your super safari' later in this chapter. I explain different types of super funds in the next section.

- **Governing rules:** A 'trust deed' (or, for a public sector fund, the governing rules in the form of an Act of Parliament) sets out the rules for running the fund. (I explain the importance of a trust deed in Chapter 7.)

- **Regulated fund:** The trustees 'elect' the *Superannuation Industry (Supervision) Act 1993* (SIS Act) — the statutory bible for all superannuation funds — to regulate the fund. (I explain the SIS Act in Chapters 9 and 11, later in this book.)

- **Complying fund:** The fund has complying fund status; that is, the fund has followed all the rules set out in the SIS Act, including complying with the fund's trust deed.

- **APRA licence or operates as a SMSF:** If the super fund is not a self-managed super fund (SMSF), then the trustee must have an RSE licence from the Australian Prudential Regulation Authority (APRA) and the fund must be registered. RSE stands for 'registrable superannuation entity'. (For information about APRA and RSE licences, refer to Chapter 1.) If you run a SMSF, your fund does not need an APRA licence, although you and the other trustees will need to be vetted by the Australian Tax Office (ATO). For details about ATO requirements, see Chapter 7.

Two key elements separate super funds from the thousands of managed funds that exist out there in the financial wild:

- The requirement that a super fund makes an election for regulation by the SIS Act.

- A super fund's complying fund status.

These two features make your super fund eligible to receive tax concessions (for info about these tax breaks, see Chapter 13), and to receive your employer's compulsory contributions and your own contributions (I discuss these contributions in more detail in Chapter 4).

If you haven't actively chosen your super fund, since 1 January 2014, your employer's compulsory SG contributions have been paid into a MySuper product chosen by your employer. A *MySuper product* is a super fund that has a single diversified investment option and simple features, which are designed to make it easier to compare super funds. I explain the role of a MySuper fund in the section 'Discovering seven fund types on your super safari' later in this chapter.

Only complying superannuation funds can receive superannuation contributions and get *concessional taxation treatment*; that is, pay lower tax rates. If you break the super rules, your SMSF could be deemed to be 'non-complying' and you potentially lose up to half of your fund assets. The stronger likelihood, however, is that if your SMSF breaks the super rules, your SMSF, or you as SMSF trustee, will be hit with financial penalties (covered in Chapters 9 and 11). Having complying fund status, however, doesn't guarantee that your fund is going to deliver positive returns.

If you want to know whether your current fund — or another fund that you're considering joining — is a complying fund, you can check a list. The government's Super Fund Lookup website (`http://superfundlookup.gov.au`) is a publicly available list of all complying superannuation funds in Australia (that is, SMSFs and super funds regulated by APRA). If you decide to set up your own super fund, your SMSF will also join this list. You can then type in your super fund's name to check that your fund is complying. If your SMSF has not yet lodged its first annual return (for info on doing so, see Chapter 12), your SMSF will be described as 'Registered — status not determined' on Super Fund Lookup. This means that the SMSF can still accept super contributions and transfers from other super funds.

Recognising Your Super Type from a Distance

Have you been hunting lately? Hunting, that is, for information about your super fund? Superannuation funds are strange beasts, really. They can change shape depending on the person or company running them. You can identify the type of superannuation fund in most cases by looking at the organisation running the fund.

Understanding the type of fund that either you belong to or you're considering joining is very important because different funds offer different benefits at varying costs.

The main purpose of your super fund is to enable you to have a better life in retirement by getting the best returns possible on your super investment. Getting good insurance coverage in your fund, or outside your fund, is an excellent idea, too (for info on insurance and super, see Chapter 24).

Super funds invest in shares, property and other investments just like you do, but super funds are often a more tax-effective option; that is, they're able to take advantage of much lower rates of tax than you may ordinarily pay on your non-super investment income (for information about super's investment rules, see Part IV in this book). Basically, a superannuation fund is a tax-effective vehicle for investing your money with special bells and whistles, and lots of rules.

Earlier in this chapter I discuss traits that identify super funds (refer to 'Appreciating a Super Fund's DNA'), but you don't need binoculars to spot one of the 537,300 or so superannuation funds in Australia, because just under 537,000 of them are *small funds*; that is, with four members or less. If you are a member of a large super fund, or considering a large super fund, then you have only 294 super funds (as at June 2014) to choose from. Just under 300 super funds may still seem overwhelming, but the good news is that there are only seven types of super fund available, which are relatively easy to spot: A SMSF, or one of six types of super funds with professional trustees. I explain these types of super funds in the following section.

Discovering seven fund types on your super safari

You can expect to find seven broad types of super funds in the super fund market, although six of these types of funds are professionally managed for you. Only one type of super fund, a SMSF, gives you total control, and also total responsibility, for your retirement savings.

The following list describes the six broad types of managed superannuation funds:

- **Industry funds:** An industry fund often caters for workers from a particular industry, but many of them are now available to anyone.

- **Company/corporate funds:** A company fund or corporate fund is ordinarily a super fund with membership only open to employees working for that company. You can't choose a company fund, but you may choose to remain in a company fund if you're an employee of the company and an existing fund member. Some company funds permit relatives of existing members to join, too.

✔ **Public sector funds:** A public sector fund is usually only available to public sector employees and, in some cases, ex-public sector employees. You can't choose a public sector fund, although some of them let you choose to remain a contributing member when you leave the public sector — in these circumstances you may be able to arrange for your new employer to contribute to your public sector fund.

✔ **Retail funds or master trusts:** *Retail super funds* are funds run by financial institutions such as banks, financial planning groups and fund managers. Anyone can join these types of funds, or master trusts. A *master trust* is an investment vehicle that pools money from individual investors or individual superannuation funds and invests this money into one or more underlying investment vehicles. You may be a member of a retail fund if your employer pays your SG contributions into a corporate master trust. A *corporate master trust* is just like a master trust for individuals but on a much larger scale. Banks and financial groups also offer what is commonly called a 'super wrap', which gives your super account access to many investment products via a single administration platform (for more info about super wraps, see the next section).

✔ **Small APRA fund — a managed form of DIY super fund:** Small APRA funds (for a definition, refer to Chapter 1) are not as popular as SMSFs, although a small APRA fund often offers the investment flexibility of a SMSF but a professional trustee runs the super fund. I explain the key differences in Chapter 1, and provide more details in 'What makes a SMSF different from other funds?', later in this chapter.

✔ **Retirement Savings Account (RSA):** A *Retirement Savings Account (RSA)* is a low-risk and low-return superannuation account provided by banks and other financial organisations. An RSA is not officially a super fund. RSAs, however, are more a parking vehicle rather than a long-term investment option. RSAs represent less than 1 per cent of all money invested in the superannuation market.

An easy way to find out what type of superannuation fund you belong to is by reading the material that your fund gives you. If possible, check your fund's website. All super funds (including SMSFs in some circumstances) must make available a detailed information booklet or *Product Disclosure Statement* about the fund — it's a document that should clearly set out information about your fund to enable you to compare your fund with similar super funds.

If you're an employee, and you have not actively chosen your super fund, then your employer's super contributions are currently being paid into a MySuper product, which will be one of four types of super funds described in the preceding list — industry fund, retail fund or master trust, corporate fund, or public sector fund. If an employee has not chosen his or her super fund (that is, the employer or an industrial agreement or award has selected the super fund) then, since January 2014, all SG contributions for this employee must be paid into a MySuper product. A MySuper product must have a single investment option, minimum insurance cover and standardised disclosure of fees. At the time of writing, there were 118 MySuper products available. For more information about MySuper, check out my website, SuperGuide (www.superguide.com.au).

Taking the wrap

If you use a licensed financial adviser to help you with your financial affairs, you're likely to be offered a 'wrap' (or 'super wrap' as it's colloquially known) as one of your super options. A *wrap* is an administration platform that operates in a similar way to a master trust — acting like a portal to potentially hundreds of managed funds. Generally, you receive a consolidated report summarising your financial position for the year, and possibly 24-hour online access to your financial information.

If you invest your super money via such a wrap, a professional trustee manages your super. Some investors may prefer holding their super investments within a wrap rather than a SMSF because they then don't have trustee responsibilities (I cover trustee requirements in detail later in this book, in Parts II and III). Some advisers place their clients in a SMSF, and then use a wrap within the SMSF. Very few wraps, however, permit investors to hold non-listed direct investments, such as residential property, within the wrap.

Usually, two main conditions apply when investing via a wrap. An investor often can access a wrap only through a financial adviser (although this requirement is being relaxed by financial providers), and an investor must pay a wrap fee in addition to any adviser fee and fund management fees.

A wrap is merely an administrative service rather than an investment portfolio. The problem with some wraps is the difficulty of working out where the cost of advice ends and the cost of administration begins.

If you use a wrap when running a SMSF, your overall investment and administration costs are likely to be higher, although if you choose a super wrap instead of running a SMSF, your responsibilities will not be as onerous.

What makes a SMSF different from other funds?

Smaller animals often survive longer in the wild than larger animals because they're able to adapt much faster to changing environments, and can more easily flee from impending danger. On the other hand, if a small animal gets trapped in a dangerous situation or makes a wrong move the tiny critter doesn't usually stand a chance, unlike its bigger neighbour.

Small superannuation funds (that is, funds with four or fewer members), operate in a similar way to these tiny animals — they can be flexible but with limited resources.

The two types of small funds — self-managed super funds (SMSFs) and small APRA funds — are managed differently. Although some of the more onerous requirements imposed on funds don't apply to small funds, the key difference between the two types of small funds is that small APRA funds are regulated by APRA, while SMSFs are regulated by the ATO (refer to 'Discovering seven types on your super fund safari', earlier in this chapter and in Chapter 1), and a small APRA fund, must have a trustee that holds an RSE licence, while a SMSF trustee doesn't require a special licence. In other words, a professional trustee company runs the small APRA fund.

The absence of a professional trustee is the key difference between a SMSF and the other types of super funds available in the super market. If you opt to run a SMSF, you take on the responsibility of running a super fund and you do this for free. Your job as SMSF trustee includes complying with the super rules, accepting super contributions and managing your super investments. Are you up for it?

The ATO regulates SMSFs, or DIY super funds (although small APRA funds can be called DIY super funds too). The members of a SMSF are also the trustees of the fund. SMSFs are very popular with owners of small companies, self-employed members of the community, and employees and retirees with large superannuation account balances.

Getting Super-Fit — Your Start-Up Kit

When you understand the basics, you can forge a strong financial future for yourself through superannuation. A weekly, monthly or quarterly contribution to a super fund can provide you with multiple investment choices and tax breaks, and potentially insurance protection if you become disabled before you retire. You can considerably boost your final superannuation benefit by making your own contributions to your fund. You may also have the flexibility to structure your contributions in a way to reduce the amount of tax that you pay.

Thanks to the Superannuation Guarantee (SG), most employed Australian workers now have at least one superannuation account, and one account is all you need. Remember, SG represents compulsory employer super contributions to a super fund that is equivalent to 9.5 per cent of an employee's salary (rate applicable from 2014–15 year until June 2021, and then gradually increases to 12 per cent by July 2025). On a $60,000 a year income, that 9.5 per cent of SG works out to be $5,700 a year — a tidy sum of money the employer is contributing on your behalf.

If you're self-employed, you don't have a fairy godmother making contributions on your behalf, but you do have access to pretty nifty tax deductions when you make your own superannuation contributions.

Considering 'big three' super decisions

At the time you join a super fund, regardless of whether you set up a SMSF or join a large fund, you ordinarily need to make important decisions about your super investments, insurance cover and level of super contributions. You can also review these decisions throughout your fund membership.

How much super you have when you retire can largely depend on how seriously you consider these 'big three' super decisions:

- ✔ **Choosing investment options (or investments).** The investment performance of your super fund is one of the main factors determining the size of your final benefit. Not all, but most, large super funds offer you several investment options and some large super funds let you choose individual share investments. If you run a SMSF, then every investment decision is up to you even if you use someone else to help you, such as a financial adviser.

✔ **Choosing the right level of insurance.** If you become ill or have an accident, paying your everyday bills is a bigger concern than saving for your retirement. Most super funds offer reasonable premiums for death and disability insurance (although there were hefty premium hikes during 2013 and 2014), and an increasing number of super funds offer income protection insurance. You can purchase insurance via a DIY super fund but note that applying for insurance as an individual, rather than via group cover offered by a large fund, can be more expensive and sometimes more difficult to obtain, if you have pre-existing health issues.

✔ **Deciding how much you want to contribute.** Contributing to your super fund is where you have the greatest control and flexibility over your super. Making voluntary contributions (see Chapter 4) can also be the difference between a penny-pinching retirement and one where you can afford some luxuries. Go for it!

Understanding your member statement

If you're considering setting up a SMSF, then your member statement from your current super fund may be the most exciting piece of paper that your fund can send you. It tells you how much super you have, what your account earnt for the year, and the items that make up your benefit.

Due to lots of government rules about the types of information super funds have to give you, and how funds must present your super information, your member statement may look as thrilling as the back of a cereal packet. Don't be fooled — it truly is exciting! Your member statement is the starting point for your retirement plans.

Your member statement is the key document that you receive from your fund. If you take the time to understand your member statement you're going to be up to date with basically everything you need to know about your current super account. Your decision about changing super funds, including starting a SMSF, can then be an informed decision.

Treat your member statement like a newspaper. You scan the headlines, read the articles that interest you and if you're in the mood, or really need to know certain information, then you read the nitty gritty. All of the information on your member statement is important, but digesting it may be easier if you tackle it in stages.

Putting your current super fund under the microscope

Before changing super funds, a prudent approach is to examine what your current super fund offers you. Your super fund's member statement shows the following key information:

✔ **Your personal details:** Check that your name, address and date of birth are correct. Also take note of your membership number. You can use this number as a reference if you change super funds.

✔ **Account balance:** Your account balance is generally easy to find on your statement. It may be called, for example, 'Your leaving benefit' or 'Closing account balance'.

✔ **Contributions:** Your statement should indicate any contributions made by your employer under the Superannuation Guarantee rules, and any salary sacrifice contributions or other employer contributions (see Chapter 4). Your after-tax contributions (if any) made to your super fund during the year should also appear on your statement.

✔ **Earnings/fund return:** Your statement includes the earning rate and the specific earnings for your account. If your super fund offers investment choice, your statement should indicate those choices, and the amounts you have decided to invest in each option. If you haven't chosen your investment options, the statement should indicate which option your super money has been invested in; that is, the default investment option.

✔ **Total fees:** Your member statement typically discloses all fees, and must disclose a dollar amount representing all the fees and costs that affected your superannuation account during the year (for more info on fees, see 'Finding Out the Facts About Fees', later in the chapter).

✔ **Death or disablement benefit (insurance cover):** There should be an item that indicates whether you have insurance cover. If you don't have insurance cover within your super fund, your death benefit is the same figure as your account balance. I discuss SMSF insurance options in Chapter 24.

✔ **Nominated beneficiaries:** Nominating who you want your super to go to if you die is especially important if you're single, remarried or in a same-sex relationship. I discuss nominated beneficiaries in more detail in Chapter 24.

✔ **Rollovers received:** If you rolled over any amounts from other super funds during the year, the amounts should appear on your statement.

✔ **Tax file number recorded:** If you or your employer haven't provided your tax file number (TFN) to your super fund, your employer's contributions and any other before-tax contributions are hit with a penalty super tax, and further, you can't make non-concessional (after-tax) contributions.

Accepting super taxes

You can save for your retirement any way you like, but superannuation is one of the more tax-effective ways, particularly if you wait until you turn 60 before retiring — superannuation benefits are tax-free for Australians aged 60 years and over (except for some retired public servants), as I explain in Chapter 19.

In addition, if your super fund is in pension phase (that is, paying you a superannuation pension), any earnings on the investments supporting your pension account in the fund are exempt from tax (see Chapters 18 and 21).

You can also enjoy the tax benefits of super long before you retire. If you pay more than 15 cents in the dollar income tax on your personal income, then you pay less tax on your superannuation earnings than if you earned the money outside super (see Chapter 13). Further, before-tax super contributions, officially known as concessional contributions, such as employer contributions and salary sacrifice contributions, are subject to a contributions tax of 15 per cent (and subject to 30 per cent contributions tax if you earn more than $300,000 a year). A contributions tax of 15 per cent is lower than the income tax payable for anyone earning more than $20,542, for the 2014–15 year.

Until June 2017, if you earn less than $37,000 a year, up to $500 of the tax paid on your employer's super contributions and other concessional contributions will be refunded to your super account. I explain how the Low Income Super Contribution works in Chapter 4.

Starting a superannuation pension

Although it is still possible under the super rules to take a lump sum in retirement, an increasing number of retirees are opting to start a superannuation pension. A superannuation pension attracts special tax concessions including tax-exempt investment earnings, subject to the individual receiving the pension taking out a minimum amount each year. A superannuation pension also receives some advantages under the Age Pension rules (see Chapter 20). I explain the retirement rules generally in Chapter 19.

You can purchase a super pension from a financial organisation or a large super fund, or you can start your super pension within a SMSF. The flexibility of SMSF pensions is a major attraction for individuals setting up a SMSF. I explain how SMSF pensions work in Chapters 21 and 22.

Finding Out the Facts about Fees

Go on, have a whinge! I hate fees, too, but what can you get in the financial world without forking out some money? The only freebies that may spring to mind are show bags at financial seminars and exhibitions, which you end up indirectly paying for anyway when you use the services of the bank or organisation that hands out the stickers, balloons and glossy brochures.

Running a superannuation fund obviously costs money and these costs are usually charged against each member's account in the form of fees. If you run a SMSF, then you're responsible for how much your super fund costs.

Your superannuation fund's investment performance (which I show you how to analyse in Part IV) is the overriding factor in determining the size of your superannuation benefit in retirement. High fees, however, can influence the level of returns your account earns each year. The higher the fees that you pay on your super, the better your fund has to perform to deliver returns that give you a decent retirement benefit.

For example, if your fund charges fees (or your SMSF costs) each year representing 3 per cent of your balance, your fund has to earn at least 3 per cent to cover the fees. If inflation is running at 2 per cent each year, your fund has to earn more than 5 per cent before it delivers a 'real return'. A *real return* is the investment return after taking into account the effects of inflation. In this example, to deliver a real return of 4 per cent, your fund needs to deliver an investment performance of 9 per cent before fees.

The reality is that you can have two funds earning identical investment returns over a 30-year period, but due to the impact of higher fees, one fund delivers a significantly lower retirement benefit.

Before you change super funds, including setting up a SMSF, check out what super fees you're paying on your current super account and compare those costs with what you expect to pay when running a SMSF. I take you through how much a SMSF costs in Chapter 6.

Choosing Another Super Fund

You don't have to be an expert in superannuation to be able to choose your own super fund, but you do need to understand the marketplace you're shopping in to choose wisely. The *super* market is a busy place with lots of fund providers, but luckily they're all selling the same thing — superannuation funds.

Choosing a suitable superannuation fund is obviously more complex than shopping for, say, a jar of jam, but both scenarios require you to make a decision about choice. Which super fund (or jam) is the best one for you?

Some clever clogs in the United States conducted a supermarket experiment about choice using two displays of jam. The display with 25 jam varieties attracted lots of window-shoppers but no-one bought the jam. Instead, customers bought from the less glamorous six-jam exhibit. The jam experiment determined that the more choice a person has, the harder the decision.

Superannuation is no different. The prospect of selecting a super fund may seem overwhelming considering the number of super funds available in the *super* market. If you do your homework, however, picking the right super fund can add thousands of dollars to your final retirement benefit — a bit like money for jam.

If you're considering changing super funds, you can start the process by asking yourself two questions:

- Do the super laws permit me to choose my own super fund?
- If the answer is yes, what are my super options?

Do you have super fund choice?

Since 1 July 2005, most Australians have been able to choose their own superannuation fund. However, whether you have fund choice depends on who you are, who you work for and where you live.

If you're an employee, you're likely to have fund choice, but it depends on the arrangement you have with your employer, or whether you're subject to certain industrial awards or agreements. An *industrial award* or *agreement* sets out your conditions of employment and often includes a provision stating that your super must be paid in accordance with that award. If you're self-employed, or a company owner, then you clearly have fund choice. As a company owner you may also have to choose a super fund for some or all of your employees.

The quickest and easiest way to find out if you have fund choice is to ask your employer. If you don't think your employer knows the answer, or you want to be doubly sure, then head to the ATO website for help on this subject.

The fund choice laws relate to the right to choose the super fund where your employer pays in the compulsory SG contributions. If you don't have fund choice over where your employer's SG contributions are directed, you can still make personal super contributions to a SMSF or other super fund of your choosing. I explain how to change super funds and redirect employer contributions to a SMSF in Chapter 7.

Deciding on your super options

When deciding whether to change super funds, you're going to be exposed to a lot of 'noise' on your super choice journey. Expect the ruckus to come from a multitude of sources — friends, TV, magazines, newspapers, advisers and the local 'expert' on everything in the known world (everyone knows one of those).

Do you stay in your existing super fund and take a greater interest in what your super fund is doing, or do you change super funds? If you change super funds, do you decide to start a SMSF, or choose a wrap, or move to another large fund?

Earlier in the chapter (refer to 'Recognising Your Super Type from a Distance'), I outlined the seven main super options available to you, and the difference between SMSFs and the other types of super options.

Unless you're already a member of a company fund (although some company super funds permit relatives of employees to become members) or a public sector fund, an employee can generally only choose from four types of super funds:

- ✔ Industry funds
- ✔ Retail funds or retail master trusts or super wraps
- ✔ Small APRA funds
- ✔ Self-managed super funds

If you decide to change superannuation funds, your super decision is all about choosing between one of the managed super fund options or a SMSF. (I explain what you need to do to change super funds in Chapter 7.)

Chapter 3

How Much Super Is Enough?

*T*he most popular question about superannuation and retirement planning is, without doubt: 'How much money is enough?'

A glib response to this question may be: 'Enough money for what?' From the many times, though, that I've been asked this question, I know that when most Australians ask it, they really want to discover the answer to: 'How much money do I need to maintain (or improve) the lifestyle I currently have until the day I die?' For some Australians, the question also includes: 'And to leave enough money to help my family after I've gone.'

Your own answer to this question depends on four main factors:

✔ The level of income that you hope to receive each year — that is, your lifestyle expectations.

✔ How long you expect to live — that is, your life expectancy.

✔ Earnings you can expect to receive on your pension account in retirement.

✔ Whether you intend to continue working and/or contributing to your super fund in retirement (I explain the implications of retiring too early in Chapter 19, and contributing while taking a pension in Chapter 22).

In this chapter, I take you through the first three factors in the preceding list. I also deal at length with the question 'How much is enough?', but you can also find much more on this topic on my website, SuperGuide (www.superguide.com.au).

Individuals who run their own super fund are generally pretty serious about planning for a comfortable retirement (I explain what 'comfortable' means in the following sections). Australians who do plan for their later years using superannuation are amply rewarded with tax-free income and tax-exempt earnings in retirement. If you take your super benefits on or after the age of 60, any super benefits including amounts paid from your self-managed super fund (SMSF) are tax-free. What's even more alluring about the superannuation system is that any earnings on super fund investments that have been invested to finance an individual's pension payments are tax-exempt. Depending on your annual income in retirement, the tax offsets on non-super income for Australians currently aged 65 years or over are also very attractive. A *tax offset* reduces the tax payable on an individual's taxable income. I explain how the retirement world works in Chapter 19, and the tax treatment of non-super retirement income on my website, SuperGuide (`www.superguide.com.au`).

In this chapter, the lump sum amounts listed in the tables are in *today's dollars*. Expressing amounts in today's dollars allows you to compare a benefit expected to be received at some time in the future with what you could buy with that money today. If you want to retire on $60,000 a year, you're likely to be thinking that the income stream represents what you can buy with $60,000 today, not what $60,000 can buy you in 10, 20 or 30 years' time. However, the effect of rising prices reduces the buying power of your money, which is why comparing amounts in today's dollars is important. For example, say you *do* retire today on $60,000 a year. Over the next five years, prices increase by a total of 10 per cent. Your annual retirement income would need to have increased by $6,000 — to $66,000 a year — to continue delivering you $60,000 in income in today's dollars.

Deciding on the Lifestyle You Want

Choosing a lifestyle is simple — you live the life you can afford. If you want a more salubrious lifestyle, you save more, earn more, win the lottery or inherit lots of money from a rich relative. The same philosophy applies to your retirement lifestyle.

Thanks to a groundbreaking study originally released in February 2004, revamped in 2010 to reflect changes in living standards (in particular, retirees' greater lifestyle expectations and changing spending patterns), and updated every three months, I can tell you, with some authority, how much money you need to live on each year in retirement, depending on the lifestyle that you want. The study, known as the ASFA Retirement Standard, measures the cost of a modest or comfortable lifestyle in retirement, in dollar terms, and adjusts these costs quarterly in line with the cost of living.

The ASFA Retirement Standard is groundbreaking because Australians now have a tangible savings target with a clear idea of what type of lifestyle that amount of money can give them in retirement. In the next section, I outline how much money you need as a lump sum on retirement to deliver you a 'basic', 'modest' or 'comfortable' life in retirement.

Comparing basic, modest and comfortable lifestyles

If you've read any of my other superannuation books (check out the section 'About the Author' at the back of this book) you probably already know that I think the ASFA Retirement Standard is fantastic because it draws a clear line in the sand for future retirees. I have adapted the findings slightly to include a 'basic' lifestyle, which is a lifestyle that simply reflects what you would receive if you had no savings and received just the Age Pension. The *Age Pension* provides a taxpayer-funded basic retirement income for those people who can't fully support themselves. I have included this 'basic' lifestyle category as a lower benchmark for your planning.

Assuming you own your own home, you need the following amounts of money, after tax, to give a single person, or a couple, a basic, modest or comfortable lifestyle:

- ✔ **Basic lifestyle (Age Pension — $22,212 a year for a single person, or $33,488 for a couple; rates applicable until March 2015, and include pension supplement and Clean Energy Supplement).** The single Age Pension represents 27.7 per cent of Male Total Average Weekly Earnings. Are you willing to live on around a quarter of an average Australian's income? Living solely on the Age Pension gives you a basic income and access to discounts on health services and energy costs. While this figure may be an amount you can survive on, many Australians don't expect to live within this level of income by choice. (I discuss the Age Pension in the section 'Living in comfort and claiming the Age Pension', later in this chapter, and in more detail in Chapter 20.)

- ✔ **Modest lifestyle ($23,363 a year for a single person, or $33,664 for a couple; latest figures available as at November 2014).** Receiving an after-tax income that's only slightly higher than the Age Pension obviously gives you a marginally better lifestyle than living solely on social security, but you can only afford low-cost activities.

- ✔ **Comfortable lifestyle ($42,433 a year for a single person, or $58,128 for a couple; latest figures available as at November 2014).** Living on this level of after-tax income means you can enjoy more recreational activities. Also, you can afford to purchase private health insurance and higher quality household goods, and travel regularly. Even so, a 'comfortable' lifestyle isn't outlandish.

Living in comfort on $42,000 (or $58,000 for a couple) a year

So what does a 'comfortable' lifestyle of $42,433 for a single person (or $58,128 a year for a couple) buy you that a 'modest' lifestyle of $23,363 a year for a single person (or $33,664 a year for a couple) can't? According to the ASFA Retirement Standard, a comfortable lifestyle means that you can enjoy leisure and recreational activities, including regular domestic travel and occasional international travel. A comfortable retirement also means that you can take out top private health cover, drive a relatively new car, update your wardrobe when needed, and replace household goods, such as a washing machine or fridge, when needed. You can also better afford utility bills than someone on a 'modest' income, and you can afford to run a mobile phone, a computer and other electronic devices.

Keeping pace with greater lifestyle expectations and changing spending patterns, the ASFA Retirement Standard shows that retirees are spending more in a number of areas to maintain a comfortable lifestyle:

- **Communications:** To cover mobile phones and the internet.

- **Private health cover:** Now assumed essential for retirees seeking a comfortable (or even a modest) lifestyle.

- **Energy:** For heating and cooling — to run ducted heating and air-conditioning.

- **Personal care:** On clothing, footwear and hairdressing.

- **Household goods and services:** For computers and electronics (which need to be updated periodically), home alarms and to conduct regular pest inspections.

- **Recreation:** For eating out and buying leisure goods such as golf clubs and fishing equipment, plus memberships to social and sporting clubs.

- **Transport:** To cover the cost of owning and running a car.

If you plan to take an income stream (pension) from a super fund, such as your SMSF, or withdraw lump sums from the super system, you can expect to pay no tax on your pension payment income provided you're aged 60 year or over. (If you're receiving super pension payments from an older public sector super fund, then you may have to pay a small amount of tax on your super pension income.) Even when you start receiving super benefits under the age of 60, with the help of good tax advice, you can earn the income amounts necessary to finance a modest or comfortable lifestyle without paying any income tax.

Living in comfort and claiming the Age Pension

If you're running your own super fund, I assume that you expect a lifestyle substantially higher than the basic lifestyle you'd get living solely on the Age Pension of $21,212 for a single person or $33,488 for a couple (rates applicable until March 2015). And, if you want a comfortable lifestyle, well, you then need to find the income from your super and non-super savings, and potentially from also claiming a part Age Pension.

If you're eligible for the Age Pension, you're going to need fewer savings when you retire. In most cases, as a single person or a couple seeking a 'comfortable' lifestyle, assuming you structure your finances appropriately, you're likely to be eligible for at least a part Age Pension. Alternatively, you may receive an income that sits between 'modest' and 'comfortable' and that gives you a greater chunk of Age Pension, which means you need less savings than what's required for a 'comfortable' lifestyle but, usually, at some sacrifice to your expected standard of living.

If you plan to retire before your Age Pension age, then you will need to rely only on your super and non-super savings to finance your lifestyle, at least until you reach your Age Pension Age. The *Age Pension age* — that is, the age that you can start receiving the Age Pension (if eligible) — is 65 years for those born before July 1952 (or an earlier age if you're a female and born before 1949). If you were born after December 1965, then your Age Pension age is 70, subject to legislation being passed. If you were born after June 1952 but before January 1966, then your Age Pension age will be somewhere between 65 and 70 years, subject to legislation. I explain the Age Pension age and other Age Pension rules, including how your Age Pension entitlements interact with your superannuation benefits, in Chapter 20.

Table 3-1 lists the lump sum amounts that you need to invest on retirement to deliver a basic, modest or comfortable lifestyle. The lump sums in Table 3-1 are based on the assumption that you retire at your Age Pension age, for example, age 67, and that your lump sum lasts for 20 years. For updated lump sum targets, including targets for other retirement ages and Age Pension ages (including ages 55, 60, 65 and 70) check out my website, SuperGuide (www.superguide.com.au).

When looking at Table 3-1, you need to be mindful of the following variables:

- ✔ The annual income and lump sum amounts that appear in Table 3-1 assume that your money is held within the superannuation system and that you're receiving tax-free super pension income. *Note:* Even when you retire under the age of 60, with the help of good tax advice, you can live off your retirement savings without paying tax (for the details on how the benefit payment tax rules work, see Chapters 13 and 19), although if you retire early you're going to need a larger lump sum to fund your longer retirement.

- ✔ The earlier you retire, the bigger the lump sum that you need to invest for your retirement. If you retire before your Age Pension age, you're going to need a bigger lump sum than those appearing in Table 3-1 because you will be retired for a longer period. If you retire before reaching your Age Pension age, then you will need to rely only on your superannuation and other savings, until you become eligible for the Age Pension, assuming you meet the Age Pension income and assets tests (for information on these income and assets tests, see Chapter 20).

Table 3-1		What Type of Lifestyle Do You Want in Retirement?				
	Single			**Couple**		
Lifestyle	**Annual Income**	**Lump Sum Needed on Retirement**		**Annual Income**	**Lump Sum Needed on Retirement**	
		No Age Pension	**Receives Age Pension**		**No Age Pension**	**Receives Age Pension**
Basic (Age Pension)	$22,212	N/A	$0	$33,488	N/A	$0
Modest	$23,363	$340,000	About $22,000 (+ Full Pension)	$33,664	$490,000	About $10,000 (+Full Pension)
Comfortable	$42,433	$615,000	At least $355,000	$58,128	$845,000	At least $405,000

Notes:

1. The lump sum amounts are in today's dollars and assume retirement at the age of 67: the lump sum will finance a retirement of 20 years, and you then live on the Age Pension only after 20 years. If you retire at age 68, then the lump sum will finance a retirement until age 88. If you retire at age 70, then the listed lump sum will finance a retirement until 90 years of age. For updated lump sum amounts see SuperGuide website (www.superguide.com.au).

2. Annual inflation rate for years in retirement is 3 per cent. Assume personal assets $25,000 apart from super pension assets.

3. If you retire before you're eligible for the Age Pension, or you're otherwise not eligible for the Age Pension, the lump sum you need to enjoy each lifestyle is a larger amount than if you were eligible for the Age Pension (see www.humanservices.gov.au *for information about the eligibility rules for the Age Pension). See 'No Age Pension' column for lump sum amounts.*

4. If you're eligible for the Age Pension (refer to 'Receives Age Pension' columns), the lump sum you need in retirement depends on how much Age Pension you expect to receive and the earnings you can achieve on your super and non-super savings. For the 'comfortable' lifestyle, part Age Pension eligibility is likely. The lump sum amount you need to invest for retirement is usually different for each person, depending on the size of the Age Pension entitlement. See sources below for assumptions.

5. Income tax isn't taken into account in this table, although, in most cases, tax is irrelevant because of the tax concessions applicable to retirees. I discuss tax and retiring in Chapters 13 and 19.

Sources: Data compiled from sources as follows:

1. Modest and comfortable annual costs/incomes (as at June 2014) —ASFA Retirement Standard. These figures, released in August 2014 (latest available at November 2014), are adjusted quarterly in line with the cost of living (check www.superannuation.asn.au *for the latest annual costs, or visit SuperGuide,* www.superguide.com.au*).*

*2. 'No Age Pension' columns. Lump sums needed when 'No Age Pension', are calculated using ASIC's 'retirement planner' calculator (*www.moneysmart.gov.au*) as at November 2014. Calculations assume 7 per cent a year return after fees and taxes (that is then reinvested) on account balance of account-based income stream (see Chapter 21). The annual income from the account-based income stream is indexed by 3 per cent a year, and runs out at the age of 87 (approximate life expectancy for a 67-year-old female). If you live beyond 87, then individual relies only on the Age Pension. Calculations don't take into account any tax payable or Age Pension. Refer to Source 1 for more details. I explain the account-based income stream in Chapter 21.*

*3. 'Receives Age Pension' columns. The lump sum amounts under 'Receives Age Pension' are calculated using ASIC's 'retirement planner' calculator (*www.moneysmart.gov.au*) as at November 2014. Calculations assume 7 per cent a year return after fees and taxes (that is reinvested) on account balance of account-based income stream (see Chapter 21). The annual income from the account-based income stream is indexed by 3 per cent a year, and runs out at the age of 87 (approximate life expectancy for a 67-year-old female). If you live beyond 87, then individual relies only on the Age Pension . The figures from 'No Age Pension' column are used as upper lump sum amount in 'comfortable' category.*

4. Age Pension amounts as at September 2014 (applicable until March 2015) (check www.humanservices.gov.au *or* www.superguide.com.au *for latest figures).*

Wanting More Than $58,000 a Year

Many people are relieved to finally know what target they need to be working towards in terms of retirement savings. A comfortable lifestyle for some Australians as defined in the preceding sections isn't what they had in mind. They were hoping for a 'very comfortable' life or even a 'lavish' lifestyle when compared to the comfortable life that they can live on when receiving just over $42,000 a year (for a single person), or roughly $58,000 as a couple.

If you fall into the 'wanting more' category, then you're probably seeking information on how much super is needed to finance much higher income levels. If this is you, keep reading this section.

The general rule when planning for retirement is: If you want a similar lifestyle to the one that you're enjoying during your working life, you need a minimum of 60 to 65 per cent of your pre-retirement income in retirement. For example, if you live comfortably on $60,000 a year and you want a similar standard of living in retirement, you probably need an income of at least $36,000 to $39,000 a year in retirement. If your pre-retirement income is $120,000 and you want to maintain that lifestyle, then you probably need at least $72,000 to $78,000 a year for retirement.

Table 3-2 lists the amount of money you need on retirement to finance an income stream at higher levels of income. The lump sum amounts shown in Table 3-2 assume a part Age Pension entitlement, where applicable. Eligibility for the Age Pension then means you need less savings in retirement. I discuss the Age Pension in more detail in Chapter 20, and I provide updated tables and extra detail on wanting a 'more than comfortable' retirement on my SuperGuide website (www.superguide.com.au).

If you receive a part Age Pension you need less super when you retire to maintain your desired retirement income. For a couple, a part Age Pension is available in the later years of retirement even when receiving $100,000 a year (indexed) over a 33-year retirement. Due to the level of assets required to finance higher incomes in retirement, or to finance a longer retirement, single people seeking more than $100,000 a year (indexed) for a 20-year retirement can expect no Age Pension entitlements, although a small part Age Pension may be available in the later retirement years when receiving $100,000 a year. For a single person seeking to finance a 33-year retirement (from age 67 to age 100), Age Pension entitlements are generally not available when seeking more than $80,000 a year (due to the level of assets required), although a small part Age Pension is available in the later retirement years when receiving $80,000 a year.

The longer you live, the more money you're going to need. Alternatively, you can just accept a lower standard of living in retirement. On average, women need to save more because they live longer than men. (I discuss how you can work out how long you're likely to live in the next section.)

Table 3-2	**How Much Super is Enough?**			
Annual Income (Including Part Age Pension)	*Lump Sum Needed if Money Runs Out After 20 Years*		*Lump Sum Needed if Money Runs Out at Age 100 (After 33 Years)*	
	Single	*Couple*	*Single*	*Couple*
$50,000	$516,000	$250,000^	$792,000	$350,000
$60,000	$735,000	$445,000	$1.07 million	$670,000
$80,000	$1.15 million	$875,000	$1.51 million	$1.33 million
$100,000	$1.45 million	$1.3 million	$1.92 million	$1.83 million
$150,000*	$2.14 million	$2.14 million	$2.83 million	$2.83 million
$200,000*	$2.88 million	$2.88 million	$3.77 million	$3.77 million

^Full Age Pension is payable for a couple owning this value of assets.

*No Age Pension entitlement at these asset and income levels.

Source: Lump sum amounts were calculated in November 2014 using ASIC's 'retirement planner' except for $150,000 and $200,000 incomes which were calculated using ASIC's 'account-based pension calculator'. For an updated version of this table, see SuperGuide website (www.superguide.com .au). Assume retirement at age 67 and reached Age Pension age. Calculations assume 7 per cent a year return net of fees on the account-based income stream account balance, and returns are reinvested. The annual income from the account-based income stream is indexed by 3 per cent a year (www .moneysmart.gov.au). Apart from super pension, assume own only $25,000 in personal assets. Lump sum amounts in table are rounded to two decimal points. (See Chapter 21 for an explanation of the account-based income stream.)

How Long Do You Expect to Live?

Discussing how long you have left on this place called Earth may be gruesome for some Australians but, if you're planning for a financially secure retirement, you need to estimate the length of your retirement, and decide whether you want to leave any money for your spouse, children or other relatives when you die.

Your average life expectancy (for the definition, refer to Chapter 2) can be measured at the time you were born or at any time during your life.

The Australian Government Actuary (AGA) compiles life tables which also measure the life expectancy of living people at their current age based on assumed mortality rates that statisticians expect people of this age to experience from now until the end of their life.

The interesting aspect to life expectancy is that the longer you live, the better your chances are of living longer — your life expectancy actually increases. For example, at birth, life expectancy for a female is around 84 years, while at the age of 55 a female can expect to live to the age of 85.5 years — 1.5 years longer than her expected lifespan at birth. When a female reaches the age of 70, her average life expectancy increases again by two years to 87.5 years (or more specifically, 87.42 years).

Life expectancy — living beyond an average life

In 1909, the average life expectancy (the number of years you're expected to live) of an Australian male was 55 years, while the average Australian female was expected to live to the grand old age of 59 years! Frightening really, but life was different then and medical discoveries, though miraculous, were infrequent in comparison to the medical advances of today.

Australia now has one of the highest life expectancy rates in the world for its non-Indigenous population. Statisticians can measure life expectancy at birth or during a person's life. Men and women born today can expect to live five years longer than men and women born 60 years ago, and the federal government's 2010 Intergenerational Report provides data to back up this evidence (for more information on this report, refer to the related sidebar in Chapter 2). The Australian Government Actuary (AGA) Australian Life Tables also measure the life expectancy of Australians at their current age, based on assumed mortality rates that statisticians expect people of this age to experience from now until the end of their life. The following table provides a sample of average life expectancies derived from the life tables.

When You're ...	Years to Live (Age) for Females	Years to Live (Age) for Males
50	35.17 (85.17)	31.43 (81.43)
55	30.53 (85.53)	26.95 (81.95)
60	26.00 (86.00)	22.63 (82.63)
65	21.62 (86.62)	18.54 (83.54)
67	19.92 (86.92)	16.99 (83.99)
70	17.42 (87.42)	14.76 (84.76)
85	7.08 (92.08)	6.03 (91.03)
100	2.74 (102.74)	2.81 (102.81)

Source: Derived from Australian Life Tables, 2005–07, Australian Government Actuary. Australian Life Tables 2010–12 due to be released in early 2015. Visit www.superguide.com.au for the updated tables, and more complete life expectancy figures. © Commonwealth of Australia, Australian Government Actuary, 2014.

You can download a copy of the life tables from the AGA's website (www.aga.au), or you can access a more specific list of average life expectancies from the age of 0 to 100 on my Superguide website, www.superguide.com.au.

If you're a man and retire today at the age of 65, you can expect, on average, to live until you are 83.5 years (18.54 more years). If you're a woman and retire today at the age of 65, you can expect to live, on average, until the age of 87 (or 86.62 years); that is, another 22 years. If you retire at age 67, you can expect your retirement to last, on average, until you are 87 (19.92 years if female) or 84 (16.99 years if male). I list some of the average life expectancies for men and women in the sidebar 'Life expectancy — living beyond an average life'.

Life expectancy figures are merely averages, which means that around one-half of the population lives longer than the average life expectancy and around one-half of the population doesn't reach the average life expectancy age. According to the 2014 interim report of the Financial System Inquiry, although most retirees risk outliving their retirement savings, 10 per cent of 65-year-old females will die before they reach the age of 77 (even though average life expectancy is 87 years), while another 10 per cent is expected to live past 100 years of age.

Have you planned for your long life in retirement? Have you also planned for the possibility that you may leave this world early? See Chapter 24 for information on what can happen to your super if you die early, and also what can happen to your super if you die after living a lovely long life.

Earning Returns for the Long Term

How long your money lasts really depends on how much you have to invest, whether you choose to invest that money in the super system, and what return you receive on your invested monies.

In Tables 3-1 and 3-2 (refer to the sections 'Living in comfort and claiming the Age Pension' and 'Wanting More Than $58,000 a Year' in this chapter), I assume a long-term return of 7 per cent after fees and taxes. Why? Well, in earlier books, I used similar assumptions, which in the past some readers questioned as being too conservative because of the boom investment markets Australia experienced from 2003 to 2007. I wonder now whether I'm to receive some comment that a 7 per cent return is too optimistic in light of relatively recent market events; for example, some super and pension accounts lost a half of their value during the 2008 calendar year. For me, however, the 7 per cent figure caters for the long-term possibility of both boom and bust investment markets, and long-term statistics prove me correct.

According to rating company Chant West, over the 22-year period since the introduction of compulsory super contributions (Superannuation Guarantee) — that is, from July 1992 to June 2014 — super accounts have delivered an annual average return of 7.2 per cent.

So, as a planning tool, I continue to adhere to an assumed rate of return of 7 per cent after fees and taxes (I explain the long-term return potential of different asset classes and investment portfolios in Chapter 15). You may choose to assume a greater (or lower) return for your own planning purposes, depending on your fund's particular investments.

The consequence of using a more conservative return as an assumption means that you need to have a larger lump sum as a starting point for a given level of income. If you assume a higher rate of return on your investments, then you can start out with a smaller lump sum upon retirement.

The financial services regulator, Australian Securities & Investments Commission (ASIC), provides several online calculators that you can use to help you work out how much money you need for your retirement. You can rely on the existing assumptions used by these calculators or you can take the opportunity to insert your own assumptions and test out the implications of earning different investments returns. To get started, go to www.moneysmart.gov.au, and try each calculator:

- ✔ **MoneySmart superannuation calculator:** This calculator gives you a snapshot of your likely superannuation situation in 20, 30 or 40 years' time, based on certain assumptions. The calculator enables you to forecast the effect on your super of making extra contributions and receiving the government's co-contribution (covered in Chapter 4), paying lower fees (see Chapter 6) or even stopping contributions for a while.

- ✔ **MoneySmart account-based pension calculator:** This calculator shows you how long your money will last if you were to withdraw specified amounts each year. You can change the amount you withdraw, the investment return that you assume for your pension investments and the costs involved in running your pension.

- ✔ **MoneySmart retirement planner:** This nifty calculator does the lot — you can insert your existing account balance, how much you earn (for Superannuation Guarantee purposes, see Chapter 4), how much you plan to contribute each year, the assumed investment return over the long-term, and the age you intend to retire. You state what level of income that you want and the calculator estimates how long your super savings are going to last, and your Age Pension entitlement (if any).

Chapter 4

Counting On Super Contributions of All Sorts

....

....

*F*or your superannuation account to exist, someone at some time has to make a super contribution. Fortunately, most Australians have an employer who's doing half the savings job for them by making compulsory Superannuation Guarantee contributions. The rest of the retirement savings challenge is up to you. Alternatively, when you don't have an employer — that is, you're self-employed or not employed — the size of your final retirement balance is totally dependent on you.

The secret to a cushy retirement is that simple, and that challenging. How big your super benefit is going to be when you retire generally depends on how much you contribute to your super fund, and strong investment earnings after fees and taxes on your super savings.

If you already have a self-managed super fund (SMSF) or you've decided a SMSF is right for you (refer to Chapter 1), then clearly you've already accepted the savings challenge — and you generally need upwards of $200,000 to $250,000 for a SMSF to be a cost-effective option. Well done!

This chapter explains your employer's super contribution obligations, the different types of super contributions that you can make, the limits on making such contributions (and what happens if you exceed those limits) and the special contribution opportunities available when saving for your retirement. I also devote a section of this chapter to a very special type of non-cash contribution known as an in specie contribution.

Superannuation contributions can also make a difference when you start taking a pension. As a bonus for readers who are already receiving a pension from a DIY super fund, or who are considering starting a SMSF pension, in Chapter 22 I explain some of the issues that you should weigh up if you also want to make super contributions to your SMSF (or you're considering starting a pension from your SMSF) while contributing to that same fund.

Superannuation Guarantee — Compulsory Super

Australia's compulsory superannuation system is an innovative policy of forced savings that means, as an employee, you have a helping hand when saving for your retirement.

The Superannuation Guarantee (SG) rules require your employer to pay the equivalent of 9.5 per cent of your ordinary wages or salary into your super fund at least every three months, although some employers pay SG entitlements monthly or fortnightly. The SG rate remains at 9.5 per cent until the end of June 2021, increases to 10 per cent for the 2021–22 year, and then gradually increases to 12 per cent by July 2025, as shown in Table 4-1.

Superannuation Guarantee doesn't mean that your employer, or the federal government, provides a 'guarantee' on your super savings. The term 'Superannuation Guarantee' simply means that your employer must pay a certain amount of money as super contributions each year, in at least quarterly instalments, into the super accounts of eligible employees.

You may be able to choose the fund that your employer pays your SG contributions into. If you have fund choice (refer to Chapter 2), you must fill in a special form known as a Standard Choice Form (SCF), if you want your employer's SG contributions to be paid into your SMSF. I explain the SCF and the process that you need to go through to ensure your employer can pay your SG entitlements into your SMSF in Chapter 7.

The SG percentage remains at 9.5 per cent until the end of the 2020–21 year, and then increases in 0.5 per cent increments each following financial year until it reaches 12 per cent from 1 July 2025. The SG rate will then remain at 12 per cent. For more details on the increase in the rate of SG contributions for later years, see my website, SuperGuide, at www.superguide.com.au.

Table 4-1	How Much SG Are You Entitled To?
Financial Year	*SG Rate (%)*
2013–14	9.25%
2014–15	9.5%
2015–16	9.5%
2016–17	9.5%
2017–18	9.5%
2018–19	9.5%
2019–20	9.5%
2020–21	9.5%
2021–22	10.0%
2022–23	10.5%
2023–24	11.0%
2024–25	11.5%
2025–26 and future years	12.0%

Are you entitled to SG?

If you earn more than $450 a month as an employee, your employer must pay SG into your super fund, at least every three months. Anyone employed for domestic or private work, such as babysitting or gardening, must also work more than 30 hours a week before an employer has to contribute SG. If an employee is under the age of 18 and working 30 hours or less, or a person is a member of the reserve forces, there's no requirement for SG to be contributed for the income the person receives for this work.

Since the 2013–14 financial year, individuals aged 70 years or over have been entitled to SG contributions assuming they satisfy the $450 a month earning requirement, and if applicable, the 30-plus hours minimum work requirement for domestic or private work. In most instances, this is great news for senior workers, but for some 70-somethings, finding a super fund for those employer contributions can be a hassle if the older person has started a super pension, or no longer has a super fund. (The policy in place before July 2013 was that an employer was not required to pay SG contributions for anyone aged 70 or over.) If you're receiving a pension from a SMSF, a solution may be to open a super account within your SMSF to accept the SG contributions, or an alternative option is to open a super account with a larger super fund (refer to Chapter 2) to accept the SG contributions.

Even when you're self-employed you still may be entitled to receive SG from one or more of your customers or clients. The rules that cover contractors are fairly complicated but, generally, if you're hired under a contract wholly or principally for your labour, and you're not free to engage other people to perform the work, you may be entitled to SG. You're never entitled to SG from your clients when you run your business as a company, although you must pay SG on behalf of your company's employee — you.

If you believe the contractors rule regarding eligibility for SG may apply to you, or you have any other questions relating to SG, you can obtain more information by phoning the ATO Superannuation Infoline on 13 10 20, or by visiting the ATO website (www.ato.gov.au) and clicking on 'Super'.

How is your SG calculated?

The law requires your employer to pay the equivalent of 9.5 per cent of what you earn from your ordinary hours of work, including over-award payments, any shift or casual loading, performance bonuses and commissions. Any payment for overtime isn't included in your income for the purposes of calculating this 9.5 per cent contribution. In addition, if you have a salary package that includes before-tax benefits, such as a car, your employer generally makes the 9.5 per cent contribution only on your cash salary.

All eligible employees have a right to SG, although the amount of SG you receive is subject to an upper income limit. Your employer must contribute 9.5 per cent of your salary only up to a maximum contribution base, which is linked to an individual's earnings. The *maximum contribution base* is $49,430 each quarter (for the 2014–15 year), which works out to be an annual income of $197,720. If your income for SG purposes exceeds $49,430 each quarter ($197,720 annualised), your employer makes your SG contributions on the basis of the maximum contribution base. The maximum contribution base is adjusted each year in line with increases in average wages. See my website, SuperGuide (www.superguide.com.au), for details on the maximum contribution base for later years.

If you believe your employer hasn't paid your SG, or hasn't paid the right amount, you can ask that your employer pay your SG contributions. If your employer fails to pay your SG, contact the ATO to investigate your concerns. You can phone the ATO Superannuation Infoline on 13 10 20 for help.

Getting Serious about Super Contributions

Creating a suitably sized retirement nest egg isn't an impossible task, but doing so does require you to make a conscious decision to get serious about your retirement planning and tax planning.

The message is very clear: If you want a comfortable retirement, you have to plan for it (for info on deciding on the lifestyle you want in retirement, refer to Chapter 3), make super contributions and take an active interest in your super savings and other investments.

While you're accumulating superannuation savings before you retire, your superannuation contributions (plus earnings on those contributions) are the lifeblood of your DIY super account. The effects of compound earnings combined with regular contributions to your super fund over many years can have a dramatic effect on your final retirement balance. The key feature of *compound earnings* is that you earn returns on your reinvested earnings, creating greater wealth. (In Part IV of this book, I explore the issues that you may face when investing your SMSF monies.)

The federal government also provides tax incentives to encourage you to contribute to your super fund, which means you can often save tax while boosting your super savings. The fanciest carrot of all dangling from the government's super tray of incentives is the promise of tax-free super for over-60s in retirement (for more information on tax-free super benefits, see Chapters 13 and 19).

Understanding the two types of contributions

You can make two types of superannuation contributions — concessional (before-tax) contributions and non-concessional (after-tax) contributions — to your super fund. Inconveniently, they sound the same, but they're two very different types of contributions.

I explain the two types of super contributions here:

✔ **Concessional contributions:** *Concessional contributions* are before-tax super contributions that provide a tax concession for the individual (or company) making the super contribution. Any concessional contributions are subject to 15 per cent tax within the super fund: This tax is commonly known as *contributions tax*. (Individuals who earn an adjusted taxable income of more than $300,000 a year pay an additional 15 per cent tax on concessional contributions.) You reduce salary or other income (or, in relation to SG, your employer reduces its income) by making that contribution, which in turn means you're subject to less tax overall, if your highest rate of income tax (marginal tax rate) is greater than the tax rate on super. If you're self-employed or not employed, you may consider making concessional contributions that you can then claim as a tax deduction against your income. Before-tax contributions such as your employer's SG contributions (refer to the section 'Superannuation Guarantee — Compulsory Super', earlier in this chapter), your personal tax-deductible contributions and salary sacrificed contributions are considered concessional contributions. I explain how the rules for concessional contributions work, including a special contributions tax refund for lower-income earners, in the section 'Making Before-Tax Contributions — Concessional', later in the chapter.

✔ **Non-concessional contributions:** After-tax contributions are officially known as *non-concessional contributions*. You may also hear them called *undeducted contributions*. Such contributions are called after-tax or non-concessional because you haven't claimed a tax deduction, or received any other type of tax concession, before making these contributions. The contribution is sourced from your after-tax income, which means the full contribution reaches your superannuation account — that is, no 'contributions' tax is deducted. I explain how you can make the most of after-tax contributions in the section 'Making After-Tax Contributions — Non-Concessional', later in the chapter.

Each type of super contribution is subject to an upper limit, known as a contributions cap. A *contributions cap* sets a limit on the amount of contributions you can make in any one year, before your contributions are potentially subject to penalty tax. If you exceed the cap, your excess contributions must be withdrawn from your super fund, or your excess contributions will be subject to penalty tax.

Instead of scaring you off from making super contributions with premature talk of penalty tax (I explain what can happen to excess contributions later in the chapter), the next few sections explain how you can make super contributions.

Business as usual for under-65s

Australians are able to make superannuation contributions until they reach age 75. Anyone under the age of 65 can make super contributions, regardless of whether they're working, retired, unemployed, bringing up children full-time, suffering an illness, or taking a long holiday.

When a person turns 65, however, they must satisfy a work test before a super fund will accept their super contributions. I explain the contributions work test applicable to individuals aged 65 years or over in the next section.

Different rules for over-64s

If you plan to make super contributions on or after reaching the age of 65, then you must satisfy a work test before contributing.

The work test for over-64s is subject to a precise definition: You must be gainfully employed on at least a part-time basis, according to the Superannuation Industry (Supervision) Regulations 1994 (SIS Regulations). What this means is that you must work for at least 40 hours in a period of not more than 30 consecutive days in the *financial year* in which you plan to make a super contribution. In Australia, the financial year runs from 1 July through to 30 June of the following calendar year.

If you're aged 65 or over, and you plan to contribute to your super fund, you must be 'gainfully employed'. The SIS Regulations define *gainful employment* to be employment or self-employment for 'gain' or 'reward' in any business, trade, profession, vocation, calling, occupation or employment. *Gain or reward* means that you receive some form of remuneration such as salary, wages, business income, bonuses, commissions or fees in return for your personal exertion.

You can satisfy the work test for any activity where you receive remuneration. This can include, for example, babysitting, lawn mowing, consulting, paid employment, cleaning, gardening, delivering advertising material to letterboxes, running a business and consulting — but not voluntary work. Any income that you receive for this work must be fully documented and declared for tax purposes.

No voluntary contributions for over-74s

The federal government places an age limit on Australians who can make contributions to super. For policy reasons, the government has decided that the age of 75 is the age that voluntary contributions to a super fund aren't for retirement purposes, but simply for estate planning purposes. However, your super fund is able to accept your contributions until the 28th day of the month after you turn 75, subject to satisfying the contributions work test.

To TFN or not to TFN

If your super fund doesn't have your individual tax file number (TFN) recorded, your employer's Superannuation Guarantee (SG) contributions are subject to an additional tax of 34 per cent (including Medicare levy), which, when added to the 15 per cent contributions tax, takes the total tax grab to 47 per cent plus 2 per cent Medicare levy. The top marginal tax rate of 47 per cent drops to 45 per cent from 1 July 2017.

Without your TFN, your voluntary concessional (before-tax) contributions, such as salary-sacrificed contributions, are also hit with this hefty tax. Your super fund cannot

accept the government's Low Income Super Contribution (LISC) without your TFN. The LISC is a refund of contributions tax payable to individuals earning less than $37,000 a year, and is payable for the 2014–15, 2015–16 and 2016–17 financial years.

Further, if your SMSF doesn't have your TFN, you can't make non-concessional (after-tax) contributions to your SMSF, or receive the government's tax-free co-contribution (if eligible). Since you run your own super fund, providing your individual TFN to your SMSF should be straightforward.

Since July 2013, an employer is still required to make Superannuation Guarantee contributions, and contributions required under an industrial award, for eligible employees aged 75 or over. However, although *you* can't make voluntary contributions to a super fund after turning 75, you can transfer super benefits from one super fund to another fund, including to a SMSF, after reaching the age of 75.

Making Before-Tax Contributions — Concessional

Concessional contributions can include your employer's compulsory SG contributions (refer to the section 'Superannuation Guarantee — Compulsory Super', earlier in the chapter), additional employer contributions such as salary-sacrificed contributions, and tax-deductible contributions made by self-employed individuals.

Concessional contributions (before-tax contributions) can be an attractive retirement savings strategy for Australians on middle and higher incomes because the maximum tax that you pay on concessional contributions is 15 cents in the dollar, unless your adjusted taxable income is more than $300,000 a year and then the tax on your super contributions is 30 cents in the dollar. (See Chapter 13 for more info on contribution taxes and other super taxes).

If you pay more than 15 per cent income tax on your personal income, then concessional contributions can be a tax-effective option. Concessional contributions are reduced by a 15 per cent 'contributions' tax upon entry to the super fund, instead of having that before-tax money taxed at your marginal tax rate. Your marginal tax rate is the highest rate of income tax that you pay on your income, which can be zero, 19 per cent, 32.5 per cent, 37 per cent or 47 per cent, plus Medicare levy. The top marginal tax rate reverts to 45 per cent, plus Medicare levy, from July 2017.

For a limited time, concessional contributions may also be tax-effective, or tax neutral, when you pay less than 15 per cent tax on personal income. For the four financial years from 2012–13 to 2016–17 years, the federal government will be paying a Low Income Super Contribution (LISC) into the super accounts of individuals earning less than $37,000 a year. The LISC is a refund of up to $500 of the contributions tax deducted from concessional contributions for eligible Australians. I explain the LISC in more detail on my website, SuperGuide (www.superguide.com.au).

If your employer pays SG contributions on your behalf, and you plan to make voluntary concessional contributions, you need to understand how the concessional contributions caps operate in order to avoid unnecessary extra tax, or unnecessary administrative hassle.

If the concessional contributions you make for the financial year exceed the annual concessional contributions cap, then you will usually end up paying income tax on the excess contributions, rather than extra contributions tax (for more info on how excess concessional contributions are treated, see the next section).

If the concessional cap fits ...

Australians are entitled to make concessional super contributions worth up to $30,000 (for the 2014–15 year) before they need to worry about excess contributions, although over-50s have access to a higher limit, as shown in Table 4-2. The $30,000 limit is known as the *general concessional cap*.

If you're aged 50 or over, you have access to a *concessional contributions cap for older Australians*, which means you can make up to $35,000 in concessional (before-tax) contributions during a financial year without worrying about excess contributions, although this higher cap is only temporary. You are eligible for the higher cap of $35,000 for a financial year (1 July to 30 June) if you are 49 years or older on the last day of the previous financial year. For example, for the 2015–16 financial year, if you're aged 49 years or over on 30 June 2015, then your concessional cap is $35,000 for the financial year running from July 2015 to June 2016.

The higher cap for older Australians of $35,000 is unindexed, and also temporary. When the general concessional cap (currently for under-50s) increases to $35,000, the higher cap for older Australians will no longer apply — one concessional cap will apply for all Australians.

Effective from July 2014, the general concessional cap increased from $25,000 to $30,000. The general cap is indexed in line with *average weekly ordinary times earnings* (*AWOTE*) and the general cap only increases in $5,000 increments. Based on recent trends in AWOTE, you can expect the general concessional cap to increase to $35,000 from July 2018 or July 2019, depending on how fast wages increase during that time. When the general concessional cap increases to $35,000, the over-50s cap will no longer be applicable.

For information on the general concessional cap for the years following 2015–16, visit my SuperGuide website (www.superguide.com.au).

Table 4-2	Concessional Contributions Cap	
Financial Year	*General Concessional Cap*	*Higher Concessional Cap for Older Australians (over-49s)*
2014–15	$30,000	$35,000
2015–16	$30,000	$35,000

Note: You are eligible for the higher concessional cap for older Australians for a financial year if you were aged 49 years or older on 30 June of the previous financial year. For confirmation of the concessional contributions cap for the 2015–16 year and indexed caps for later years, visit the ATO Superannuation website (www.ato.gov.au/super), or visit SuperGuide at www.superguide.com.au.

Your employer's SG contributions, salary sacrifice and personal tax-deductible contributions also count towards your concessional contributions cap.

If you exceed your concessional (before-tax) contributions cap, your excess contributions will count towards your assessable income and be subject to your marginal tax rate, plus you will incur an *excess concessional contributions charge* (*ECCC*) to recognise that you're paying income tax on the excess contributions at a later date than other income. You'll also receive a 15 per cent tax offset to account for the 15 per cent contributions tax already paid on the excess contributions within your super fund.

You have two choices in how you deal with the excess concessional super contributions: You can have up to 85 per cent of the excess concessional contributions returned to you (the remaining 15 per cent of the contribution has been deducted as contributions tax), which can help you pay the extra income tax. Or, you can keep the super contributions within the super fund, and instead pay the additional income tax from your personal savings. I explain how the excess contributions rules operate in the sidebar 'Nightmare on super street: Excess contributions', later in the chapter.

If you retain the excess concessional contributions in your super fund, note that those concessional contributions will then also count towards your non-concessional (after-tax) contributions cap (see the section 'Making After-Tax Contributions — Non-Concessional'). If you withdraw the excess concessional contributions, then they will not count towards your concessional cap, and nor will they then count towards your non-concessional contributions cap.

Taking advantage of salary sacrifice

For many employees, a salary sacrifice arrangement is a popular option. A *salary sacrifice arrangement* means including concessional (before-tax) super contributions as part of your salary package, which then reduces your taxable salary while increasing your super savings.

Contrary to the literal meaning of the term 'salary sacrifice', you're not truly sacrificing any salary when you have a salary sacrifice arrangement in place (although your SG entitlements may be affected by the reduction of salary). Your salary is reduced, at least on paper, for the purposes of paying less income tax, and the portion of your salary that you're not paying income tax on is redirected to your super fund. These super contributions are treated as employer contributions and, like all concessional contributions, are subject to a contributions tax of 15 per cent (or 30 per cent if you earn an adjusted taxable income of more than $300,000), rather than your marginal tax rate.

A salary sacrifice arrangement is a contractual agreement with your employer to adjust your salary package. You trade part of your future salary or wages for an additional concessional (before-tax) superannuation contribution. Any salary sacrifice arrangement that you agree to can only relate to future salary — that is, salary that you're still to earn. You can also salary sacrifice performance bonuses if the agreement regarding your salary sacrifice is entered into before you become entitled to your performance bonus.

Other tax-deductible contributions

If you don't have an employer, or your employment income represents only a small part (less than 10 per cent) of your total income, you may be able to claim a tax deduction for your super contributions.

If you're self-employed or not employed, you can claim a tax deduction for super contributions. Ordinarily, you can claim a tax deduction for personal super contributions under one of the following circumstances:

- ✔ You're self-employed and not working under a contract principally for your labour
- ✔ You're not employed; for example, you're a full-time investor
- ✔ You satisfy the 'maximum earnings as an employee' condition

To meet the *maximum earnings as an employee* condition, you can receive part of your income as an employee, but less than 10 per cent of your 'total income' (that is, assessable income, plus reportable fringe benefits plus 'reportable employer super contributions') from employment as an employee. *Assessable income* is generally gross income before any tax deductions are allowed, and includes salary and wages, dividends, interest distributions from partnerships or trusts, business income (including personal services income), rent, foreign source income and net capital gains. *Reportable employer super contributions* are non-compulsory employer contributions that the employee is capable of influencing, such as salary sacrifice contributions or other discretionary employer contributions. Compulsory SG contributions do not count towards 'total income' for the 10 per cent rule.

Tax-deductible super contributions and other concessional contributions are subject to 15 per cent contributions tax within a super fund (and 30 per cent tax is imposed on your concessional contributions if you earn an adjusted taxable income of more than $300,000 a year). If you pay more than 15 cents in the dollar in income tax, then claiming a tax deduction for super contributions can be tax effective for many taxpayers.

Before making any super contributions, check with your accountant or the ATO to confirm your eligibility for claiming a tax deduction. For example, an individual under the age of 18 years can claim a tax deduction for super contributions only where his or her income is derived from carrying out a business or, in certain circumstances, from being an employee.

If you wish to claim a tax deduction for a super contribution, you must notify your super fund in writing. As both a trustee and member of a SMSF, it may seem silly to have to formally notify yourself of the intention to claim a deduction, but you must always remember that you're wearing two hats — member and trustee (to understand the SMSF trustee role, see Chapters 8 and 9). Theoretically, the trustee (you) isn't aware of your intention to claim a tax deduction for your contributions until you inform the trustee.

You must lodge a *Notice of intent to claim a tax deduction for super contributions or vary a previous notice* (section 290-170 notice) with your SMSF. You can obtain copies of the notice and instructions on how to complete the notice, from the ATO (publication number NAT 71121). You must receive acknowledgment of receipt of the notice from your SMSF (you) before you lodge your individual income tax return. The trustee (you) then uses the notice, to determine the treatment of the contributions for benefit component purposes, and to report the nature of the contributions in the SMSF's annual return. (I explain lodging your fund's annual return in Chapter 12.)

Splitting contributions with your spouse

Depending on the rules of your SMSF, you may be able to split your future concessional contributions with your spouse. Splittable contributions include both your employer's SG contributions and your voluntary concessional contributions. Typically, one spouse makes the super contribution, which is then split and paid into two separate super accounts after deducting the contributions tax. The contribution that you split counts towards your concessional contributions cap, not your spouse's cap, and you spouse must be under the age of 65. You can find more info about splitting super contributions with your spouse on the ATO website (www.ato.gov.au/super) or on my website, SuperGuide (www.superguide.com.au).

Splitting super contributions is not the same concept as splitting super benefits, which can only be done when a couple separates. (For more info on what happens to super benefits when a couple divorces or separates, see Chapter 23.)

Making After-Tax Contributions — Non-Concessional

When you make non-concessional (after-tax) contributions, you place money in an environment where earnings are ordinarily taxed at a much lower rate than would be the case for earnings outside the super fund. Super fund earnings are taxed up to 15 per cent (see Chapters 13 and 18) compared to marginal income tax rates of up to 47 per cent plus Medicare levy on individual earnings outside the super environment. The top marginal tax rate reverts to 45 per cent plus Medicare levy from July 2017.

You can make up to $180,000 (indexed) (for the 2014–15 year) in non-concessional contributions each year — officially called the *non-concessional contributions cap* — to your super fund, before you need to worry about the excess contributions rules.

Nightmare on super street: Excess contributions

Since 1 July 2013, if you exceed your concessional or non-concessional cap, the consequences are generally administrative inconvenience and a small financial charge. Before July 2013, the consequences of exceeding one or both caps could be financially devastating.

If you exceeded your concessional cap for the 2012–13 year, or earlier years, then your excess concessional contributions were hit with excess contributions tax of 31.5 per cent, in addition to the usual 15 per cent contributions tax payable on the contributions.

The government did show some mercy after much complaining from the super industry and complaints from commentators like myself, by allowing a first-offence waiver. From 1 July 2011 and until 30 June 2013, individuals who exceeded the concessional contributions cap by up to $10,000 could request that the excess contributions were refunded to them. You could only seek a refund if you had exceeded the concessional cap for the first time, and you exceeded the cap by no more than $10,000.

Another sting for the super saver is that those excess concessional contributions also count towards your non-concessional (after-tax) cap. Before July 2013, if you exceeded your non-concessional contributions cap, the excess contributions were hit with the top

marginal tax rate plus Medicare levy (which was a total of 46.5 per cent), even when your marginal tax rate was much lower.

Today, the consequences of exceeding your concessional cap involve extra income tax rather than onerous penalty tax. Your excess contributions will count towards your assessable income and you will have to pay income tax on those contributions since they are treated as part of your regular income. You will also incur an excess concessional contributions charge to recognise the delay in paying income tax on this income.

More good news is that since 1 July 2013, excess non-concessional contributions can now be withdrawn from a super fund without financial penalty, although the super fund earnings associated with those excess contributions count towards your assessable income and will be subject to your marginal tax rate. However, if you choose to leave your excess non-concessional contributions within your super fund, then your super contributions made on or after 1 July 2014 will be subject to the top marginal tax rate (47 per cent plus Medicare levy of 2 per cent) even when your marginal tax is lower.

You can find more information about excess contributions and the contributions caps on my SuperGuide website (www.superguide.com.au).

The annual non-concessional (after-tax) contributions cap of $180,000 (for the 2014–15 year) is to remain fixed at six times the ongoing concessional (before-tax) contributions cap. What this 'fixing' means is that the after-tax cap increases only when the concessional contributions cap increases.

If you earn less than $18,200 in a year (or $20,542 when you take into account the low income tax offset), you have no real income tax advantages when investing via a superannuation fund, unless you're eligible to take advantage of the government's co-contribution scheme. Under the co-contribution scheme, the federal government places up to $500 of tax-free super money into your super fund when you make up to a $1,000 non-concessional contribution, and you satisfy the eligibility rules. I explain how you can take advantage of this scheme in the section 'Cashing in on co-contributions', later in the chapter. If you earn less than $37,000, you may also be eligible for the Low Income Super Contribution, which involves the government refunding up to $500 of the contributions tax deducted from your, or your employer's, concessional contributions (for more details on this low income contributions tax refund, see my SuperGuide website at www.superguide.com.au).

Using the bring-forward rule

If you're under the age of 65, you have some flexibility in how you make the most of the annual $180,000 (for the 2014–15 year) non-concessional contributions cap. You can bring forward up to two years' worth of contributions, which allows you to make up to $540,000 at any time, over a three-year period, including $540,000 in one year, although the opportunity only triggers when you contribute more than $180,000 in the first year, as shown in Table 4-3. This is called a _bring forward,_ using the bring-forward rule, which is explained in this section.

Anyone under the age of 65 on 1 July of a financial year can take advantage of the bring-forward rule during that financial year even if they make the super contributions after turning 65. In Australia, a financial year runs from 1 July through to 30 June.

If you were under 65 on the 1 July of a financial year, but you intend to make a super contribution during that financial year and after turning 65, you can still take advantage of the bring-forward rule for that year if you satisfy a work test before making the super contribution. You must work for at least 40 hours in a period of not more than 30 consecutive days in the financial year in which you plan to make the super contribution. For more details about the work test, refer to the section 'Different rules for over-64s', earlier in the chapter.

Table 4-3	How the Bring-Forward Rule Works			
Contributions in …	*2014–15 Year*	*2015–16 Year*	*2016–17 Year*	*2017–18 Year*
Example 1	$540,000	–	–	$180,000
Example 2	$200,000	$200,000	$140,000	$180,000
Example 3	$540,000	–	–	$540,000
Example 4	$360,000	$180,000	–	$180,000

Note: The table assumes that the non-concessional contributions cap remains at $180,000 for the 2017–18 year, although average wage increases may trigger a lifting of the cap by 2017–18 to $210,000, but this is unlikely. As soon as you trigger a bring forward, you can't take advantage of any increase in the non-concessional cap that takes place while that bring forward is in operation.

You can't play catch-up with the bring-forward rule if you fail to utilise your non-concessional cap for one or more years. A bring forward can relate only to contributions for two future years, not past years.

The annual non-concessional (after-tax) contributions cap applies to each person. A couple has the potential to make non-concessional contributions of up to $360,000 (indexed) ($180,000 each) every year. Under the bring-forward rule, a couple can make up to $1,080,000 (indexed) in non-concessional contributions in one year, every three years, based on the $180,000 cap applicable for the 2014–15 year.

When you contribute more than $180,000 in non-concessional contributions in one year, you automatically trigger the bring-forward rule for the following two years (refer to Examples 1, 2 and 4 in Table 4-3), assuming you are under the age of 65 on 1 July of the financial year in which you're contributing.

For instance, if you make a $540,000 non-concessional (after-tax) contribution to your super fund during the 2014–15 year, say on 1 May 2015, you're bringing forward two years of contributions for the purposes of the non-concessional contributions cap (refer to Examples 1 and 3 in Table 4-3). If you make a $360,000 after-tax contribution during the 2014–15 year, say on 1 May 2015, that brings forward one year of contributions, and it means you trigger the bring-forward rule for the next two years (refer to Example 4 in Table 4-3).

If you make non-concessional (after-tax) contributions that exceed yourannual non-concessional contributions cap of $180,000 (for the 2014–15 year) (if age 65 or over) or your $540,000 bring-forward limit (if under 65), the excess contributions can now be withdrawn from your

---

Aged 63 or 64 and about to retire?

If you're aged 63 or 64, you can take advantage of the bring-forward rule without satisfying the over-65 work test rules (refer to the section 'Different rules for over-64s', earlier in the chapter) that normally apply to contributions that cover future years. For example, John is 63 and decides to bring forward his annual non-concessional contributions cap. He makes a $540,000 after-tax contribution. Although the contribution partly represents his cap for a period of time when John is 65, he doesn't have to satisfy a work test before contributing, because the contribution is made while he is under the age of 65.

---

super fund, and earnings associated with the excess contributions are included in your personal income and taxed at your marginal tax rate. If you choose to retain the excess contributions within your super fund, then your excess contributions will be subject to the top marginal tax rate of 47 per cent plus Medicare levy, and 45 per cent plus Medicare levy from July 2017. The harsh approach taken to excess non-concessional contributions retained in a super fund is similar to the tough rules that were in place before July 2013 (refer sidebar 'Nightmare on super street: excess contributions', earlier in the chapter).

Cashing in on co-contributions

The federal government's super co-contribution scheme makes non-concessional (after-tax) contributions more attractive for those earning less than $49,488 (for the 2014–15 year). The grand plan behind the government's super co-contribution scheme is to encourage those on lower and middle incomes to save for their retirement. Depending on how much income you earn in a year, your super balance can receive a boost of up to $500 as a tax-free government co-contribution when you make a non-concessional contribution of up to $1,000.

To be eligible for the tax-free co-contribution, you must be aged 70 or under at the end of the income year (financial year) in which you make the after-tax (non-concessional) contribution.

Do you want a guaranteed 50 per cent return?

Think about this option. Before your super contribution is even invested, you earn 50 cents for every dollar that you contribute. That figure represents a 50 per cent return on the contribution before you invest the money.

Here's how the co-contribution works:

- ✔ For those earning less than $34,488 (for the 2014–15 year), the government promises to co-contribute 50 cents tax-free for every after-tax dollar an individual contributes to a super fund, up to a maximum of $500. In other words, if you contribute $1,000, you get a $500 freebie from the government. If you make a $500 contribution, the government pays $250 into your super fund.

- ✔ If your assessable income (plus reportable fringe benefits plus reportable employer super contributions) is more than $34,488 (for the 2014–15 year), your co-contribution entitlement reduces by 3.33 cents for every dollar you earn over $34,488, until it cuts out entirely at $49,488. For example, if you earn $40,000 and you make a $1,000 non-concessional super contribution, the government's maximum contribution of $500 is reduced by $182, giving you a co-contribution of $318. Remember, reportable employer super contributions are non-compulsory employer contributions that the employee is capable of influencing, such as salary sacrifice contributions or other discretionary employer contributions.

You must receive a portion of your income from work as an employee, or from self-employment, to take advantage of the super co-contribution scheme. You may not be eligible if you're unemployed, taking time out from the workforce or a full-time investor.

To qualify for a co-contribution, you must also earn 10 per cent or more of your total income from work as an employee, or from carrying on a business, or from a combination of both. Business income includes income from any profession, trade, gainful employment or vocation. The income used for testing against the income threshold of $49,488 (for determining the amount of co-contribution) is net business income, while the income used for the 10 per cent work test (for determining eligibility for co-contribution) is gross business income.

Receiving your bonus contribution

Your SMSF must include in the fund's annual return (see Chapter 12) the details of all contributions made to the fund. You don't receive your co-contribution until the ATO processes your super fund's return for the year, and the ATO receives and processes your individual tax return for the year in which you make your non-concessional (after-tax) contribution. The co-contribution should be paid into your super account within 60 days of the ATO receiving both your tax return and your super fund's return. You can also expect to receive a letter from the ATO explaining your co-contribution payment.

If you want to take advantage of the super co-contribution scheme, you can find out more by phoning the ATO Superannuation Infoline on 13 10 20 or by visiting the ATO website (www.ato.gov.au/super), or by visiting my SuperGuide website (www.superguide.com.au).

Contributing for your spouse may earn a rebate

Another small opportunity when making super contributions is the possibility of claiming a tax offset by making a non-concessional contribution to your spouse's super fund account. If eligible, you can claim the *spouse super contributions tax offset*, which means you can claim an 18 per cent tax offset for non-concessional contributions of up to $3,000 made on behalf of your spouse. Your spouse can be a de facto partner, including same-sex partner. Your spouse must be earning an adjusted income of no more than $13,800 in a financial year, and the maximum offset of $540 is payable when your spouse earns $10,800 or less. For more information about this offset, see the ATO website (www.ato.gov.au/super).

Special Contribution Rules

Every rule generally has an exception and the super contribution rules are no exception — pardon the pun. Three of the most significant exceptions or qualifications to the contributions rules are

- ✔ Additional non-concessional contribution limit for some small business capital gains
- ✔ No limit on contributions sourced from settlements for suffering personal injury
- ✔ Special rules for certain transfers of overseas benefits

The general rule that applies when making non-concessional (after-tax) contributions is: For the 2014–15 year, individuals can contribute no more than $180,000 (indexed) a year, or $540,000 (indexed) when using the bring-forward rules. Two exceptions apply, however: If you run a small business or if you receive a settlement for suffering personal injury, you may be able to contribute additional after-tax money into your super fund. I explain these two exceptions in more detail in the next sections.

If you plan to transfer a superannuation benefit from an overseas fund into your SMSF, your benefit may be subject to tax, or subject to the non-concessional contributions cap. I recommend you talk to an adviser (to source one, see Chapter 5) who understands the requirements for such transfers. You can find more information about transfers from overseas on the ATO website, and on my website, SuperGuide (www.superguide.com.au).

Running a business

When you run a business, you may be eligible for an additional lifetime limit of $1.355 million (for the 2014–15 year) in non-concessional (after-tax) contributions, from the disposal of qualifying small-business assets. This additional limit is officially known as the *capital gains tax cap* (*CGT cap*).

The rationale behind this additional $1.355 million (indexed) limit for small business is that many self-employed people choose to build up the value of their business as a way of providing for their retirement, rather than contributing to a super fund. If you're eligible for certain small business CGT exemptions, you can access the CGT cap. I explain the main small business CGT exemptions, called small business entity concessions, in Chapter 13.

Before, or when, you make the super contribution, you must formally notify your super fund that you plan to take advantage of the CGT cap. Notification ensures the contribution is reported against your CGT cap and not against your regular non-concessional (after-tax) contributions cap.

Talk to an independent adviser who understands the super and tax rules before you take advantage of the CGT cap. The eligibility rules for the CGT cap are strict and can be complex, and a good independent adviser (for help finding one, see Chapter 5) can provide expert advice in this area.

Suffering permanent disability

If you receive a settlement from a personal injury claim, you may be able to contribute that settlement as an after-tax contribution in addition to the annual $180,000 (indexed) non-concessional cap or bring-forward cap of $540,000 (indexed) (applicable for the 2014–15 financial year).

Non-concessional (after-tax) contributions that are sourced from personal injury claims aren't subject to contribution limits. Two legally qualified medical practitioners, however, must certify that, as a result of the injury, you're unlikely ever to be gainfully employed in a capacity for which you're reasonably qualified.

The non-concessional contributions from a personal injury payment must be part of a structured settlement, or an order for a personal injury payment, or a lump sum workers compensation payment. You must also notify your super fund, using a special ATO form, that you're making the contribution under the personal injury payment exemption before, or when, making the contribution. You can obtain a copy of the form *Contributions for personal injury* (NAT 71162), from the ATO website (www.ato.gov.au) or by phoning the ATO on 13 10 20.

If you receive a settlement for suffering personal injury, talk to an independent adviser who understands the super and tax rules.

Investigating Asset Contributions to Your SMSF

Money, that is, hard cash, isn't the only contribution that you can make to your SMSF — you can contribute investments to your fund as well. Making a contribution to a super fund in the form of an asset is known as an *in specie contribution*.

In most cases, your fund can't normally purchase or use an asset that a fund member owns (see Chapter 15 for special investment rules), and this restriction would normally cover in specie contributions. Fortunately for members of SMSFs, specific exceptions to this general restriction apply.

For the time being, you have a lot of flexibility in the type of investments you can transfer as contributions to your DIY super fund. These include:

✔ Listed shares, debentures and options

✔ Interests in managed funds

✔ An office or factory, or any other business real property

✔ Farm property

Your fund's trust deed (for information about SMSF trust deeds, see Chapter 7) must permit in specie contributions, and you can choose to make concessional (before-tax) or non-concessional (after-tax) contributions as in specie contributions. Any contribution that you choose to make, however, is still subject to the contributions caps (refer to the sections 'If the concessional cap fits ...' and 'Making After-Tax Contributions — Non-Concessional', earlier in the chapter).

If you transfer an asset into your SMSF, you need to be mindful that such a transfer is considered a change of ownership and may trigger the capital gains tax (CGT) rules for your personal tax situation. The value of an in specie contribution is deemed to be whatever the market value of that asset is at the time of transferring the asset into your SMSF. If the asset transfer triggers a profit on the sale of the asset, you may have to pay income tax on the capital gain. The tax liability is your personal liability and not your SMSF's tax bill. Depending on the size of your potential tax bill, you can offset all or part of your CGT liability by making concessional (before-tax) superannuation contributions in the year that you incur the CGT.

A popular strategy to minimise a CGT bill is to reduce any tax on capital gains by treating the transfer as a concessional (before-tax) contribution rather than as a non-concessional (after-tax) contribution, or rather than as a direct purchase of an asset by your SMSF. The most common version of this strategy is where you make substantial tax-deductible contributions (assuming you're eligible to make such contributions and subject to the concessional contributions cap) in the year when you realise significant taxable capital gains.

Note: You can only claim deductions for super contributions against assessable income (such as employment or business income, investment income and taxable capital gains).

Chapter 5

Getting the Right DIY Super Advice

Most Australians seek some type of professional advice at different stages in their life — they may visit doctors for medical conditions, lawyers for estate planning and property conveyancing, and accountants for tax advice.

An increasing number of Australians now recognise that when planning for retirement, they may need an expert eye to review their savings plans. If you're running a self-managed super fund (SMSF), you're more likely than most to seek out experts to assist you with your retirement planning — including planning for what happens to your savings after you're gone (for information on looking after your family, see Chapter 24). I cover your main advice options in this chapter.

Keeping It Clear and Simple

Superannuation has a lot of complicated rules, but the principles behind super are simple — money goes into your DIY super account, your fund trustees (you!) invest that money and your account balance grows over time. On retirement, you receive a lump sum or, more likely, a superannuation pension (for details about the pension phase, see Chapters 21 and 22), which you hope is enough for you to live on.

The ultimate aim when running your SMSF is to deliver your fund members (including you) a reliable income in retirement, while ensuring you follow the super and tax rules.

You can make this task easier by maximising your tax advantages and ensuring your money is invested in assets that grow in value over time. You also want your SMSF to be a cost-effective retirement savings option (I discuss how much a DIY super fund costs in Chapter 6). Getting the right advice can help you achieve this goal.

Keep those simple principles in mind when you next chat to your financial adviser, lawyer, accountant or fund administrator. A *fund administrator* is a service provider that the trustees of a SMSF can appoint to manage the administration, compliance and, usually, the reporting requirements of the fund.

Getting On the Super Soapbox — Independent Advice

The term 'independent' is used a lot in the financial services industry, often inappropriately. I've met very few individuals in the industry who are truly independent — they can't afford to be because they have to make a living by providing you with a service or by selling you something.

What everyone means when they talk about 'independence' in the financial services industry is that the expert you're relying on is working for *you* only rather than a financial product provider, who may be paying the adviser's wages, or providing the adviser with incentives to sell selected products developed by the financial product provider.

In my experience, the level of independence of an adviser or expert is an inverse relationship to the complexity of the advice or products being offered. What I mean by this line of comparison is that, as a rough rule: The more an advising firm confuses clients by offering complex investment products, the less likely that firm is independent.

Only a special category of financial adviser can call herself an independent adviser. According to the *Corporations Act 2001*, a self-described independent adviser must operate free from restrictions and conflicts (relationships or associations) relating to the financial products she recommends, or financial services that she provides. According to section 923A of the *Corporations*

Act 2001, a licensed financial adviser (or her representative) can only call herself 'independent' or 'impartial' or 'unbiased' when the financial adviser does *not* receive any of the following:

- ✔ Commissions (apart from commissions that are rebated in full to the adviser's clients)

- ✔ Volume-based remuneration (that is, forms of remuneration calculated on the basis of the volume of business placed by the person with the issuer of a financial product)

- ✔ Other gifts or benefits from an issuer of a financial product that may reasonably be expected to influence the financial adviser

Based on statistics released by the Financial System Inquiry during 2014, only 15 per cent of financial advisers are fully independent (under the *Corporations Act 2001* definition). That is, the other 85 per cent of financial advisers are aligned with financial institutions, banks and other wealth managers. When you take into account that Australia has around 18,000 financial advisers, this means only around 2,700 Australian advisers are in a position to call themselves independent.

Financial advisers who are considered independent under the *Corporations Act 2001* may still be able to charge asset-based fees, although this issue is contentious within the financial planning industry. Asset-based fees are charged on the premise that the more money you have invested, the more your adviser can charge for his or her services, even if no more time or expertise is involved in providing you with advice. One section of the financial advising industry believes that independent financial advisers should only charge a fee for services rendered, rather than charge asset-based fees.

According to the Independent Financial Advisers Association of Australia (IFAAA), a financial adviser can only pass the IFAAA's Gold Standard of Independence if the financial adviser:

- ✔ Isn't affiliated with a product manufacturer, namely, a bank, insurance company or investment company

- ✔ Doesn't receive commissions or incentive payments of any sort, including insurance commissions, unless the adviser refunds these amounts to the client

- ✔ Doesn't charge asset-based fees; that is, a fee based on a percentage of client assets under advice, or under management

Retirement planning is about strategies and tax management rather than financial products. However, the implementation of any retirement plan usually involves actual investments, including where applicable, financial products. Check that your adviser appreciates the difference between a retirement plan and recommending financial products.

I believe an independent, qualified financial adviser focused on the best interests of the client, along with excellent tax advice from an accountant, can be valuable partners for any individual or family creating a long-term wealth creation plan. For more info about what independent advice means, and how to find an independent adviser, see my website, SuperGuide (www.superguide.com.au).

Who Can Give Advice about DIY Super Funds?

The comforting but, sometimes, annoying feature of running a SMSF is that if any aspect of running your own fund is too difficult — administration, investment, financial reporting — you can bet an expert is at the ready to take the hassle of that work off your hands — for a price. Experts who can help you establish and run your SMSF include accountants, licensed financial advisers, lawyers, insurance brokers (for arranging life insurance cover) and stockbrokers (for buying and selling shares).

My suggestion to you is this: Be very clear about what type of advice you need for your SMSF. Under no circumstances allow an adviser or product promoter to bamboozle you with package deals, with free this and free that and slick promotions (such as free overseas travel, as one recently demised financial planning firm offered to selected clients). Ah ... so you're trying to guess which firm I'm referring to? Okay, here's a clue — the fallout from the firm's collapse was certainly not a storm in a teacup.

If you rely on experts when running your fund, what you need from them is specialist assistance when making decisions, such as advice when

- ✔ Setting up your DIY super fund (see Part II)
- ✔ Making decisions about your fund's compliance and reporting obligations (see Chapters 11 and 12)
- ✔ Considering the tax consequences of your super contributions and fund investment decisions (see Chapters 4, 13 and 18)
- ✔ Drafting your fund's investment strategy (see Chapters 14 and 15)

✔ Choosing specific investments (see Part IV)

✔ Considering taking a superannuation pension — also known as a superannuation income stream (see Chapters 21 and 22)

✔ Planning for what happens to your super after you die (see Chapter 24)

Under the super rules, you must appoint an approved SMSF auditor to conduct your SMSF's annual audit. You may also need to use an *actuary* (a specialist who evaluates superannuation risks and opportunities using financial analysis) when you start taking a superannuation pension — where you continue contributing to your fund while taking a pension from that fund and you don't separate the assets financing your pension. For this, your fund must obtain an actuarial certificate. The actuary provides an *actuarial certificate* that confirms your fund's annual return on investments, and what proportion of those investments and returns relate to assets financing your pension. I discuss the role of auditors in the section 'Appointing an auditor', later in this chapter, and explore actuaries and pensions in Chapter 22.

If you're planning to set up a SMSF, find an adviser who is knowledgeable on SMSFs and can structure your financial affairs, and can assess the viability of a SMSF — from both a tax and retirement perspective. Your adviser needs to take into account your existing business structure (if any) and financial and family circumstances.

Some SMSF specialists belong to the Self-Managed Super Fund Professionals' Association of Australia (SPAA), although the majority of SMSF specialists are accountants belonging to the main accounting bodies. I provide more info on the two main accounting bodies in the next section, and details about SPAA in 'Finding a (licensed) financial adviser' later in this chapter. You can also check out my SuperGuide Directory (www.superguide.com.au/directory), for potential SMSF service providers.

Asking an accountant

Qualified and experienced accountants are a useful first point (and usually continuing point) of contact when seeking advice on financial affairs. They spend three to four years at university, and the motivated ones complete a postgraduate qualification supervised by their profession. They also belong to professional associations that strictly regulate them, such as CPA Australia and Chartered Accountants Australia and New Zealand. The best thing about them, in relation to super advice, is that they're normally very good on tax issues, because many accountants are also registered tax agents.

You can use a *registered tax agent* to help you complete and lodge your SMSF's annual returns. These tax agents are the only qualified experts who can charge for lodging tax returns and for providing tax advice (although some financial advisers have a special exemption until December 2015 to provide tax advice without being registered tax agents). You can check that your accountant/tax agent is registered as a tax agent, or your financial adviser is registered as a tax (financial) adviser, by visiting the Tax Practitioners Board website (www.tpb.gov.au).

If you want an accountant to advise you specifically on financial products and services, your accountant must hold an Australian Financial Services Licence or be an authorised representative of a licence holder. A financial product includes investing in a managed fund (where many investors pool money into one investment vehicle) or specific shares on the stock market. If your accountant refers you to a third party who is licensed, she needs to disclose whether she receives a payment for this referral.

A self-managed superannuation fund is seen as a financial product, so anyone advising on this product requires a licence, or requires an exemption under the *Financial Services Reform Act 2001*. Until 30 June 2016, accountants are granted exemptions from requiring a licence when advising clients on setting up and running SMSFs. From 1 July 2016, any accountant seeking to provide financial advice on superannuation products, including SMSFs, must hold at least a 'limited' Australian Financial Service Licence (AFSL). Remember, however, that not all accountants have expertise in SMSFs. Even so, in my opinion, because of the tax implications of SMSFs, accountants who specialise in superannuation are possibly better suited to advising on SMSFs than many more generalist licensed financial advisers.

From 1 July 2016, an accountant needs a limited AFSL to advise on:

- ✔ SMSFs

- ✔ A client's existing superannuation holdings

- ✔ A 'class of products', such as superannuation, securities (such as shares), general insurance, life risk insurance, basic deposit products and simple managed investment schemes

Your accountant doesn't need a licence, or exemption, to give your SMSF:

- ✔ Tax advice, if a registered tax agent

- ✔ Broad asset allocation advice — that is, a recommendation about how you can allocate your SMSF money into different types of asset classes such as shares, property, cash, fixed interest and alternative assets (see Chapters 14 and 15 for more information on asset allocation)

> ✔ Traditional accounting advice, such as advising on risk management (but not recommending insurance products) and fund reporting

> ✔ Administration services, including compliance, reporting and tax management (but *not* investment advice)

If you're seeking an accountant, the two main accounting bodies have easy-to-use search facilities on their websites. CPA Australia has an excellent search service called 'Find a CPA' that also allows you to search for CPAs with financial planning expertise (www.cpaaustralia.com.au), whereas Chartered Accountants Australia and New Zealand (CAANZ) has a 'Find a Chartered Accountant' facility on its Australia website (www.charteredaccountants.com.au). Other accounting associations include the National Institute of Accountants, the Association of Taxation and Management Accountants, and the National Tax and Accountants Association.

Finding a (licensed) financial adviser

A large number of financial advisers specialise in retirement planning. Seen as a holistic approach to investing, retirement planning involves assessing your financial background, current financial position, insurance needs, and your financial goals and aims. Although you're seeking advice as a SMSF trustee, an adviser should consider your financial circumstances outside your super fund, too.

Investing the assets of your SMSF is a big responsibility (as I explain in the chapters in Part IV of this book). You may want advice on your fund's investment strategy, what shares to invest in, whether to use managed funds or what alternative investments are available. If you're seeking advice on specific investments, make sure you choose a licensed financial adviser.

Expect proper disclosure

A licensed financial adviser should give you a written Financial Services Guide before dealing with you. The *Financial Services Guide* (*FSG*) explains what services the adviser offers, how she operates, in what form and how much your prospective adviser gets paid, how she deals with customer complaints, and any interests, associations or relationships that may influence the advice the adviser gives you.

After you choose a licensed adviser, any *personal advice* (where the adviser has considered your fund's particular circumstances) that the adviser gives your SMSF must also be provided in a written Statement of Advice. The *Statement of Advice* (*SOA*) should explain the advice your adviser gives your fund, the reasons for providing you with the advice and how much your adviser gets paid.

Your adviser must also disclose any interests that may influence her recommendations; for example, if she can only recommend financial products from a specific financial organisation, then she must disclose that her advice is influenced by this connection, and that any recommendations she makes are limited to the products supplied from this specific organisation.

If your adviser recommends that your SMSF invest in any financial products, then your adviser should give you the Product Disclosure Statement for each product she recommends. A *Product Disclosure Statement* (*PDS*) explains the key features of a financial product, including the fees charged and the expected risks and returns of the financial product.

If you're relying on a licensed financial adviser to set up and run your super fund for you, check that your adviser understands the SMSF rules, and has a tax background or works with a registered tax agent (typically an accountant) who can provide the tax expertise. If you're using an accountant who's also a licensed financial adviser, your accountant must also supply you with a FSG and SOA when providing advice on financial products to you personally or in your capacity as trustee of your super fund.

Expect transparency from your fund's adviser

All financial advisers charge for their services even when no money changes hands. Your adviser can charge your SMSF an upfront fee or she may arrange a regular deduction from your SMSF account, or the advice fee may be charged via a payment from a financial product provider, if you agree.

If you visit a financial adviser who charges a fee for giving advice, you can expect a fixed fee for the financial plan, and perhaps an additional fee for the implementation of the financial plan. If you then choose to remain with the adviser on a long-term basis, you may pay either an annual fee for ongoing advice or an hourly fee on an as-needs basis, or possibly a retainer fee (in monthly or quarterly instalments). Some financial advising firms charge a percentage of a client's assets — for example, 1 per cent — that the financial adviser is looking after, and many of these advisers then cap that fee when the assets are valued at a certain amount.

When using a financial adviser, you may find you're paying an additional fee for administration services. Most financial advisers lock their clients into a *platform*, also known as a wrap or wrap account, which is consolidated reporting, but for a fee. As I outline in Chapter 2, a wrap is an information collection service that bundles all of your investments — direct shares, bank accounts, term deposits and managed funds. A wrap service records all transactions, prices, brokerage, any GST, dividends paid, tax payable and other similar items. By using a platform, you may also be able to access managed funds at a cheaper rate, although, as with any packaged financial product or service, your choice of investments is limited to what the platform provider chooses to offer. (I also briefly discuss wraps in Chapter 1.)

Finding a decent financial adviser means doing your homework before selecting one. You need to do your due diligence before selecting an adviser for your SMSF. As a starting point here are six organisations that may assist you in locating a licensed financial adviser:

- ✔ The Independent Financial Advisers Association of Australia (IFAAA) provides a list of all of its members, namely independent financial advisers, on its website (www.ifaaa.com.au).

- ✔ Many licensed advisers, but certainly not all, belong to the Financial Planning Association of Australia (FPA). A Certified Financial Planner (CFP) or *CFP professional* is a member of the FPA and holds the highest financial planning designation — based on tertiary qualifications, the CFP certification examination and a level of experience. Ask the adviser if he's a member of the FPA, and what his links are to major financial organisations. Alternatively, you can find out if your adviser is an FPA member by phoning the FPA on 1300 626 393 or visiting the FPA website (www.fpa.asn.au/find-a-planner) and using its 'Find a Financial Planner' service.

- ✔ The Association of Independently Owned Financial Professionals (AIOFP) requires any member to hold their own Australian Financial Services Licence, and not to be owned by a financial institution. According to the AIOFP website, an AIOFP *Certified Financial Strategist* (*CFS*) must work for an independently owned financial practice, charge on a fee-for-service basis, and have a minimum of three years' experience as a financial adviser. You can use its 'Find an Adviser' (www.aiofp.net.au/about-aiofp/find-a-general-adviser) to find a CFS or one of AIOFP's general members.

- ✔ The Association of Financial Advisers (AFA) is another organisation representing financial advisers. You can use its Find An Adviser service (www.afa.asn.au/findanadviser) to locate a licensed adviser in your area and/or who has the specialist expertise that you're seeking.

- ✔ CPA Australia also has a specialist financial planning designation — CPA (FPS) — which is in addition to the accounting qualification that a CPA must hold. You can find a CPA-qualified financial planner by visiting the CPA Australia website (www.cpaaustralia.com.au) and clicking on Find a CPA.

✔ The SMSF Professionals' Association of Australia (SPAA) represents the SMSF industry but also offers SMSF specialist accreditation that enables accountants, financial advisers, lawyers and other experts to advertise their SMSF expertise. You can use SPAA's Find a Professional search facility by visiting this link: www.spaa.asn.au/trustees/find-a-professional.aspx.

Looking up a lawyer

A lawyer can assist you with drafting your DIY super fund's trust deed, which is also known as the 'governing rules'. A trust deed outlines how your super fund must operate and what you as trustee can and can't do (for an in-depth definition on trust deeds, along with info on how to set up a DIY super fund, turn to Chapter 7). Lawyers are also useful people to consult when you're considering what happens to your super, and super fund, after you die (see Chapter 24), or if you have a dispute between the trustees of your fund, or you have the misfortune to endure a divorce. I discuss divorce and super in Chapter 23, and also on my website, SuperGuide (www.superguide.com.au).

Appointing an auditor

Your DIY super fund must appoint an auditor to conduct two audits — a financial audit and a compliance audit — on your SMSF, at the end of each year. A *financial audit* checks that your fund's accounts are accurate. A *compliance audit* checks that you're running your fund in line with the superannuation laws.

You can appoint only an approved SMSF auditor to conduct these audits. An *approved SMSF auditor* must be registered with the Australian Securities and Investments Commission (ASIC), which provides the auditor with a unique SMSF auditor number (SAN). A registered approved SMSF auditor must satisfy minimum qualification and experience requirements, and pursue continuous professional development. I explain the role of your fund's auditor in more detail in Chapter 12.

Relying on the regulator

The Australian Taxation Office (ATO) is the main regulator of SMSFs, although the Australian Securities & Investments Commission (ASIC) oversees the licensing of financial advisers and the registration of approved SMSF auditors.

The ATO has a curious role as regulator of SMSFs — the ATO also performs an education function. The ATO helps SMSF trustees understand their trustee duties and responsibilities, while monitoring compliance with the super laws, and imposing penalties when necessary.

Be warned that any SMSF trustee who fails to make a genuine effort to comply with the super rules, or who deliberately breaks the rules, can expect financial penalties, prosecution or even the loss of the right to run their own super fund. I explain the ATO's policing role in Chapters 9, 11 and 12.

If you have a compliance question specific to your SMSF, the ATO can now provide you with specific advice, in the form of a private ruling, about how the super laws apply to your situation. The ATO also provides general rulings and determinations on different aspects of the super rules. I refer to some of these general rulings and determinations later in this book, in Appendix B.

Opting for Administration Assistance

If you're so inclined, you can meet all of your super fund's administration and compliance obligations (apart from your fund's audit) yourself; or, you can work with your adviser, or advisers, on your trustee obligations, including recording and tracking your investment transactions.

Alternatively, you can choose to appoint a fund administrator; that is, a professional administration company that worries about the administrative and compliance issues of your fund, which allows you to focus on the investments of your SMSF, and the strategic direction of your fund. Or you can use an administrator for some of your SMSF obligations only. I explain the many options when running your super fund in Chapters 6, 7 and 10.

Many SMSF administration companies also provide investment wrap accounts or have arrangements with organisations that provide wrap accounts. I explain wraps in the section 'Finding a (licensed) financial adviser', earlier in this chapter.

Unhappy with Your DIY Super Advice?

Good advice normally pays for itself. Sometimes, however, an adviser may not meet a client's expectations. If this happens to you, you may want to make a complaint. You can approach your adviser directly and express your concern or, if that option doesn't resolve the issue, you can take the matter further. You can make complaints about the following types of advisers in the following way:

- ✔ **Actuary:** You can phone the Actuaries Institute (AI) on (02) 9233 3466, or you can make a complaint via the AI website (www.actuaries .asn.au). I explain the role of actuaries in Chapter 22.

- ✔ **Accountant:** You can contact the professional association the accountant belongs to (refer to 'Asking an accountant' earlier in the chapter for the names of the main professional bodies and websites for CPA Australia and CAANZ).

- ✔ **Approved auditor:** If you have a complaint about an approved SMSF auditor in relation to your fund's audit, you can report the auditor to ASIC by phoning 1300 300 630 (for more information about the role of an approved SMSF auditor, see Chapter 12).

- ✔ **Financial adviser:** You can take your complaint to the Financial Ombudsman Service. The *Financial Ombudsman Service (FOS)* administers the Financial Industry Complaints Service and several other dispute resolution schemes within the financial services sector. You can contact the service via phone (1300 780 808) or via its website (www.fos.org.au), although you must complain directly to your adviser in the first instance. If you suspect your financial adviser of committing fraud, then you should complain to ASIC, and report the activity to the police.

- ✔ **Lawyer:** You can make a complaint to the Law Society in your state.

- ✔ **Tax agent:** First, check that your accountant/tax agent is a registered tax agent, or your financial adviser is a registered tax (financial) adviser, by visiting the Tax Practitioners Board website (www.tpb .gov.au). You can access a complaint form via the website, or by phoning 1300 362 829 for assistance.

If you're unhappy with the treatment you receive from the ATO — that is, you believe you're being treated unfairly or unreasonably — in the first instance you can complain to the ATO by phoning 1800 199 010 or making a complaint in writing. If you're dissatisfied with how your complaint is treated you can contact the Taxation Ombudsman (TO) by phoning 1300 362 072 or visiting the TO website (www.ombudsman.gov.au).

Part II

Setting Up a DIY Super Fund

Five Tips before Starting Your SMSF Show

- ✔ **Chat to an expert:** A DIY super fund is not for everyone. You need to ensure that setting up a SMSF is appropriate for your financial and personal circumstances, and more importantly, that you're suited to running your own fund.

- ✔ **Do your super sums:** Running a SMSF costs money and some costs are fixed regardless of the size of your super account. At the least you have to pay for a fund auditor, an annual levy to the ATO and pay investment transaction costs. If you plan to hire someone to help you run your SMSF, then you need to budget for this cost too.

- ✔ **Talk to your employer:** For most Australians, the primary contributor to any super account is an employer, unless you're self-employed. Before you start the SMSF set-up process, chat to your employer about your plans and ensure that you submit all the necessary paperwork to enable employer super contributions to be redirected to your SMSF.

- ✔ **Decide on a super contributions strategy:** The prospect of making super contributions into your super fund is a no-brainer. But you need to decide whether to make extra super contributions, in addition to your employer's super contributions. You also need to decide if you'll transfer super benefits from your previous super fund to your SMSF.

- ✔ **Keep in mind your trustee investment obligations:** Investing your SMSF money is the serious end of your retirement planning, and it's your responsibility as a SMSF trustee. Don't wait until your SMSF is set up to ponder how you'll invest your fund's assets and monitor their performance.

Check out www.dummies.com/extras/diysuperau for a free article about setting up a DIY super fund.

In this part ...

✔ Appreciate the costs involved in setting up and running a self-managed super fund (SMSF), including appointing a corporate trustee, and the additional fees involved when appointing a fund administrator to help you with some, or all, of your trustee tasks.

✔ Understand the 10 main steps involved in setting up a SMSF, including what you need to do to ensure your employer's super contributions are paid into your SMSF.

✔ Understand the implications of choosing an individual trustee compared with a corporate trustee.

✔ Be prepared to sign a special document declaring that you understand your SMSF responsibilities and you promise to follow the super rules.

Chapter 6

How Much Does a SMSF Cost?

In This Chapter

▶ Getting help from an administrator or accountant

▶ Calculating the cost of your fund's start-up

▶ Estimating your fund's ongoing expenses

▶ Allowing for one-off fund costs

*H*ow much does it cost to run your DIY super fund? A glib answer may be: 'How long is a piece of string?' But a more precise answer is, 'It depends!' Seriously, how much your super fund costs to run depends on whether you appoint experts to help you, and how often you buy and sell investments.

In most cases, the more money you have in your super account, the cheaper it becomes to run your own DIY super fund. The reason that bigger means cheaper is that running a self-managed super fund (SMSF) involves some costs that are payable regardless of the size of your super account, such as fund establishment costs (including the trust deed), the ATO supervisory levy of $259, and the annual fund audit (although the audit often can cost more for larger SMSFs).

The costs involved in establishing (and running) your fund are important because fund expenses affect your long-term investment returns. For example, according to ASIC, if your fund incurs 2 per cent in total fees each year rather than, say, 1 per cent in fees each year, for 30 years, then your super benefit is going to be 20 per cent smaller because of that additional 1 per cent in fees. In plain language, the extra fees can reduce a potential $600,000 benefit into a $480,000 benefit over a 30-year period.

In this chapter, I take you through the costs involved in setting up a SMSF and the annual expenses that you can expect to incur when running your fund. I also explain some of the one-off costs that your fund may need to budget for, such as specific financial advice and trust deed updates.

Appointing an Administrator or Accountant ... or Not

How much your SMSF costs to run depends on whether you truly do it yourself or whether you hire one or more helpers to make your life easier. Don't be embarrassed if you're considering outsourcing elements of your SMSF, such as fund administration. An increasing number of SMSF trustees are using professional administrators, although many more outsource the fund administration to their accountants. (I explain the outsourcing decision in Chapter 7, and go into detail about fund administration in Chapter 10.)

Some individuals, however, get great satisfaction from doing all things administrative themselves; and good luck to you if you're one of those individuals. But doing something yourself still requires the use of experts at critical moments. For example, if you're renovating the house, only a mad person does the electrical work without an electrician. In fact, it's illegal. Having said that, I'm certain a DIY renovator is out there, somewhere, fiddling optimistically with strange wires. Running your own fund is very similar. You can save yourself money and have greater control over the process by setting up, and running, a DIY super fund yourself, but you're likely to need a qualified adviser (refer to Chapter 5) to guide you along your way at critical points: For example, before setting up your fund, and when starting a superannuation pension. Your accountant and/or financial adviser can be your first point of expert contact.

Even when you do (nearly) everything yourself when running your SMSF, you still have to pay the ATO supervisory levy of $259, plus you must appoint an approved SMSF auditor to audit your super fund (I show you how, in Chapter 12). Your fund is also subject to transactions costs when investing (see the section 'Calculating investment costs and related expenses', later in the chapter), and insurance premiums (Chapter 24) that you may pay within your super fund. All super fund members, whether in a SMSF or large fund, must also pay tax (see Chapters 13 and 18) on fund earnings while accumulating savings for retirement, and on concessional contributions (refer to Chapter 4).

SMSF Start-Up Costs

Setting up your SMSF can cost you, typically, anywhere between nothing and $3,000-odd dollars and sometimes more, depending on the sign-on incentive offered by the SMSF service provider, the level of service you want, the amount of advice you receive, whether you choose to have a company as trustee of your fund (I cover the trustee's role in Chapter 8), and how much time is spent on tailoring your fund's trust deed.

If you're seeking a no-frills set-up with individual trustees and a fairly standard trust deed, then it is possible to set up a SMSF for around $1,100, and some providers even offer this service for free. If you're seeking a more pointy-end service, such as a customised trust deed, a corporate trustee and full service set-up, then your set-up costs could reach $3000-plus. In most cases, SMSF providers charge under $2,000 for the more tailored SMSF set-up, including the appointment of a corporate trustee. Table 6-1 summarises your fund's possible set-up costs.

Table 6-1	Set-Up Costs for DIY Super (Estimates)	
Trust Deed Only	*Full Set-Up (Including Trust Deed) for Individual Trustees*	*Additional Cost, if Appointing a Corporate Trustee*
$110–$1,100	$0–$2,200	$880–$1,100*

* Corporate trustee costs include an ASIC registration fee of $457 and an annual ASIC fee of $45 (see Chapter 8).

Source: Analysis of public information from 32 SMSF service providers.

The difference between the lower and upper end of the cost ranges in Table 6-1 generally relate to the absence of advice and hands-on assistance (at the lower end), and more hand-holding and advice at the upper end of the cost ranges. For example, a trust deed that costs just $110 is ordinarily a standard deed provided as part of a do-it-yourself fund establishment kit, while a trust deed that costs up to $1,100 is usually drafted and tailored specifically for your needs by a solicitor, in conjunction with your adviser.

Some service providers are quoting a basic service in setting up a DIY super fund for less than $500 or even for free! At that price, expect a standard trust deed, no corporate trustee, no advisory support and no bells or whistles. Alternatively, a service provider that states it can set up your fund for under $500 may be providing this service at a substantial discount as a means of enticing you to use the provider's other services. The costs of offering such cheap set-up costs are ordinarily recouped by charging more for other ongoing services, or charging advisory fees on one-off services related to your super fund.

The basic steps in setting up a superannuation fund are the same whether you're establishing a large fund or a small fund. To give you an idea of what you can get for your money when using a service provider, flick to Chapters 7 and 8 for the main steps.

Costing trust deeds and trustees

A fairly standard trust deed on its own can cost around $400 to $500, and even more when you use a solicitor to tailor the trust deed for your specific needs. Even so, quite a few service providers supply DIY super fund kits for around $500. The kit includes a trust deed, standard documents necessary to set up your SMSF, and a page of instructions — not unlike flat pack furniture, where you buy a bundle of ready-to-assemble material and instructions to put it all together. You can purchase and implement the DIY super fund kits on your own or in conjunction with your financial adviser. Remember to factor in the cost of your adviser's time.

At least fourteen out of the many hundreds of SMSF administrators operating in Australia offer to set up your fund for free, including throwing in your fund's trust deed for free, usually if you sign on for the company's administration service for at least 12 months, or two years (see the next section, 'Opting for the DIY package deal', for more details).

If you appoint trustees as individuals (rather than as a company), you can expect to establish a SMSF for the cost of between nothing and $2,200, depending on the sign-on incentive (if any) offered by the service provider, the cost of your trust deed and the level of advice you require. Using a corporate trustee for your SMSF means you may fork out an additional $880 to $1,100 when establishing your fund, and expect some extra ongoing costs each year. However, before you ditch the idea of a corporate trustee because of cost, I suggest you read Chapter 8, where I explain what's involved when you take on the role of trustee and the advantages and disadvantages of using a company as your fund's trustee.

Opting for the DIY package deal

Many fund administrators package the set-up costs for a SMSF with the first year's administration (and compliance) fees, which can be an attractive option if you understand what the package covers. If you choose this option, ask what the annual administration fee for the second year and future years is expected to be, and what services the annual fee includes, and what it doesn't include. I explain your fund's **C**ompliance, **A**dministration, **R**eporting and **T**ax (CART) obligations in Part III of this book.

Some SMSF service providers may offer a financial incentive for you to sign on for the package deal. For example, more than one SMSF provider offers to set up your SMSF for free, subject to you appointing that provider as your administrator and tax agent for 12 months, or two years, and using the administrator's preferred bank and online stockbroker. Other SMSF service providers offer a set-up freebie, or offer a discounted price for setting up a SMSF, if you take up the company's annual administration service and other SMSF-related offerings. Sounds pretty good doesn't it? Remember, nothing is for free in the financial services world; so, work out exactly what your needs are, what you get for your money, and what money changes hands before choosing an adviser or provider based simply on cost.

Benchmarking your SMSF's running costs

When working out the running cost of your SMSF, your best approach is to have some type of benchmark to compare against your own fund's costs. As a ballpark figure, a low-cost professionally managed large super fund charges around 1 per cent of an individual's account balance as fees, although many large super funds charge close to 2 per cent of account balances in fees and other costs. If you choose your own investment options within a large super fund, you may find that your chosen investment option has higher investment fees than you realise.

On a $500,000 account balance, total running costs for your SMSF of 1 per cent equals $5,000, 2 per cent equals $10,000, and 3 per cent equals $15,000 in fees. On a $200,000 account balance, 1 per cent equals $2,000, 2 per cent equals $4,000 and 3 per cent equals $6,000.

If reducing the costs associated with your super savings is the main driver for setting up your SMSF then, logically, your SMSF needs to be cheaper than the super fund you currently belong to, or cheaper than the other super alternatives in the marketplace (refer to Chapter 2 for all of your super fund options). For example, if you're in an existing large fund that charges 2 per cent, a SMSF is going to be cost-effective for you when your fund's total costs are less than 2 per cent of your account balance. Alternatively, you can opt for a large fund such as an industry fund or retail fund that charges lower fees than your existing fund.

Budgeting for Annual SMSF Costs

Before you start organising the set up of your SMSF (covered in Chapter 7), you need to choose between running your SMSF yourself or paying an administrator (or accountant) to do most of the job for you. In the following sections I deal with the costs associated with administering your super fund, such as the tasks you must do as SMSF trustee to comply with the super rules, including recording and reporting information. I also explain some of the transaction costs your fund may have to pay when investing.

When running a SMSF, your fund is subject to annual expenses, which involve fixed costs such as the ATO's supervisory levy, and variable costs such as transaction costs related to investing your super contributions and accumulated fund earnings. Your SMSF's annual costs, generally, can be broken up into four categories:

✔ Administration/compliance costs

✔ Investment transaction costs

✔ Insurance premiums (see Chapter 24)

✔ Taxes (see Chapters 13 and 18)

Choosing from the administration menu

If you plan to do as much as possible yourself in the way of administration, your annual costs can be kept to a minimum. Even so, your fund must still pay the annual $259 ATO supervisory levy, arrange for an approved SMSF auditor to conduct the annual audit (at least $330 and up to $1,200 or maybe more, depending on your super fund's complexity), and allow for your fund's investment transaction costs.

Table 6-2 outlines the possible running costs of a SMSF when fees are charged based on a flat rate, or based on the size of the fund balance, or based on the number of fund transactions. Some SMSF providers cap the fees as soon as a super fund reaches a certain size. For example, I'm aware of one SMSF provider that charges a flat administration fee of 1 per cent of a fund's account balance, which is capped at a maximum fee of roughly $5,000 a year regardless of the size of the fund.

Don't go running to your adviser yet! The cost of your fund may be considerably more than the costs shown in Table 6-2, depending on the complexity or activity of your DIY super fund. For example, the cost of complying with the super rules and administering your fund doesn't take into account any investment costs you may incur, such as brokerage on share transactions, and management fees on managed funds (if any). Note that many of the SMSF providers allow for transaction costs by charging you a higher administration fee when you have frequent investment transactions. Also, you may pay more if your SMSF is paying a pension (for information about running a super pension, see Chapter 21).

Table 6-2	Annual Administration/Compliance Costs for DIY Super (Estimates)		
Fund Charges Based On ...	*Flat Rate Option*	*Size of Account Balance Option*	*Number of Transactions for Year Option*
Full administration service (including reporting, audit, tax return)	$700–$6,600	**Example 1:** 1% of account balance up to maximum cost of $5,000 **Example 2:** $2,000 minimum, up to balance of $200,000, then up to $3,500 for balance up to $400,000, and $4,000 for balance up to $500,000	$1,000–$4,000, or more if hundreds of transactions
Year-end reporting only + audit + tax return lodgement	$500–$2,200	Included in package fee	Included in package fee
Audit only	$330–$1,200	Included in package fee	$330–$1,200
Additional Costs ...			
ATO supervisory levy	$259	$259	$259
ASIC return, if corporate trustee	$45–$243	$45–$243	$45–$243

Source: Analysis of public information from 32 SMSF service providers.

Calculating investment costs and related expenses

You, or anyone, incur costs when investing, whether you invest within your super fund or outside the super structure. For example, when you buy property you have to pay stamp duty, and when you sell property you usually have to pay a commission to a real estate agent. And, if you invest in a managed fund, you pay the financial organisation promoting the fund an annual fee, and possibly an entry fee.

In short, investment costs aren't unique to superannuation funds. The important point to highlight, however, is that many budding DIY super trustees fail to factor in the costs of investing (and any investment advice) when working out the costs of running a SMSF.

If you're in a typical large super fund, the investment transaction costs aren't directly linked to your annual account fees because the super fund holds the investments collectively on behalf of all fund members. The one exception to this scenario is where you have chosen an investment option that permits you to directly invest in shares, and then your account is charged for each share transaction.

Some people use a wrap service to bundle together all their SMSF investments. A wrap service (also called a wrap account or platform; refer to Chapter 5) records all transactions, prices, brokerage, any GST, dividends paid, tax payable and other similar items. Many SMSF administration companies offer investment wrap accounts. Ordinarily, by using a wrap account, you can access information regarding your investments instantaneously, via a secure website.

The administration costs can skyrocket for your SMSF when you use a wrap investment account in conjunction with a professional administration company, and then you need to factor in your other investment costs and possible financial advice. The costs of running your SMSF with a wrap service can be anywhere up to $7,000 or $8,000 a year for a fund balance of $200,000. In percentage terms, that works out to be around 4 per cent of fund assets. The actual cost can depend on the complexity of your fund and the frequency of investment transactions. By comparison, the cost of running most SMSFs is nowhere near $7,000 for a SMSF with an account balance of $200,000. Shop around to ensure you pay for only what you need.

Many advisers offer wraps as an alternative to running your own super fund. If you use a *super wrap* (for a definition of this type of service, refer to Chapter 2), the wrap operator is the trustee, which means it looks after the compliance and administration responsibilities. Some wraps are rip-offs, while other wraps can be a viable alternative to a SMSF when you're looking for investment flexibility, but don't want the hassle of compliance and administration responsibilities. Do your homework and calculate the annual costs before you choose the wrap option.

Accounting for One-Off Costs

Although most costs associated with SMSFs are annual or ongoing costs, certain decisions that you make within your super fund trigger one-off costs. Some of the one-off costs that your SMSF may be up for include:

- **Trust deed updates:** On occasion, when major changes occur in the super rules or you wish to do something significant in your fund (for example, start a transition-to-retirement pension — covered in Chapter 21), your trust deed may need to be updated. Costs vary, but updates can cost from $110 to $880, and even more if you decide to replace all the terms of the trust deed. I discuss trust deeds in Chapter 7.

- **Financial advice:** Expect an hourly rate from $200 to $550, depending on the type of advice you need, and the type of adviser that you use. For some super funds, advice is an annual cost. For other funds, advice is sought at critical times; for example, when a member is planning to retire. Often, providing financial advice is where the cheaper administrators make their money. For more info on getting financial advice, refer to Chapter 5.

- **Starting a pension:** Taking a pension from your SMSF involves some paperwork and specific decision making. A service provider may not charge anything for you to start a pension, but more likely the provider can charge anywhere from $110 to $990 (and sometimes more) for activating a pension (see Chapter 21).

- **Lump sum benefit payments:** Although pension payments are regular events, lump sum payments are usually one-off or irregular (for more info on lump sum payments from your SMSF, see Chapter 19). If you use an administrator, expect a cost of between $110 and $330 for the recording and compliance work when a lump sum is paid.

- **Actuarial certificates:** If you plan to contribute to your super fund — while taking a pension — you may need an actuarial certificate each year (see Chapter 22). An actuarial certificate states what proportion of your fund's investment returns and assets relate to your pension. Expect a cost from $150 to $550.

✔ **Pension commutation:** In some cases, you may want to stop your pension, that is, activate a pension commutation, and return your account to accumulation phase. (I explain stopping your SMSF pension in Chapter 22.) You can expect an administrator/accountant to charge you between $220 and $880 for the commutation, and expect closer towards the higher range if you want to then start a new pension.

In some circumstances, a certain cost may be ongoing — but only for certain fund members or a specific stage in a member's life. For example, expect to pay more when your super fund is paying you an income stream (pension) because most administrators charge an additional fee — from $330 and up to $1,100 — for the extra paperwork. If you shop around, you may find an administrator who charges the same amount regardless of whether your fund is in accumulation phase or paying you a pension.

Chapter 7

Simple Steps to SMSF Start-Up

'*D*o you mean that I have to complete all of this paperwork?' is an occasional response to the reality of setting up a self-managed super fund (SMSF). You may be surprised (or not) to learn that the interest in DIY super from some individuals wanes when faced with the prospect of actually making it happen. A common response from such individuals is: 'Setting up a DIY super fund seems so complicated', or 'It seems too difficult for me to do'.

Not so! Setting up a DIY super fund can be fiddly, but certainly not difficult. Realistically, you can be running your super fund within two or three weeks of making the decision to set up a SMSF.

Even when you delegate the set-up task to a SMSF service provider, you need to be aware of the steps involved in setting up your super fund. You're the fund trustee and responsible for everything to do with your fund, and you must sign some important documents during the set-up process, even when you arrange for someone else to do the legwork.

In this chapter, I explain the steps involved in setting up a SMSF. You can do everything yourself or, if you can't be bothered with the paperwork, you can hire someone to do the job for you.

Knowing When to Go Solo or Seek Help

A perennial theme when running your own super fund is deciding when you need assistance. Popular outsourcing options include appointing an accountant or a fund administrator. I discuss the costs of appointing an administrator compared to doing nearly everything yourself in Chapter 6, and I explain your outsourcing options and what a fund administrator can do for your SMSF in Chapter 10.

You don't always need to appoint someone to administer your SMSF. However, you can find an expert to assist your super fund at any stage — when setting up (to complete steps in this chapter), starting a pension (see Chapter 21), winding up your SMSF (see Chapter 24), and for any other aspect of your fund's operation.

Your options when running your own super fund are:

✔ Go solo with everything (except your fund's audit) — you set up your fund yourself, administer the fund, meet all of your fund's compliance and reporting obligations (see Chapters 11 and 12), and invest your super monies (see Part IV).

✔ Outsource your fund's set-up — but then run the fund yourself.

✔ Outsource nearly everything (set-up and running the fund) — but you choose and make your fund's investments.

✔ Set up your fund yourself — but outsource your administration, compliance, reporting and investment responsibilities.

✔ Set up your fund yourself *and* invest your fund's super monies — but outsource your fund's administration, compliance and reporting responsibilities.

✔ Outsource everything to a service provider, such as a fund administrator or a financial adviser — the set-up, administration, compliance, reporting and investment.

Setting Up Your SMSF in Simple Steps

So, you're ready to set up your SMSF. If you're considering such a strategy, you've obviously determined that a SMSF is right for you (refer to Chapter 1). I also assume that you've explored the costs involved in setting up, and running, a SMSF (refer to Chapter 6). A SMSF has a legal structure known as a trust, which means that when setting up your fund, you must satisfy important requirements under trust law, and under the super rules.

According to the ATO publication, *Setting up a self-managed super fund* (NAT 71923), a *trust* is an arrangement 'where a person or company (the trustee) holds assets (trust property) in trust for the benefits of others (the beneficiaries). A super fund is a special type of trust, set up and maintained for the sole purpose of providing retirement benefits to its members (the beneficiaries).' I explain the 'sole purpose' requirements of a super fund in Chapter 9, and the practical application of these requirements in Chapter 11.

A super fund receives special tax treatment under the tax rules, which means your SMSF also must satisfy special conditions to obtain those tax concessions. Beyond the legal and tax obligations, you then need to cater for the compliance issues of accepting contributions, recording transactions and investing your super money.

To meet your legal, tax and compliance obligations you can expect, at a minimum, to take the following steps. What usually occurs is that many of the steps I outline in this list (and throughout the rest of this chapter) are proceeding concurrently:

1. **Draft a trust deed (and choose a name).**

2. **Appoint the trustee (individuals or corporate).**

3. **Admit members (and supply Product Disclosure Statement).**

4. **Sign the ATO SMSF trustee declaration.**

5. **Open a bank account.**

6. **Establish accounting and administrative procedures.**

7. **Accept contributions.**

8. **Apply to be regulated (and other preliminary matters).**

9. **Draft your fund's investment strategy.**

10. **Prepare your fund for investing.**

Depending on your individual circumstances, you may decide to add extra steps, such as appointing an adviser (refer to Chapter 5), and/or appointing an administrator (see Chapter 10). You may also consider moving your existing super benefits, held in another fund, into your new SMSF. I discuss transferring your existing super benefits, in the section 'Changing Super Funds', later in the chapter.

All trustee decisions affecting your super fund need to be documented, including decisions relating to setting up the fund — such as appointing trustees, admitting members, opening the fund's bank account and formulating the fund's investment strategy. In particular, you need to ensure that the ten steps — refer to the preceding bulleted list, and the details set out in the following sections — have been 'minuted' as part of the initial trustee meeting. As SMSF trustee, you need to keep minutes from trustee meetings (including minutes of trustee decisions) for at least ten years.

Step 1: Draft a trust deed (and choose a name)

The *trust deed* is your DIY super fund's rule book. The trust deed also gives you, as trustee, the power to operate your fund. Everything you do as trustee is governed by your fund's trust deed. Examples of the types of provisions that you need to have in your trust deed are

- The power to appoint and remove trustees
- Detail of the powers of the trustees
- The power to open a bank account on behalf of the fund
- Detail on conditions for accepting contributions
- The power to appoint professional advisers to assist in running the fund
- The power to formulate an investment strategy
- Detail of the types of investments your fund can invest in
- Detail on conditions for benefit payments to members
- The power to wind up the fund

A trust deed is a legal document, and drafting a deed is legal work, which means only a lawyer can charge for such a service. Some SMSF experts argue that lawyers don't understand SMSFs; so, instead, you need to rely on a specialist SMSF adviser when drafting a trust deed to set up your fund. What do I think? My opinion is that SMSF advisers don't generally understand the intricacies of trust law and a lawyer is the best person to draft a deed, as long as the trust deed reflects what you (and your adviser, if you have one) instruct the lawyer to include in the trust deed.

Choose a lawyer who regularly works with SMSF advisers, or choose a SMSF adviser (if you want one) who regularly works with a SMSF specialist lawyer. Although SMSF advisers may use a standardised trust deed for their clients, the key is to ensure that the trust deed caters for what you intend to do in your fund. For example, if you plan to invest in artwork or other types of collectibles, you need to ensure that your trust deed permits such investments (see Chapter 15). I explain trust deed costs (and any deed updates) in Chapter 6.

Before you launch your own SMSF show, you need to consider what name you're going to use for your super fund. The fund's name appears in the trust deed and in all fund documents. You can choose any name you like, although many SMSF trustees opt for their own names: For example, the Trish Power Super Fund (which, if you're curious, isn't the name of my SMSF). If you opt for a corporate trustee (see Chapter 8), you can name the company in a similar way to the fund: For example, Trish Power Super Fund Pty Ltd (again, no, that's not my SMSF's name). Some trustees choose names linked to their business, or company name. Choosing a fund name peculiar to you and the other members can minimise the chances of your adviser (or the ATO) confusing your fund with another SMSF.

After you receive your fund's draft trust deed, and the trustees have been appointed (see the next section), you must ensure the trust deed is properly executed according to your state (or territory) laws: You must sign and date your fund's trust deed — and in most states this step must be witnessed — and, if applicable, arrange for the deed to be stamped at the state revenue office in your state (or territory).

If you choose to have a corporate trustee (see the next step, and Chapter 8), then you must ensure that your trust deed allows for a corporate trustee. You must also set up the trustee company before you can execute your trust deed.

Step 2: Appoint the trustee (individuals or corporate)

All members of your SMSF have to become trustees of the fund, and you can have no more than four individual members; or you can choose to have a corporate trustee. If you opt to have a corporate trustee, then all members of your SMSF must become directors of the trustee company.

You appoint the trustees of your SMSF around the same time that you establish your trust deed, and each appointment must be in accordance with your SMSF's trust deed. Each trustee must consent to the appointment in writing.

Before you establish your deed then, you need to decide whether your fund is going to have individual trustees or a corporate trustee. A *corporate trustee* is a trustee incorporated as a company (and made up of directors), and performs the same role as an individual trustee, but collectively. And, as I mention in the preceding section, if you want a corporate trustee, you must set up the trustee company before you can execute your trust deed.

In Chapter 8, I explain who can and can't be a SMSF trustee, your responsibilities as trustee, and what you need to consider when choosing between an individual trustee and a corporate trustee.

Step 3: Admit members (and supply Product Disclosure Statement)

Your role as SMSF trustee is separate from your role as SMSF member. As SMSF trustee, you must admit members to your SMSF, which generally involves a member completing an application form of sorts. The type of paperwork you choose to use to admit fund members is up to you or the fund's trust deed. Although, if you're using a SMSF service provider to help you, then you're likely to be using a template application form provided by your SMSF administrator. Except when you are the only member of your SMSF (see Chapter 8), all of your fund's trustees must be members. At this stage, you should record each fund member's tax file number (TFN), and other personal details. I explain the importance of TFNs in Chapter 4.

You may need to ensure that each fund member (including you!) receives a Product Disclosure Statement (PDS), before joining the fund. The PDS your fund's trustees (including you) give to your fund members (including you) needs to disclose the key features of your SMSF, including the expected fees and the possible risks when running this type of fund. Large super funds must supply a PDS to each fund member. Supply of a PDS may not be necessary for SMSF members, however, where each fund member is aware of how the super fund operates, and the costs involved. However, many SMSF advisers recommend providing a PDS to each SMSF member as a standard procedure, regardless of the level of member knowledge. Although this approach may seem like overkill, particularly if you're a hands-on trustee/member, I strongly suggest providing a PDS to a fund member commencing a pension via the fund (see Chapter 21 for information on running a SMSF pension), or where an adviser/administrator is heavily involved in helping you run your fund.

Step 4: Sign the ATO SMSF trustee declaration

As a new trustee (or new director of a corporate trustee) of a SMSF, you must sign the ATO's *Self-managed super fund trustee declaration* within 21 days of becoming a SMSF trustee (or director). By signing the SMSF trustee declaration, you're acknowledging that you understand you're responsible for ensuring your super fund complies with the super laws.

The trustee declaration is an extremely important document for SMSF trustees. I devote a whole chapter (Chapter 9) to explaining the contents of the declaration, which includes statements about your trustee duties and investment restrictions affecting your fund.

You don't send the trustee declaration to the ATO. Your fund must keep the SMSF trustee declarations, signed by your fund's trustees, as part of the fund's records, and make it available to the ATO, if requested.

Step 5: Open a bank account

Your SMSF must hold assets on trust for members, and any cash assets must be held in a bank account. Your super fund needs to have its own bank account, separate from your business or personal bank accounts. When opening your account (or accounts), the bank usually requires a copy of the executed trust deed to verify your identity as trustee (and ASIC registration, if a corporate trustee) and to confirm the existence of the super fund. The financial organisation may ask for further documentation such as your fund's tax file number (TFN). For info on how to obtain a TFN for your SMSF, see the section 'Step 8: Apply to be regulated (and other preliminary matters)', later in this chapter.

Under no circumstances can you mix your fund's super money with your non-super money (see Chapters 9 and 11). Penalties may apply if you do.

Step 6: Establish accounting and administrative procedures

An important consideration for any SMSF trustee is how you plan to process and store your fund's paperwork (such as keeping minutes of trustee meetings, accepting contributions and recording investment transactions). As trustee of your SMSF, you also must keep accurate accounting records.

A prudent measure for any budding trustee is to set up your fund's reporting systems before accepting any contributions, and before your fund makes any significant decisions. Often, new trustees skip this step and come back to establishing procedures later. If you're planning to do your own administration, and you run a very simple fund with cash contributions, and irregular and straightforward investments (such as listed shares and cash), establishing procedures can generally be done at any stage in the set-up process.

In Part III of this book, I explain the issues you need to consider when developing processes for your fund, such as appointing an administrator to worry about this for you.

Step 7: Accept contributions

Your SMSF is legally established when trustees are appointed, the trust deed is executed and the fund holds assets in trust for the benefit of members. For a new super fund, holding assets means a fund member making a super contribution, or redirecting employer or personal super contributions, or transferring super benefits from another fund. (I explain how to redirect super contributions, or benefits, in the section 'Changing Super Funds', later in the chapter.)

A super contribution can be a cash contribution or an in specie contribution — a non-cash contribution that may take the form of listed shares and certain other assets (I explain in specie contributions, along with the other types of contributions, in Chapter 4). When accepting contributions, your fund must follow the contribution rules, be mindful of any investment restrictions (see Chapter 15) and follow the terms of your trust deed or other fund rules.

 Legally, the trustees of a fund should make a decision on whether to accept a contribution whenever a fund member makes a contribution. The decision to accept a contribution should be recorded in minutes along with the member's name, details of the type of contribution (refer to Chapter 4), and a statement confirming that the fund member is permitted to make contributions under the super rules. You can include as much information as you believe is necessary for the proper operation of your fund, including arranging for the member to complete a contribution form.

Under the super rules, in most cases, you must allocate contributions to the relevant fund member's account within 28 days after the end of the month that you receive them. As a SMSF trustee, generally, you should be allocating contributions immediately because this 28-day rule is really catering for large super funds that deal with thousands of super contributions every month.

Step 8: Apply to be regulated (and other preliminary matters)

As trustee, you must 'elect' for the *Superannuation Industry (Supervision) Act 1993* (SIS Act) to regulate your super fund and you must make this election within 60 days of establishing your fund. The SIS Act is the statutory bible for all super funds.

By choosing to become a regulated fund, your fund can then become a *complying fund*, which entitles your super fund to receive tax concessions (see Chapter 13) — a financial reward from the government for accepting the SIS Act as your super guide. Securing the complying fund status also means that you, and your employer, can claim tax deductions when making contributions (refer to Chapter 4) to your fund.

You make the election for your super fund to be regulated by the SIS Act by completing an *Application for ABN registration for superannuation entities* form (NAT 2944), which is also the form to use to apply for your fund's ABN, TFN and for GST:

- ✔ **Australian Business Number (ABN):** Using the ATO's definition, the *ABN* is a public number that gives businesses in Australia a single identification number to use when dealing with a range of government departments and agencies. The ABN doesn't replace your super fund's tax file number. Your super fund's name then appears on the ATO's Australian Business Register (see www.abr.gov.au) and the Super Fund Lookup search facility (see http://superfundlookup.gov .au). The ATO can take up to 28 days to send your fund's ABN.

- ✔ **Tax file number (TFN):** The ATO allocates a TFN and an ABN to all super funds that register with the ATO. Your super fund's TFN is different from your individual TFN, or the individual TFNs of other trustees.

- ✔ **GST registration (if applicable):** The *goods and services tax (GST)* is a flat 10 per cent tax on most goods and services in Australia. Most SMSFs don't need to register for GST, unless the fund has an annual turnover of GST-applicable supplies of greater than $75,000. Most typical SMSF investments are not considered taxable supplies for GST purposes. You may consider registering your fund for GST, if your fund is planning to purchase or lease a commercial property (see Chapter 17) where GST is payable, or your fund incurs a lot of brokerage when trading shares. ***Note:*** Your fund can only claim 75 per cent of any GST refundable.

According to the ATO, you lodge your election to become a regulated fund when you've legally established your fund; that is, after your trust deed is signed and the first contribution is made. Presumably, the ATO means after your trust deed is executed, that is signed and witnessed, and the first contribution is made. (Each trustee must also have signed a SMSF trustee declaration before lodging the election.) ***Note:*** From a practical (rather than legal) point of view, if a fund member is planning to make a cash contribution (rather than a non-cash contribution — refer to Chapter 4), then your fund must have an operating bank account to bank the cash (refer to the earlier section 'Step 5: Open a bank account') before accepting contributions ('Step 7: Accept contributions'). When opening a bank account, the bank ordinarily requires a copy of the signed/executed deed. As I mention at the start of this section, many of the set-up steps outlined in this chapter proceed concurrently.

You can apply for your fund to be regulated (and apply for an ABN, TFN and register for GST) via the internet by visiting the Australian Business Register (ABR) (www.abr.gov.au). Or, you can download a copy of the form from the ATO website (www.ato.gov.au) or you can request a copy of the *Application for ABN registration for superannuation entities* (NAT 2944) form by phoning the ATO on 1300 720 092, and then follow up by mailing the completed form to the ATO.

Step 9: Draft your fund's investment strategy

As trustee of your SMSF, you're responsible for investing your fund's assets and monitoring the performance of those assets. You must invest in accordance with your fund's investment strategy, and drafting this strategy is one of the most important tasks facing a SMSF trustee. I explain what you need to consider, and the steps involved in drafting your fund's strategy in Chapters 14 and 15.

Your DIY super start-up kit

The ATO releases publications to help SMSF trustees understand their responsibilities, such as:

✔ *Running a self-managed super fund* (NAT 11032)

✔ *Paying benefits from a self-managed super fund* (NAT 74124)

✔ *Winding up a self-managed super fund* (NAT 8107)

I suggest you order, and then store these publications in your new DIY super library, along with this book, *DIY Super For Dummies*, 3rd Australian Edition. To order these ATO publications, check out Appendix B at the end of this book.

Step 10: Prepare your fund for investing

As trustee, you must research your investment choices, and complete any paperwork necessary to enable you to invest on behalf of the fund. For example, you must ensure that any assets you buy are held in your name as 'trustee' if you have individual trustees, or in the name of the corporate trustee. I explain the special investment rules peculiar to super in Chapter 15.

Before You Pop the Champagne ...

A DIY super trustee's job is never really done. Although you may have set up your fund, you still have three important tasks remaining. You need to:

✔ **Appoint an approved SMSF auditor:** You must appoint an auditor who, after the end of each financial year, reviews whether your super fund's financial accounts are accurate, and assesses whether your fund has complied with the SIS Act. I explain the role of your fund's approved SMSF auditor in Chapter 12.

✔ **Make a death benefit nomination:** You can nominate your superannuation dependants, or your estate, to receive your super benefit in the event that you die. See Chapter 24 for information about death benefits.

> ✔ **Redirect your super contributions to your SMSF:** An important step in your SMSF retirement savings plan is to ensure that your SMSF can receive your super contributions. In the next section, 'Changing Super Funds', I explain how to instruct your employer to pay SG (and other employer contributions) into your SMSF, and how to arrange for the transfer of super benefits from other funds.

Changing Super Funds

Your SMSF needs to be operational before it can accept super contributions or transfers of super benefits from other super funds. Now that you have set up your SMSF, you need to ensure that your super entitlements are redirected or transferred to your SMSF.

Redirecting SG contributions to your fund

If you're an employee and you have the right to choose where your employer pays your Superannuation Guarantee (SG) contributions (refer to Chapter 4), you can arrange for your employer to pay your SG contributions to your SMSF.

You must complete a Standard Choice Form, then return it to your employer. A *Standard Choice Form* (*SCF*) is a special form that your employer must give to eligible employees, informing the employee about her options under the fund choice rules. Your SMSF must be established, and ready to accept contributions from your employer, before you complete the SCF. You insert your SMSF details in Part A of the SCF, providing certain information including your SMSF's name, address and contact number, your fund's ABN, your fund's bank details and your fund's Electronic Service Address (ESA), for accepting your employer's contributions. I explain how to obtain an ESA in the next section, 'Receiving employer contributions in SuperStream form'. You can ask your employer for a SCF or you can download the SCF (NAT 13080), with instructions, by visiting the 'Individual' section of the ATO website (www.ato.gov.au).

You must also supply the letter from the ATO confirming that your fund has elected to be a regulated super fund (refer to the section 'Step 8: Apply to be regulated (and other preliminary matters)', earlier in the chapter) to your employer. Your employer must then pay your SG contributions into your SMSF within two months of receiving the SCF. I explain the fund choice rules briefly in Chapter 2, and in more detail on my website, SuperGuide (www.superguide.com.au).

Receiving employer contributions in SuperStream form

Before you complete the Standard Choice Form (refer previous section), you must obtain an *Electronic Service Address* (*ESA*) to enable your SMSF to receive a contribution data message from your employer. In the past, an ESA was not necessary, but since SuperStream was introduced, all SMSFs receiving super contributions from employers must have an ESA. *SuperStream* is a suite of reforms to make the super industry more efficient, including making employers and super funds submit payments and data electronically in standard form.

The ESA allows your employer, or the employer of another member of your fund, to send data electronically to your SMSF, including:

- ✔ Employer details (sender)
- ✔ Employee details (SMSF member)
- ✔ Contribution types (concessional and non-concessional) and amounts
- ✔ Payment details, which includes a unique payment reference number (PRN)

You can appoint a SMSF messaging provider to set up an ESA for your SMSF. The ESA allows your fund to receive data via a secure electronic distribution network using the SuperStream standard, and which translates the information into a format that SMSF trustees can readily access. According to the ATO website, there are at least 10 SMSF messaging providers available to all SMSFs, and around 20 providers offering ESAs to existing SMSF clients only. You can access these lists by visiting this link: www.ato.gov.au/ super/superstream/in-detail/contributions/smsf-messaging- service-providers. If you're planning to use a fund administrator to run your SMSF, or you've already appointed a fund administrator, then it's likely an ESA has already been allocated to your fund. If not, ask your administrator about obtaining one.

Redirecting salary sacrifice contributions

You need to make arrangements with your employer so that your salary-sacrificed contributions (refer to Chapter 4) are also paid into your SMSF. Unlike SG contributions, where your employer *must* pay into your chosen fund when you have the right to choose your super fund, your employer could deny you the right to redirect your salary-sacrificed contributions into your SMSF. Such a refusal by an employer is unlikely (and mean spirited), but possible.

If you're a member of a super fund where your final retirement is known (that is, you belong to a *defined benefit fund*), your employer may be making additional contributions on your behalf that you could lose if you leave the fund. If this situation applies to you, seek financial advice before closing the door on your old super fund.

Transferring current benefits

In most cases, you can transfer your existing benefits into your SMSF. You need to complete the ATO portability form, *Rollover initiation request to transfer whole balance of superannuation benefits to your self-managed super fund* (NAT 74662), and provide a certified copy of your proof of personal identification, such as your driver's licence or passport. Your existing super fund may require additional information to verify that you are the trustee and member of the SMSF that you claim to be. Your existing fund must then transfer your benefits within three business days of receiving a properly completed form. If you intend to make a partial transfer of your super benefit to your SMSF, then you can't use the ATO form; instead, you must use a form supplied by your existing fund.

Find out the implications of moving your super benefits including the impact on any life insurance benefits that you have within your existing fund, and any possible exit fees that your existing fund may charge. Moving to a SMSF may mean that you pay more for your life insurance cover than what you paid in a larger fund. If you have a health condition, you may even have difficulty securing adequate insurance cover. You may be able to transfer only part of your super benefits to protect your existing insurance cover. Flick to Chapter 24 for more on insurance.

Chapter 8

Individual Trustees versus Corporate Trustee

*I*f you want your superannuation savings held in a self-managed super fund (SMSF), you must become a trustee of your fund. As *trustee*, you look after a fund, a SMSF, that has the legal structure of a trust, and you run the SMSF and make decisions on behalf of fund members — including you! Ordinarily, all trustees must be members of your SMSF, and all members must be trustees. In other words, you can't be a member of a SMSF without also being a trustee of that fund. This means you wear two hats — SMSF trustee and SMSF member.

A trustee can be an individual or a company. A *corporate trustee* is a company incorporated under the law that then acts as trustee for the fund. If you choose to have a corporate trustee for your SMSF, then you're appointed as a director of that company.

In this chapter, I cover who can and can't become a DIY super trustee. I explain the difference between individual trustees and a corporate trustee, and what you need to consider if you choose to use a corporate trustee. I also detail the special trustee rules that apply to single member SMSFs.

Drawing a Line between Trustee and Member

The distinction between, say, Trish Power as SMSF trustee and Trish Power as SMSF member may seem trivial in such a small fund but, legally, the role of trustee is a separate and very important responsibility. In fact, as a new trustee, you must sign a special declaration within 21 days of becoming a trustee stating that you understand your responsibilities as a superannuation trustee. (I take you through the SMSF trustee declaration and your trustee responsibilities in Chapter 9.)

You can have no more than four members in a SMSF, which means also you can have no more than four individual trustees, or no more than four directors of a corporate trustee. And in case you're wondering, you can't receive any remuneration for taking on the job of SMSF trustee.

Meeting the Standards of a SMSF Trustee

Anyone can become a SMSF trustee. Well … almost anyone. Your age, your home address, your financial history and your criminal history (if any) can affect your eligibility to be a superannuation trustee.

Trustees of SMSFs must be 18 years of age or over, although children under the age of 18 can still be members of a SMSF. A parent or guardian can be a SMSF trustee for a member who is under the age of 18. If the child is a fund member due to receiving a death pension upon the death of a fund member (see Chapter 24), then the child's *legal personal representative* — that is, the executor of the estate of the deceased fund member (which can be a parent) — acts as SMSF trustee for the child. ***Note:*** Before admitting a child under the age of 18 as a member, a parent should chat to an accountant or financial adviser (refer to Chapter 5) to ensure that such an option is clearly in the financial best interests of the child, and also perhaps to review whether such an option is in the best financial interests of the parents.

You cannot be a SMSF trustee if you are a disqualified person. You're considered a *disqualified person* if you have been convicted of an offence involving dishonesty, you're an undischarged bankrupt or you have previously broken a serious superannuation law. (I explain these situations later in the chapter.) If you become a disqualified person while you're a

SMSF trustee, then you must resign as trustee. You then have six months to restructure your SMSF to ensure it remains complying, or transfer your assets to an APRA-regulated fund. (For more info on APRA-regulated funds, refer to Chapters 1 and 2.)

Protecting your residency status

If you're living overseas or plan to be out of Australia for an extended period, you need to be aware of the superannuation residency rules. For your SMSF to receive tax concessions, your fund must meet the definition of 'Australian superannuation fund' at all times during the income year to be considered a complying fund for tax purposes.

Your super fund must satisfy these three tests to be considered an *Australian superannuation fund* for an income year:

✔ **Your SMSF is established in Australia or any asset of the fund is located in Australia.** According to the ATO, a SMSF is established in Australia when the trustee receives and accepts the initial super contribution in Australia.

✔ **Central management and control of the fund is 'ordinarily' in Australia.** This generally means that high-level decision making (such as drafting your SMSF's investment strategy and reviewing your fund's investments) is conducted within Australia, rather than just the more mundane (but still important) administrative tasks. Depending on your individual circumstances, you can satisfy this limb of the test even when the SMSF trustees are temporarily overseas for up to two years, and potentially longer.

✔ **Active members must be Australian residents.** Your SMSF has at least 50 per cent of your SMSF's assets linked to active members and the active members are Australian residents, or your SMSF has no active members. An *active member* is a member who makes contributions to the fund or who receives contributions from an employer or other person, and those contributions are paid into the member's SMSF account.

To explain the last two points, consider this example: Beth and George run a two-member SMSF, which is invested in Australian shares and cash. Each member is entitled to 50 per cent of the assets of the fund, based on member account balances. George takes up a job opportunity in Dubai for 18 months, while Beth stays behind to look after the kids. Six months into the contract, George is offered a permanent position and decides to stay. The ATO considers him no longer an Australian resident. George has made no contributions to the SMSF while he was away and he has no intention of making any contributions. But Beth remains an Australian resident and continues to make super contributions to the SMSF. Therefore the fund meets the definition of 'Australian superannuation fund' because the control of the fund is in Australia. A few months later, Beth then decides to move the family to Dubai permanently. The couple's SMSF is at risk of failing the Australian superannuation fund definition, because although neither Beth nor George intend to make super contributions while living in Dubai, the permanent move to Dubai infers that central management and control is no longer 'ordinarily' in Australia.

If your SMSF fails the Australian superannuation fund definition, your fund may have to pay the top marginal income tax rate of 47 per cent (and reverting to 45 per cent from July 2017) on its assets and earnings, rather than 15 per cent tax on fund earnings and no penalty tax on the assets of the fund. The ATO suggests that before your SMSF faces this situation, a trustee/member can appoint a legal representative as trustee while temporarily overseas to maintain the fund's residency status, or convert the fund into a small APRA fund, or roll over his or her super benefits into a large commercially available super fund (refer to Chapter 2). Chat with an adviser about your options because if your SMSF accepts contributions from a non-resident member, the residency status of your fund could be jeopardised. (To find a suitable adviser, refer to Chapter 5.)

No employer/employee relationships

Your super fund isn't considered a SMSF when you have a fund member who is employed by another fund member, unless the two members involved are relatives. According to the super rules, a 'relative' is a fund member's:

✔ **Spouse:** A spouse includes a de facto partner of the same sex or different sex, who, although not legally married to the SMSF member, lives with the person on a genuine domestic basis in a relationship as a couple.

✔ **Parent, grandparent, brother, sister, uncle, aunt, nephew, niece, lineal descendant or adopted child of the member, or of the member's spouse:** A relative can include the former spouse of the member, or a spouse of the relatives mentioned here — that is, individuals colloquially known as an 'in-laws'.

Example: Maria and her younger brother, Joe, run a franchise supermarket together in the western suburbs of Melbourne. Maria is the owner of the business, and she employs Joe to look after the day-to-day management of the supermarket. They're members/trustees of the same SMSF. Although Joe is an employee of Maria, they're related, which means they can both be members/trustees of the same SMSF. Maria is considering offering a long-term and loyal employee, Frida, the opportunity to join their SMSF. Frida is unrelated but 'like family' according to Maria. However, under the super rules, Frida is ineligible to join the same SMSF as her employer.

No dishonesty offences

Generally, you can't be a SMSF trustee if you've been convicted of an offence involving dishonest conduct. You're then considered a disqualified person, which precludes you from the role of SMSF trustee. The term 'dishonest' is fairly broad and can mean different things for different individuals but, generally, this includes convictions involving fraud, lying, perjury or theft — and prison time can automatically prevent you from taking on the role of trustee. *Note:* Dishonesty offences include providing false information on your tax return and travelling on a train without paying for a ticket.

If you do have a criminal record involving dishonesty, then a SMSF is probably not for you. At times, however, the ATO can show compassion. If you consider your dishonesty offence was relatively minor — not an offence involving serious dishonest conduct — you can apply in writing to the ATO for a waiver from the 'disqualified person' rule.

A criminal fine greater than $20,400, or prison time of two years or more for dishonest conduct, is automatically considered an offence of serious dishonest conduct. In a 2011 ATO Interpretative Decision (ATO ID 2011/24), the ATO considered a waiver application from an individual who had been convicted to two years' jail for dishonest conduct but had been released before he served the two years. Although the applicant's time in prison was less than two years, the ATO deemed that the gravity of the offence was the most important factor in determining whether an individual was a prudential risk to a superannuation fund. The legislation (paragraph 126B (2)(a) of the SIS Act) specifies 'penalty actually imposed for the offence', rather than actual time spent in prison.

No undischarged bankrupts

If you can't properly manage your own financial affairs, then don't expect to become a SMSF trustee. You can't be a SMSF trustee if you're an *insolvent under administration*, which is more commonly known as an *undischarged bankrupt*. If you've been declared bankrupt, or you've entered a personal insolvency agreement (to avoid bankruptcy), you're considered a 'disqualified person', which means you can't become a SMSF trustee until your bankruptcy is discharged.

Previously naughty trustees

You can't be a SMSF trustee if you've ever been subject to a civil penalty order under the super laws or you've previously been disqualified from being a superannuation trustee by the ATO (or by APRA). If you've been subject to a *civil penalty order*, then you've seriously breached important super rules such as the sole purpose test (see Chapter 11) or the borrowing rules (see Chapter 16) or the in-house asset rules (see Chapter 15).

Deciding between Individual Trustees or a Corporate Trustee

For your SMSF, you can choose between appointing individual trustees or appointing a corporate trustee. A SMSF can have up to four individual trustees, while a corporate trustee can have up to four directors.

According to the ATO, around three-quarters of all SMSFs have individual trustees, and the remaining 25 per cent use a corporate trustee, which in my view simply reflects the fact that a corporate trustee is more expensive and hence not as popular as the cheaper option of individual trustees.

Individual trustees are regulated under the pension powers within Australia's Constitution, while a corporate trustee is subject to the *Corporations Act 2001*. The main implication of this distinction is that a SMSF with a corporate trustee can pay benefits as a lump sum or as an income stream. A SMSF with individual trustees must state in its trust deed that the fund is established for the sole or primary purpose of providing *old-age pensions* (which are private retirement income streams rather than the government-supplied Age Pension). A fund with individual trustees can still pay benefits as a lump sum, but the deed must have a specific clause allowing such payments.

For individual trustees, a change of trustee also means that all fund investments have to be re-registered using the names of the remaining trustees. Also, if you intend to purchase an investment property within your SMSF, then a corporate trustee may be simpler for fund administration and for properly identifying the SMSF as owner of the asset (for more info on rules regarding investments, see Chapter 15).

Having a corporate trustee means your SMSF ordinarily costs more to set up and to operate each year (for information on costs, refer to Chapter 6). Choosing a corporate trustee, however, can mean less administrative hassle when a fund member leaves or dies. For example, upon the death of an individual trustee of a two-trustee fund, the remaining trustee has to act swiftly to ensure that the fund meets the trustee rules for a single member fund — you can't have a sole individual trustee for a SMSF, although you can have a single director trustee company. (I explain the rules applicable to single member funds in the section 'Single Member SMSFs: A Special Case', later in the chapter.)

If you intend your SMSF to be multi-generational, that is, a SMSF that your children, and possibly grandchildren, can join over time, the initial costs of setting up and running a corporate trustee can be worth the expense.

The ATO provides an excellent table highlighting the pros and cons of individual and corporate trustees in its publication *Setting up a self-managed super fund* (NAT 71923). Table 8-1 summarises the ATO's analysis.

Table 8-1	Comparing Individual and Corporate Trustees	
	Individual Trustees	*Corporate Trustee*
Setting up your fund		
Administrative costs	Less costly	More costly because of initial set-up and annual company costs
Single member funds	Must have two individual trustees	Can have a single director of trustee company
Governing rules (trust deed)		
	Must follow fund's trust deed and super laws	Must follow trust deed, super laws, company's constitution and *Corporations Act 2001*

(continued)

Table 8-1 *(continued)*

	Individual Trustees	*Corporate Trustee*
Ongoing administration and reporting		
Administration	Less reporting obligations and simpler to administer, although increased paperwork to change trustees	Easier to administer ownership of assets, and easier to keep fund assets separate from personal or business assets
Reporting	Must appoint auditor, lodge SMSF annual return and pay ATO levy	Must appoint auditor, lodge SMSF return and pay ATO levy, and must also lodge company return and pay ASIC levy
Changes to trustees and members		
Fund assets	Held in name of all individual trustees 'as trustees'. When change of trustee, change name on all ownership documents	Held in name of company 'as trustee'. When change of directors, no change in names on ownership documents
Move to single member trustee	If two-trustee fund and one dies, need to appoint a second trustee for SMSF to continue	If two-director trustee company and one director dies, can continue with one director
Reporting	Notify ATO within 28 days of change in trustees/members	Notify ATO and ASIC within 28 days of change in directors
Paying benefits to members		
	Fund can pay benefits as pensions, and lump sums if trust deed specifically allows lump sums	Fund can pay benefits as lump sum or income stream

Source: Adapted from table appearing in ATO document Setting up a self-managed super fund *(NAT 71923).*

Choosing a Corporate Trustee

If you've opted for a corporate trustee, your two choices are:

✔ **Superannuation Trustee Company:** The most effective (and cheaper) type of trustee company for SMSFs is a type of *special purpose company*, more specifically known as a *Superannuation Trustee Company (STC)*. The sole purpose of such a company is to act as a trustee of a regulated superannuation fund. The company's constitution must have a clause prohibiting the company from distributing income or property to its shareholders. Further, the company can't be used for any other purpose, such as operating the family business. If you use a special purpose company as trustee, the ASIC levy for the annual company tax return costs $45.

✔ **Trading company and/or multi-purpose company:** You can use a new (or existing) multi-purpose company as the trustee company for your SMSF. You may run a business using a corporate structure, or you may use a corporate trustee for your family trust. Although many thousands of SMSFs happily operate with family trading companies as trustee, it seems to me that mixing business with your retirement planning objectives may end in tears. The directors of the existing company must meet the requirements of a SMSF — no more than four directors, and each company director must be a member of the SMSF — and must not be an employee of another member unless related, nor be a disqualified person. Further, the ASIC levy when lodging annual returns for regular companies is $243, compared with $45 for a STC.

Use ASIC Form 201, *Application for registration as an Australian company*, to register your company. The ASIC lodgement fee in this instance is $457. You can download Form 201 from the ASIC website (www.asic.gov.au).

Alternatively, you can arrange for a fund administrator to set up your trustee company for you. Costs range from $880 to $1,100, including ASIC's $457 fee. You may find a fund administrator that is able to set up your company for less, but check what the service fee includes.

Single Member SMSFs: A Special Case

If you plan to run a SMSF with just you as a member, you must satisfy special trustee rules.

If you choose to have individual trustees for a single member SMSF, you must have two trustees, one being you. The other individual trustee can't be your employer, unless your employer is a relative (for details about these rules, refer to the section 'Meeting the Standards of a SMSF Trustee' earlier in this chapter). Typically, the second trustee is a close relative such as wife or husband, or adult child, because only someone who loves you would ordinarily take on the responsibility (and liability) of a trustee role.

Taking on the responsibility of trustee without reward isn't an attractive option for many individuals (even for relatives), when you're not even a member of the fund that you're looking after. What often happens is that many single member SMSFs have a second individual trustee who is a relatively passive trustee, and not actively involved in the fund's decision making.

Before you can be appointed as a SMSF trustee, you must consent in writing to your appointment, which is especially important for individuals who agree to become a non-member trustee for a single member SMSF. Likewise, all other trustees (or directors of a corporate trustee) must consent to their individual appointment as trustee or director. Trustee appointments must then be minuted at a trustee meeting and the fund must notify the ATO of any trustee changes within 28 days. Each new trustee must also read and sign the SMSF trustee declaration (see Chapter 9).

A more practical option for a single member SMSF is to opt for a corporate trustee. You can have a corporate trustee with a sole trustee director or with two directors, the other director not being your employer unless that employer is a relative. For example, even where your wife or husband is your employer, they can still be a director of your SMSF's trustee company.

Chapter 9

Trustee Declarations and Other Promises

*Y*our role as a self-managed super fund (SMSF) trustee isn't a dress rehearsal: You must take it seriously from day one. Some DIY super spruikers claim running your own fund is as simple as purchasing a DIY super fund kit, buying a few shares and enjoying the tax benefits of super. Committing to a SMSF, however, can be considered nearly as significant as getting married, but usually not as expensive.

If you're willing to put in the time to understand the rules, the prospect of complying with the superannuation laws shouldn't deter you from setting up your own fund. If you do find the compliance side too intimidating, though, service providers can look after your administration and compliance obligations (for these details, see Chapter 10).

Outsourcing your obligations doesn't remove your ultimate responsibility as trustee of your own fund. As trustee of your SMSF, you carry the can if something goes wrong. Even if you hire a specialist company to look after your SMSF's administration and compliance, and investment obligations, in the end, you're responsible for what happens in your fund.

In this chapter, I explain what you need to think about before signing the ATO's *Self-managed super fund trustee declaration*. I take you through the contents of this important document, namely, understanding your trustee responsibilities. I also explain what happens if you break your trustee promises.

If you set up your SMSF before July 2007, then you were not required to sign the SMSF trustee declaration at the end of this chapter because, back then, the document did not exist. Even so, as an experienced SMSF trustee, it's still worth checking out the trustee declaration at the end of this chapter, because the document is an excellent reminder of your responsibilities as a SMSF trustee.

Signing the Trustee Declaration

When setting up your SMSF, or as a new trustee of an existing SMSF, you must sign a document — the *Self-managed super fund trustee declaration* (NAT 71089) — within 21 days of becoming a SMSF trustee, stating that you 'understand [your] duties and responsibilities as a trustee or director of the corporate trustee of the self-managed superannuation fund named on this declaration ...'

The declaration is a curious document because its purpose is simply to confirm that you understand your responsibilities as fund trustee. As trustee, you're still subject to these responsibilities even when you don't sign the document. If you don't sign the trustee declaration, however, you may be subject to penalties, such as a $1,700 fine that you have to pay from your personal savings rather than from your super account. If your fund breaks the super rules, you (or your fund) can be subject to very serious penalties. I explain what these penalties can be in the section 'Breaking Your Trustee Promises', later in the chapter.

I provide a copy of the SMSF trustee declaration (NAT 71809) in Figure 9-1 at the end of this chapter. Alternatively, you can download the SMSF trustee declaration from the ATO website: `https://www.ato.gov.au/Forms/ Trustee-declaration---for-new-trustees---directors-of- corporate-trustees-of-SMSFs/`

Before you sign the trustee declaration, you must read the ATO fact sheet *Self-managed super funds — key messages for trustees* (NAT 71128). This fact sheet basically states that you're responsible for managing your fund even when you use a professional to help you manage your SMSF. The fact sheet also explains that you must understand your trustee duties and responsibilities, which include

✔ Ensuring your SMSF is maintained for the purpose of providing retirement benefits, which is more commonly known as meeting the sole purpose test. I explain what this test means later in the chapter in the section 'Meeting the Sole Purpose Test, Always'.

✔ Drafting the fund's investment strategy and making investment decisions (see Part IV in this book).

✔ Accepting contributions (refer to Chapter 4) and paying benefits (see Chapters 19, 21 and 22).

✔ Appointing an approved SMSF auditor for each income year (see Chapter 12 for reporting requirements).

✔ Lodging annual returns with the ATO and keeping fund records (also in Chapter 12).

✔ Advising the ATO of any change in trustees, directors or members within 28 days of the change. (For more information on these obligations, refer to Chapter 8.)

When signing the SMSF trustee declaration, you must ensure you insert the full name of your fund at the beginning of the declaration. You must then sign and date the declaration on page 2 of the form, and ensure you have a witness to your signature who also signs and dates the form.

Keeping Mindful of Your Trustee Duties

As a SMSF trustee, you need to understand that a super fund is a trust, which is a legal structure that enables you and any other trustees to invest money on behalf of the fund members; in this case, for the retirement of members. The trustee's responsibility to fund members is known as a *trust relationship*. You, as trustee, own the investments in your superannuation fund but, you, as fund member, have a *beneficial interest*. In other words, as trustee, you're required to look after the investments on behalf of all fund members, not just your interest in the fund, and ensure all trustee decisions are in the best interests of fund members. The trust relationship is heavily backed up by the *Superannuation Industry (Supervision) Act 1993* (SIS Act).

The SMSF trustee declaration reminds you that for the duration of your trusteeship, the SIS Act and trust law also require you to

✔ Act honestly in all matters relating to your SMSF.

✔ Exercise the same degree of care, skill and diligence as you'd expect from an ordinary prudent person.

✔ Act in the best interests of all fund members.

The SMSF trustee declaration also highlights that the SMSF trustee should then run the fund according to the terms of the fund's trust deed (refer to Chapter 7), and in line with the super rules, including:

✔ **Meeting conditions of release:** Ensuring that the members of your SMSF can only access super benefits if they meet a legitimate condition of release (see Chapter 19).

✔ **Avoiding dodgy benefit payment schemes:** Okay, the SMSF trustee declaration does not use the word 'dodgy' but it does warn you to refrain from entering into transactions that circumvent restrictions on the payment of benefits.

✔ **Separating assets:** Keeping your fund's assets separate from your own assets — for example, your personal bank account can't be confused with your fund's bank account (for your compliance obligations, see Chapter 11).

✔ **Protecting assets:** Taking appropriate action to protect your fund's assets — for example, ensuring you have evidence that proves ownership of fund assets, such as ensuring ownership is in the name of the corporate trustee or, where individual trustees, in the name of individuals 'as trustees'. I explain this requirement in Chapter 15.

✔ **Making no improper contracts:** Not entering into any contract (or any other action) that would hinder you from performing your role as trustee — for example, you can't use your fund's assets as security for a margin loan.

✔ **Providing access to information:** Allowing all fund members to have access to fund information, including details about the fund's financial situation, the fund's investments and individual benefit entitlements.

Meeting the Sole Purpose Test, Always

Your SMSF must meet the sole purpose test when managing the fund, in particular, when investing your fund's money. The *sole purpose test* can arguably be considered the underlying moral basis for superannuation trustee behaviour.

What the sole purpose test means for you as a trustee is that a superannuation fund must be maintained for at least one of the following primary (or core) purposes:

✔ Payment of benefits on or after retirement from gainful employment (see Chapter 19)

✔ Payment of benefits to members when they reach the age of 65 (I explain this condition of release in Chapter 19)

✔ Payment of benefits when a member dies (see Chapter 24)

According to section 62 of the SIS Act, the sole purpose test also permits additional benefits to fund members for an ancillary purpose, including in the following circumstances:

✔ Termination of a member's employment with an employer who made contributions for that member

✔ Termination of employment due to physical or mental ill health

✔ Member's death after retirement or after reaching the age of 65 (death benefits paid to dependants or a legal representative)

Using your SMSF assets to finance, say, an overseas holiday or to finance your personal art collection, can only end in tears — very costly tears. If your SMSF is found to breach the sole purpose test, the penalty can be a fine of up to $340,000 as an individual trustee and possible imprisonment for up to five years. The ATO may also deem your fund to be non-complying. I discuss the penalties that apply if you break your trustee promises in the next section.

Thou shalt not breach the sole purpose test. I explain the ins and outs of this important SMSF commandment in Chapter 11, and list my ten commandments of DIY super in Chapter 26.

Taking Note of Three Important Challenges

In late 2012, the ATO made three important changes to the SMSF trustee declaration to reflect certain areas that were of a concern to the government. So, when you sign the declaration you also declare that you understand the following trustee responsibilities:

✔ **Drafting and reviewing an investment strategy:** You must prepare, implement and regularly review an investment strategy that reflects the risk, return, diversification, liquidity and insurance needs of your SMSF members (see Chapters 14 and 15 for an explanation of these concepts).

✔ **Considering insurance cover:** When drafting and reviewing the fund's investment strategy, you must decide whether the trustees should hold insurance cover, or not, for one or more fund members (see Chapter 24).

✔ **Understanding the absence of government financial assistance:** You must also make a specific declaration that you are aware that you do not have access to the government's financial assistance program that's available to trustees of funds regulated by the Australian Prudential Regulation Authority (APRA) , such as small APRA funds (refer to Chapter 1).

Breaking Your Trustee Promises

Failure to comply with the SIS Act and the SIS Regulations is known as a *contravention* of the super rules, and can ordinarily result in some type of punishment or compliance action.

The ATO regularly reminds individuals that, as trustee of your SMSF, you must act in accordance with: Your fund's trust deed; the SIS Act and the SIS Regulations; the *Income Tax Assessment Act 1997*; the *Tax Administration Act 1953*; the *Corporations Act 2001*, and other general rules, including tax and trust laws.

Responsibility lies squarely with you when the ATO knocks on your door and decides your SMSF has room for improvement. If you break the super rules and the ATO finds out, you can't blame your accountant, your fund administrator or your financial adviser for your predicament. You can't even blame your fellow trustees, although they're also likely to be punished by the ATO. You may have a right of action against one or more of your service providers (refer to Chapter 5), but the ATO targets you, as trustee, if you choose to ignore the super rules.

The ATO assumes *all* trustees are fully informed and fully active in your fund's decision-making process. Ignorance is no excuse, and you can face hefty financial penalties, or even jail, for pleading ignorance.

Reacting to your auditor's concerns

If your SMSF breaches the super rules in the first 15 months of operation, your fund's auditor must report any breach to the ATO if the value of the breach is greater than $2,000, regardless of whether the breach is minor from a compliance point of view.

For SMSFs in existence for more than 15 months, your fund's auditor must follow strict guidelines when reporting breaches of the super rules. If your auditor identifies a breach of the super rules, you need to take immediate steps to rectify the breach. In certain circumstances, the auditor will also report the breach to the ATO. The ATO is also notified if the auditor is concerned about your fund's financial position. I explain your fund auditor's role in more detail in Chapter 12.

Asking for administrative penalties

You, as SMSF trustee, may be personally liable for administrative penalties in the form of cash fines if you (as super fund trustee) break the super rules, such as when your fund

- ✔ Fails to advise the ATO of a change of trustee or other changes in the fund ($3,400 fine for each trustee)

- ✔ Fails to keep and maintain fund records ($1,700 fine for each trustee for each breach)

- ✔ Fails to lodge returns on time ($1,700 fine for each trustee)

- ✔ Provides false and/or misleading statements (fines ranging from $3,400 to $10,200)

For more information on how to ensure you don't break these super rules, see Chapters 11 and 12.

Allowing for rectification and education directions

If your fund breaches the super rules (that is, your fund contravenes the SIS Act), the ATO may shower some mercy upon you and issue you with a rectification order or an education order or both. Or, the ATO may fine you *and* force you to change your naughty ways.

The ATO can issue a *rectification direction*, which means the ATO has the power to force you to fix the consequences of a breach of the super laws by your super fund. Although only introduced since July 2014, it is expected that a rectification direction will require a SMSF trustee to undertake very specific action within a specific timeframe and the SMSF trustee will have to provide the ATO with evidence of compliance.

The ATO can also force you to attend mandatory trustee education by giving you an *education direction*. Again, this ATO power was only introduced from July 2014, but it's expected that such a direction will require a SMSF trustee to undertake a specific course within a specific time frame and that the SMSF trustee provides evidence to the ATO of having completed the course.

If you receive an education direction, you will also be required to re-sign the SMSF trustee declaration. (I explain the rectification direction, education direction and other SMSF penalties in more detail in Chapter 11.)

Dealing a death blow to SMSF trustees

The ATO takes a dim view of SMSF trustees who either deliberately breach the super rules or who don't care whether they comply with the rules or not. The ATO is also unimpressed with SMSF trustees who fail to make a genuine effort to rectify a breach, when a contravention is discovered. Depending on how naughty you're found to be, the ATO may prosecute you and/or you may lose the right to be a superannuation fund trustee. The ATO can

✔ **Suspend or remove you as a SMSF trustee:** If the ATO suspends all the trustees of your SMSF, the ATO appoints a trustee during the period of suspension — and the ATO can direct the acting trustee to operate in a certain way.

✔ **Disqualify you:** If you're disqualified (refer to Chapter 8), you can no longer be a SMSF trustee — now, and in most cases, the future.

✔ **Impose a fine on you:** For example, if you breach the sole purpose test (refer to the section 'Meeting the Sole Purpose Test, Always', earlier in the chapter, and see Chapter 11), you can be fined up to $340,000 as an individual trustee. You can be penalised up to $17,000 for failing to formulate an investment strategy for your fund (see Chapter 15).

✔ **Throw you in jail:** Breaching the sole purpose test by illegally accessing your super benefits can mean facing jail for a term of up to five years.

Losing your fund's complying status

Punishing the members of a super fund is usually a last resort but, if a contravention is particularly serious, you can expect your SMSF to be declared a *non-complying fund*. For example, if all the SMSF trustees were complicit in the contravention, then, in that situation, such a severe punishment is more likely.

A non-complying fund can't access the tax concessions applicable to complying super funds. Even worse, a super fund that loses its complying status is hit with penalty tax — your fund is liable to pay 47 per cent tax on the taxable income of the fund, and 47 per cent tax on the assets (excluding non-concessional contributions) of your fund. The penalty tax rate of 47 per cent reverts to 45 per cent from July 2017.

Defending decent SMSF trustees

Becoming a SMSF trustee means joining a select and very influential group of Australians. More than 1 million Australians, or just over 4 per cent of Australia's population, control around a third of the $1.8 trillion or so held in superannuation accounts, according to the ATO. That's a big deal!

The rest of the super industry can't quite accept the spectacular growth of the SMSF sector, warning Australians of unscrupulous individuals who want to make money from redirecting your super savings to a SMSF. And such SMSF scammers do exist, but the majority of individuals working in the SMSF sector are legitimate service providers.

In the recent past, the Australian government has expressed nervousness that so much of Australia's retirement security rests in the hands of so few Australians. Hang on! Apart from the 534,000 or so SMSFs holding a one-third share of all super money, most of the remaining two-thirds of super money is held in fewer than 300 large funds, which is controlled by fewer than 3,000 trustees and invested by roughly 130 investment managers (although around 30 investment managers invest the bulk of the super money held by the large super funds). Shouldn't the government be similarly concerned that the retirement savings of the remaining 23 million or so Australians is in the hands of so few?

Even more concerning is that some of the largest super funds are interrelated through the use of common fund managers and asset consultants. Ah, but the discussion of potential 'trustee' risk and 'fund manager' risk associated with large funds just has to be shelved for a different book.

An important difference between running a SMSF and running a large super fund, however, is that the trustees of large super funds (such as industry funds and retail funds) are licensed by the Australian Prudential Regulation Authority (APRA). APRA has imposed prudential requirements on trustees of large funds, which aren't generally imposed on SMSF trustees — such as the requirement to regularly report to APRA how the super fund manages risk. In many cases, large funds are also licensed by the Australian Securities & Investments Commission (ASIC). A super fund requires an Australian Financial Services Licence when the fund offers financial products or financial advice. I explain licensed financial advice in Chapter 5.

Lack of prudential supervision over SMSFs isn't the only concern that has bothered the government and some sections of the super industry. The government also believes that many SMSF trustees arrange for accountants or financial advisers to set up their fund, and then arrange for these service providers to run the fund on the trustees' behalf without much involvement by the fund trustees. In other words, some sections of the super industry, and to a lesser extent, the government, believe that too many SMSF trustees aren't taking such an important role seriously enough.

This concern from government and the broader super industry is one of the main reasons the government now requires SMSF trustees to sign the ATO SMSF trustee declaration when they start a SMSF.

Source: Originally published on consumer website www.superguide.com.au. *Copyright Trish Power. Reproduced with permission.*

Australian Government
Australian Taxation Office

Self-managed super fund trustee declaration

I understand that as an individual trustee or director of the corporate trustee of

Fund name

I am responsible for ensuring that the fund complies with the *Superannuation Industry (Supervision) Act 1993* (SISA) and other relevant legislation. The Commissioner of Taxation (the Commissioner) has the authority and responsibility for administering the legislation and enforcing the fund's compliance with the law.

I must keep myself informed of changes to the legislation relevant to the operation of my fund and ensure the trust deed is kept up to date in accordance with the law and the needs of the members.

If I do not comply with the legislation, the Commissioner may take the following actions:
■ impose administrative penalties on me
■ give me a written direction to rectify any contraventions or undertake a course of education
■ enter into agreements with me to rectify any contraventions of the legislation
■ disqualify me from being a trustee or director of a corporate trustee of any superannuation fund in the future
■ remove the fund's complying status, which may result in significant adverse tax consequences for the fund
■ prosecute me under the law, which may result in fines or imprisonment.

Sole purpose
I understand it is my responsibility to ensure the fund is only maintained for the purpose of providing benefits to the members upon their retirement (or attainment of a certain age) or their beneficiaries if a member dies. I understand that I should regularly evaluate whether the fund continues to be the appropriate vehicle to meet this purpose.

Trustee duties
I understand that by law I must at all times:
■ act honestly in all matters concerning the fund
■ exercise skill, care and diligence in managing the fund
■ act in the best interests of all the members of the fund
■ ensure that members only access their super benefits if they have met a legitimate condition of release
■ refrain from entering into transactions that circumvent restrictions on the payment of benefits
■ ensure that my money and other assets are kept separate from the money and other assets of the fund
■ take appropriate action to protect the fund's assets (for example, have sufficient evidence of the ownership of fund assets)
■ refrain from entering into any contract or do anything that would prevent me from, or hinder me in, properly performing or exercising my functions or powers as a trustee or director of the corporate trustee of the fund
■ allow all members of the fund to have access to information and documents as required, including details about
  – the financial situation of the fund
  – the investments of the fund
  – the members' benefit entitlements.

I also understand that by law I must prepare, implement and regularly review an investment strategy having regard to all the circumstances of the fund, which include, but are not limited to:
■ the risks associated with the fund's investments
■ the likely return from investments, taking into account the fund's objectives and expected cash flow requirements
■ investment diversity and the fund's exposure to risk due to inadequate diversification
■ the liquidity of the fund's investments having regard to the fund's expected cash flow requirements in discharging its existing and prospective liabilities (including benefit payments)
■ whether the trustees of the fund should hold insurance cover for one or more members of the fund.

Accepting contributions and paying benefits
I understand that I can only accept contributions and pay benefits (income streams or lump sums) to members or their beneficiaries when the conditions specified in the law and the fund trust deed have been met.

Investment restrictions
I understand that, as a trustee or director of the corporate trustee of the fund, subject to certain limited exceptions specified in the law, I am prohibited from:
■ lending money of the fund to, or providing financial assistance to, a member of the fund or a member's relative (financial assistance means any assistance that improves the financial position of a person directly or indirectly, including the provision of credit)

NAT 71089-08.2014   Page 1

Figure 9-1:
SMSF
trustee
declaration
(page 1 of 2).

■ acquiring assets (other than business real property, listed securities, certain in-house assets and acquisitions made under mergers allowed by special determinations or acquisitions as a result of a breakdown of a relationship) for the fund from members or other related parties of the fund

■ borrowing money (or maintaining an existing borrowing) on behalf of the fund except in certain limited circumstances (while limited recourse borrowing arrangements are permitted, they can be complex and particular conditions must be met to ensure that legal requirements are not breached)

■ having more than 5% of the market value of the fund's total assets at the end of the income year as in-house assets (these are loans to, or investments in, related parties of the fund – including trusts – or assets subject to a lease or lease arrangement between the trustee and a member, relative or other related party)

■ entering into investments that are not made or maintained on an arm's length (commercial) basis (this ensures the purchase or sale price of the fund's assets and any earnings from those assets reflects their market value).

Administration

I understand that the trustees of the fund must:

■ keep and retain for at least 10 years
  – minutes of all trustee meetings at which matters affecting the fund were considered (this includes investment decisions and decisions to appoint members and trustees)
  – records of all changes of trustees, including directors of the corporate trustee
  – each trustee's consent to be appointed as a trustee of the fund or a director of the corporate trustee
  – all trustee declarations
  – copies of all reports given to members

■ ensure that the following are prepared and retained for at least five years
  – an annual statement of the financial position of the fund
  – an annual operating statement
  – copies of all annual returns lodged
  – accounts and statements that accurately record and explain the transactions and financial position of the fund

■ appoint an approved SMSF auditor each year, no later than 45 days before the due date for lodgment of the fund's annual return and provide documents to the auditor as requested

■ lodge the fund's annual return, completed in its entirety, by the due date

■ notify the ATO within 28 days of any changes to the
  – membership of the fund, or trustees or directors of the corporate trustee
  – name of the fund
  – contact person and their contact details
  – postal address, registered address or address for service of notices for the fund

■ notify the ATO in writing within 28 days if the fund becomes an Australian Prudential Regulation Authority (APRA) regulated fund.

DECLARATION

By signing this declaration I acknowledge that I understand my duties and responsibilities as a trustee or director of the corporate trustee of the self-managed superannuation fund named on this declaration (or if the fund's name changes, that name). I understand that:

■ *I must ensure this document is retained for at least 10 years or while I remain a trustee or director of the corporate trustee (whichever is longer) and, if I fail to do this, penalties may apply.*

■ *I may have to make this document available for inspection by a member of staff of the ATO and, if I fail to do this, penalties may apply.*

■ *I do not have access to the government's financial assistance program that is available to trustees of APRA regulated funds in the case of financial loss due to fraudulent conduct or theft.*

Trustee's or director's name

Trustee's or director's signature

Date

Day / Month / Year

Witness' name (witness must be 18 years old or over)

Witness' signature

Date

Day / Month / Year

SENSITIVE (when completed)

Figure 9-1:
Continued
(page 2 of 2).

Part III
Running Your Self-Managed Super Fund

Five Things to Check When Appointing a Fund Administrator

- ✔ **Years of experience in the SMSF sector:** Experts can have dozens of years of experience in superannuation, or may have just entered the SMSF space. Do your due diligence on who'll be working on your SMSF, and ensure your prospective administrator has the expertise and the systems to service your fund.

- ✔ **Scope of administration service agreement:** When appointing a SMSF administrator, you'll be asked to sign an administration service agreement, which covers the scope of what your administrator will do for your SMSF. Read the agreement carefully before signing.

- ✔ **Administration schedule of fees:** The fee schedule often forms part of the administration service agreement. Check the fee schedule to see what's covered in any fixed administration fee, and what services are additional costs. ATO annual levy fees are extra.

- ✔ **Total SMSF package or separate investment administration:** Be clear with prospective administrators about your expectations in terms of managing your fund's investments. Many administrators offer an administration platform for SMSF investments and collate all SMSF paperwork on your behalf, while others separate SMSF compliance from investment administration, in various forms.

- ✔ **Complaints resolution process:** Does your prospective administrator have a published complaints resolution process if something goes awry with the administration process? Many SMSF administration providers don't publish this information, which means you have to actively seek the answer to this question yourself.

Check out www.dummies.com/extras/diysuperau for a free article about running your own SMSF.

In this part ...

✔ Appreciate that you must steer your fund's super CART — that is, your fund's **C**ompliance, **A**dministration, **R**eporting and **T**ax management responsibilities.

✔ Understand the options available if you want to delegate part, or all, of your SMSF trustee duties (but not responsibility) to a service provider.

✔ Work out the best way to successfully run your SMSF according to the super laws.

✔ Get a short course on how the tax rules on super apply to your super fund, and your super benefits.

Chapter 10

Finding a Fund Administrator, or Not

As a self-managed super fund (SMSF) trustee, the question you need to ask is: Who is going to steer your super CART? CART is an acronym I coined to help you get your head around the mandatory aspects of running a DIY super fund — that is, your **C**ompliance, **A**dministration, **R**eporting and **T**ax management responsibilities.

One of the biggest decisions you need to make when running a SMSF is whether you steer the entire CART yourself, or you delegate all or just part of your workload to a professional administrator, an accountant, or to another service provider. In Chapter 5, I examine the main experts available to help you with running your SMSF, including the option of appointing a fund administrator. In Chapter 6 I consider the costs of running a SMSF, including the cost of possible outsourcing options, and in Chapter 7 I list your six main administration options.

In this chapter, I explain your outsourcing options in more detail. I take you through what you need to consider when making a decision to delegate part, or all, of your CART responsibilities, particularly your administrative obligations.

Taking Aim at SMSF Administration

In practical terms, your fund's administration tasks support many of your fund's compliance, reporting and tax management obligations. You may find that your fund's service provider classifies many of your fund's compliance and reporting obligations under the general category of 'administration', which is fair enough because many CART responsibilities overlap. You can read more about your compliance obligations in Chapter 11, your recording and reporting commitments in Chapter 12, and tax management responsibilities in Chapter 13.

You also need to think carefully about whether you plan to invest your super monies yourself, or whether to appoint an investment adviser to assist your fund. For many SMSF trustees, the main reason for using a professional administration company is that the service provider can worry about the administrative and compliance issues of your fund — allowing you to focus on the investments of your DIY super fund. I discuss investing your DIY super money in Part IV, later in this book.

Debunking the DIY Super Myth

The practice of calling self-managed super funds (SMSFs) 'DIY super funds' upsets the regulator, and also concerns many of the service providers making a living from helping individuals set up, and run, SMSFs. The key message emanating from the SMSF industry is that you can't possibly do it all yourself; you need professionals to help you run your super fund because of the myriad **C**ompliance, **A**dministration, **R**eporting and **T**ax obligations (or CART obligations) associated with SMSFs. True or false? This key message from the industry is true ... and is, strictly speaking, false (more on this debate in the next section, 'Going It Alone').

The debate about terminology, however, is merely a fruitless distraction about semantics. Most Australians who consider running their own super understand that 'DIY super' is a term used to distinguish from the large funds (refer to Chapter 2) that have professional trustees and an administration team looking after your super benefits for you. The greater concern is whether those individuals who take on the responsibility of running a SMSF have the skills to do so; and, if they don't have the expertise, whether they know when to call in the experts.

After setting up a SMSF (refer to Chapter 7), your main CART obligations for your SMSF are

✔ Acting in accordance with super and tax laws (see Chapter 11)

✔ Acting in line with your fund's trust deed (see Chapter 11)

✔ Complying with the sole purpose test (refer to Chapters 9 and 11)

✔ Accepting super contributions (refer to Chapters 4, 13 and 22)

✔ Investing in accordance with your fund's investment strategy and super's special investment rules (see Part IV)

✔ Preparing minutes of trustee meetings and decisions (see Chapter 12)

✔ Keeping accurate accounting records, including recording all contributions (Chapter 4), expenses (Chapter 12), tax paid (Chapter 13), investment transactions (Chapters 15 and 18) and other transactions throughout the year

✔ Paying income streams (pensions) and fulfilling the legal requirements, including tax obligations, associated with an income stream (if your fund is paying a pension) (see Chapters 13, 18 and Part V)

✔ Preparing annual financial reports — operating statement and statement of the fund's financial position (see Chapter 12)

✔ Arranging for the audit of your fund's financial accounts and statements (see Chapter 12)

✔ Preparing and lodging, by due date, the fund's annual return, which contains the annual tax return, regulatory return (SIS compliance information) and member-specific transaction information (see Chapter 12)

✔ Paying the supervisory levy of $259, and tax liability when due

Questions about appropriate skills equally apply to SMSF service providers. The SMSF industry is relatively new, which means quality administrators aren't always easy to find. Before your SMSF appoints an administrator or other type of service provider to assist you with your SMSF, check that the adviser or administrator has several years of experience with SMSFs, or that the individuals who own the business have been in the SMSF space for a few years. (I discuss choosing an adviser in more detail in Chapter 5.)

The compliance and administration checklist for SMSF trustees (see Appendix A, at the end of this book) illustrates what's involved in running your SMSF on your own, or what you can expect from your fund's administrator if you choose to delegate your CART obligations.

Going It Alone

Are you required to use experts when running your own fund? Strictly speaking, you need only appoint a registered approved SMSF auditor (see Chapter 12) to audit your fund.

Under the superannuation laws, SMSF trustees (like all other superannuation trustees) are permitted to set up and administer a super fund on their own, including looking after the investment side of the fund, and paying retirement benefits.

If you're prepared to dedicate sufficient time and research to the role of SMSF trustee, the possibility is there for you to look after your fund's CART obligations, which can keep costs to a minimum. If a trustee doesn't pay for investment advice or other services, then the only essential costs to consider are investment transaction costs, audit fees for the annual review of the fund, the annual supervisory levy of $259 and an annual ASIC levy (if corporate trustee). (I discuss the costs of running a SMSF in Chapter 6.)

SMSF trustees who are intent on doing everything themselves, ordinarily don't draft their own fund's trust deed, though. In most cases, such individuals still buy a trust deed from a solicitor, or from an administrator who has arranged for a solicitor to draft a standard deed. I explain the importance of your fund's trust deed in Chapter 7 (and the cost of a trust deed in Chapter 6).

If you plan to prepare all of your fund's records, including member benefit statements, benefit payment summaries and *year-end reports*, such as your fund's operating statement and statement of financial position (see Chapter 12), your best chance at complying with the super rules is to use specialist SMSF software. You can learn more about the different types of SMSF software available by doing a search for **SMSF software** on the internet. If your fund is relatively simple (say, a single member fund or a fund with no members in pension phase), you may only require a simple spreadsheet program such as Excel, but make sure that you correctly track your members' super contributions (refer to Chapter 4) and benefit components (see Chapter 19).

Often, the stumbling block for those seeking to independently run a SMSF is in meeting the fund's reporting requirements, including year-end reporting and the lodgement of fund returns. The actions taken by such SMSF trustees generally fall into two main categories:

✔ **Delegate year-end reporting and return lodgement.** You may choose to complete all of your fund's administration, compliance and recording obligations, apart from your fund's year-end accounts, and preparation and lodgement of your fund's annual return. If you get an accountant to do your year-end reporting, you may find it cheaper over the longer term to use the same reporting program that your accountant uses. If you run a simple fund, with only a handful of transactions, and you don't have to prepare any major reports (such as benefit payment reports) during the year, then the accountant may be happy to rely on your own software or hard copy records when producing the financial reports, and completing and lodging your fund's tax and compliance return. You then need only to satisfy your auditor's demands.

✔ **Do everything and give final accounts and fund records to approved auditor.** If the only expert that you intend to use when running your super fund is an approved SMSF auditor, then you must prepare your own fund reports (including year-end reporting and member benefit reporting), and prepare and lodge your fund's annual return. Over the longer term, costs are usually cheaper if you use the same reporting program that your fund's auditor uses because he or she can more easily include your fund in the practice's annual SMSF auditing program. In some cases, an auditor may require you to use a certain software program as a condition of appointment.

The fees quoted by a service provider for a stand-alone fund audit are generally higher than the audit fee quoted as part of a complete compliance and administration service, although there are competitively-priced stand-alone audit services from SMSF audit specialists (refer to Chapter 6 for SMSF costs).

Delegating Your CART Obligations

As a SMSF trustee, you have total control over how you run your fund. Generally speaking, you can choose from one of three different approaches when meeting your SMSF trustee obligations:

✔ You can do everything yourself, apart from using an approved SMSF auditor (refer to the previous section).

✔ You can delegate all of your trustee tasks to a service provider.

✔ You can delegate only part of your trustee workload.

Delegating your SMSF's trustee to-do list means finding a suitable SMSF adviser, or another type of SMSF service provider, for your fund. Besides choosing accountants and financial advisers who specialise in SMSFs, you can also access several online and/or face-to-face service providers. These providers can support your fund with establishment services, ongoing administration and compliance services, and one-off transactions.

Many of these providers have relationships with adviser groups and some are also owned by financial organisations. Some stand-alone administrators have even diversified into selling financial products to SMSF trustees. At least one SMSF administrator develops and operates investment products (as fund manager) that they then recommend to SMSF clients. After all, as soon as a firm has your fund's administration contract, you're a captive audience!

If you decide to go extreme and opt for a complete package, you get an administration service for your compliance and reporting requirements, a financial adviser, a wrap account for your investments (refer to Chapter 5), a tax agent, an approved SMSF auditor and a relationship manager to hold your hand while the service provider 'steals' your money. Huh? Only kidding about the theft comment, but you can be charged a lot of money if you sign on for one of these complete package deals. For example, on a $400,000 account balance, sometimes these super-duper-complete-service arrangements can cost you up to $16,000 a year, or 4 per cent of your account balance, and even more! However, you can find other full-service (excluding financial advice) providers in the marketplace who promise to charge you no more than 1 per cent of your account balance, while other SMSF administration providers may charge you even less, depending on your account balance.

Alternatively, if you wish to be more hands-on, you can opt for administration assistance for, say, one aspect of your fund's operation, such as financial reporting (Chapter 12) or tax management (Chapter 13). Or perhaps, you want a service provider to set up your fund for you, but then you want to do the rest yourself. In Chapter 7, I explain the steps involved in setting up a SMSF.

You can't delegate your ultimate responsibility as SMSF trustee. You can appoint a fund administrator to look after all, or part, of your CART obligations, but you remain responsible for what happens in your SMSF if something goes wrong (refer to Chapter 9).

Seeking service quotes

Do some research on what services are available for SMSFs. Chatting to your adviser (if you have one) is usually the best option; however, most SMSF administrators have websites that give you general information on what you need to do to set up a SMSF and the estimated costs involved.

You can find a lot of DIY super-related sites by typing in **DIY super administration** or **SMSF administration** into internet search engines such as Yahoo! or Google or Bing and checking out the content links on the main page, and the advertised links at the top or right-hand side of the web page.

The types of services offered by SMSF administrators can be confusing. In Appendix A, I include a comprehensive list that illustrates what you can expect from your fund's administrator if you choose to delegate your CART obligations.

If you're opting for a package deal, the better administration option depends on *what* the administrator gives you for your money, and whether the package meets all of your retirement planning needs. You can compare which service provider delivers the better value, by asking each administrator/adviser to itemise the following:

- ✔ Advice component (if any)
- ✔ Establishment costs (including trust deed)
- ✔ Running costs such as administration, annual audit and reporting
- ✔ Any other costs included in the fee
- ✔ Any other costs that may arise that are *not* included in the fee

I suggest you also ask the administrator/adviser to separate the costs relating to running your SMSF and the cost of other advice (if any) relating to non-super assets. I discuss the merits of financial advice in Chapter 5, and the costs of running a SMSF in Chapter 6.

Appointing your administrator

Before a fund administrator/accountant can assist you with your SMSF, you must sign a contract, that is, an *administration service agreement*, outlining the services that are to be delivered. Any agreement should clearly list what the administrator plans to do for your fund, the fees involved, and the time frames for delivery.

The trustees (or directors, if your fund has a corporate trustee — refer to Chapter 8) of your SMSF must decide to appoint the fund administrator at a trustee meeting. This decision must be minuted, and a copy of the administration service agreement must be stored with your fund's records.

In many cases, a specialist fund administrator can require you to use a bank account from a preferred financial organisation. The reason for requiring you to use a specified bank account may be for administrative efficiency; although, in some cases, the fund administrator receives a commission from the financial organisation for opening a certain number of bank accounts. The bank account (such as a cash management account) may also be linked to certain online stockbrokers, which means you may have to use your fund administrator's preferred stockbroker. Again, your fund administrator may receive commissions for bringing new business to the stockbroker. Before signing any agreement, ask your fund administration company what arrangements it has in place (if any) with related service providers.

Don't Be a Clever Clogs on Tax

A superannuation fund is a tax-friendly investment vehicle, which means, in effect, every superannuation decision — contribution, investment, benefit payment — has tax implications.

Even if you intend to do everything yourself when running your SMSF, get advice from a registered tax agent, usually an accountant, on key decisions regarding your super fund. Here's why: One gentleman I was chatting to at a seminar (who was very experienced in running his fund) had cost his wife and himself nearly $50,000 in unnecessary taxes because he hadn't understood the tax implications of his fund investment decisions.

In nearly all cases, only a registered tax agent can charge a fee for dealing with your fund's tax affairs, which includes completing and lodging your fund's annual return and may include providing advice on tax-driven superannuation strategies. Note that some financial advisers have a special exemption until December 2015 to provide tax advice without being a registered tax (financial) adviser. The exemption means that a financial adviser can continue to charge for tax-related advice, provided she notifies ASIC that she intends to become registered as a tax (financial) adviser. Alternatively, if she does not intend to become a registered tax (financial) adviser by December 2015, then any tax-related advice she provides must be accompanied by a disclaimer explaining to her client that the client not rely on that tax advice, and that the client should seek advice from a registered tax agent.

To avoid nasty tax surprises for your SMSF, and for you, use a tax expert for tax-related matters (such as superannuation strategies), or use an adviser who works closely with an accountant/registered tax agent.

Revving Up Arrangements for Retirement

Running a SMSF in retirement is a radically different proposition from running such a fund while you're working. If you're taking a pension from your SMSF, then you must withdraw minimum amounts each year. If you're under the age of 60, then you probably have to deduct income tax from your pension payments. You may also continue contributing to the fund, which means the administration of your SMSF is a little more complicated. I explore running a SMSF during your retirement in Part V of this book.

Chapter 11

Do the Right Thing — Compliance

In This Chapter

▶ Following the super laws and your trust deed

▶ Understanding the eight main areas of super compliance

▶ Flaunting the super laws leads to financial penalties and more

▶ Maintaining your super fund for the sole purpose of providing retirement benefits

*M*ention the term 'compliance' and most individuals get fidgety while they wait for their eyes to glaze over. Compliance seems like a boring concept for many people, but complying with the super rules is the key to a successful self-managed super fund (SMSF).

Compliance with the super rules, however, is merely a means to an end. The 'end' or purpose of your SMSF isn't simply to stay on the right side of the law (although that's a good thing to do), but to save for your retirement in a 'concessionally taxed' environment. *Concessionally taxed* means paying less tax or even no tax.

Okay then: If you want a tax-friendly retirement vehicle for your savings, delivering you tax-free super from the age of 60 and other tax concessions, you have to follow some special rules — that's compliance!

In this chapter, I take you through some of the big-ticket compliance items that the ATO is particularly evangelical about monitoring, before dishing up the dirt on trustee penalties. I then deal with all the fuss surrounding the number one commandment in superannuation: You must comply with the sole purpose test (SPT).

Just in case you're considering skipping this chapter, you may be interested in knowing that as a SMSF trustee the ATO assumes you know the super rules and that you run your SMSF in line with those rules, including the SIS Act, the tax laws and your fund's trust deed. The SIS Act, outlined in the following section, is the statutory bible on super. You can't say: 'I'm not to blame; my accountant looks after all of that for me.' If you're particularly naughty, you may be disqualified from acting as a SMSF trustee, or incur a fine the size of a lotto win (think $340,000!), or lose the tax concessions for your SMSF, or even land yourself in jail.

... Because It's the Law

Nearly everything written about compliance in this book can be linked back to superannuation law, tax law, corporations law or trust law.

According to the ATO, as a SMSF trustee, you must act in line with the following legal documents and laws:

- ✔ **Your fund's trust deed:** As a trustee, you must act in accordance with your trustee responsibilities as set out in your fund's trust deed. The trust deed is your fund's rule book — a very important document.

- ✔ **Trust law:** Your SMSF is a trust, evidenced by your fund's trust deed, which means your fund is subject to trust law. As trustee, you're subject to general trustee duties, some of which are listed in the SMSF trustee declaration that you sign when you become a SMSF trustee. I explain the contents of this declaration in Chapter 9.

- ✔ **Super laws:** The superannuation laws are set out in the *Superannuation Industry (Supervision) Act 1993* (or SIS Act), the main legislation governing super, and the associated *Superannuation Industry (Supervision) Regulations 1994*. The SIS Act also imposes minimum requirements on trustees, which are general trustee duties under law (refer to the preceding point), and these duties are deemed to be included in a SMSF's trust deed.

- ✔ **Tax laws:** You can find the main tax laws relating to superannuation in the *Income Tax Assessment Act 1997* and the *Tax Administration Act 1953*, although your fund is subject to other tax laws, too.

- ✔ **Corporations law:** If you have a corporate trustee, your fund is subject to the *Corporations Act 2001*, and must report annually to the Australian Securities & Investments Commission (ASIC), as I explain in Chapter 8. As a corporate trustee, you must also follow your company's constitution.

Monitoring the Must-Do's

As a SMSF trustee, you must follow special rules that generally cover eight main areas of compliance:

- ✔ **SMSF definition:** Your SMSF must have fewer than five members, and all members must be trustees (or trustee directors, if your fund has corporate trustee) of the SMSF. A SMSF member can't be an employee of another member unless they're relatives, and no SMSF trustee can receive payment for performing the role of trustee. I explain the SMSF definition more fully in Chapter 1, and the eligibility requirements of trustees in Chapter 8.

- ✔ **Administrative and reporting obligations:** Your fund must meet its administrative and reporting obligations, including lodging SMSF returns by the due date (refer to Chapters 10 and 12).

- ✔ **Trustee declaration:** A new SMSF trustee must sign a statement, called the *SMSF trustee declaration*, confirming that the trustee understands the responsibilities and duties involved in running a SMSF. In Chapter 9, you can find a copy of the trustee declaration. In that chapter I also highlight some of the issues that a SMSF trustee needs to think about before signing the declaration.

- ✔ **Sole purpose test (SPT):** Your super fund is set up for the sole purpose of providing retirement benefits to members, rather than, for example, providing an antique roadster for weekend driving. I briefly discuss the SPT in Chapter 9, and in detail in the section 'Thou Shalt Comply with the Sole Purpose Test', later in this chapter.

- ✔ **Contribution rules:** You must satisfy the contribution rules, for example, if a member is aged 65 years or over, they must satisfy a work test before contributing. I take you through the contribution rules in Chapter 4.

- ✔ **Investment strategy and investment restrictions:** As SMSF trustee, you must formulate and implement an investment strategy for your fund, and regularly review this strategy. You also must be mindful of the special investment restrictions applicable to super funds when making your fund's investments. I take you through what you need to consider when drafting your fund's investment strategy in Chapters 14 and 15, and the investment restrictions that apply to super fund investing in Chapters 15, 16 and 17.

- ✔ **Benefit payment rules:** You must comply with the benefit payment rules; for example, ensuring a condition of release is satisfied before paying a lump sum or pension from your super fund. In Part V, I explain the rules that apply when paying super benefits from a SMSF.

- ✔ **Registered approved SMSF auditor:** You must appoint an approved SMSF auditor, registered by ASIC, to conduct two audits — a financial audit and a compliance audit — on your SMSF, at the end of each year. I explain why your fund must be audited in Chapter 12, along with who can be appointed an 'approved SMSF auditor' and what the role of auditor involves.

If your SMSF fails to comply with any obligations in its first 15 months of operation (from date of fund establishment), your fund's auditor must report any breach to the ATO if the value of the single breach is greater than $2,000, regardless of whether the breach is minor from a compliance point of view. For SMSFs in existence for more than 15 months, your fund's auditor must follow strict guidelines when reporting breaches of the super rules (see Chapter 12).

The ATO regularly issues public rulings (see Appendix B) on your SMSF obligations and other documents covering significant topics. You can also seek a private view, known as a *private ruling*, from the ATO. In such an instance, the ATO provides written advice to trustees on how the super laws apply to a specific transaction or arrangement. The ATO also issues product rulings on SMSF investment products.

Penalising Pesky Trustees

Not so long ago, the ATO took more of an educative approach, rather than punitive approach, when dealing with breaches of the super laws by SMSF trustees. This gentle approach was partly due to recognition of the fact that many SMSF trustee errors were unintentional and could usually be rectified, and be prevented in the future by the ATO (or the SMSF's auditor) drawing attention to the error. The soft compliance approach taken by the ATO was also partly due to the fact that before July 2014, the ATO had limited options when imposing penalties. The limited penalties available before July 2014 could be financially and personally devastating for the SMSF trustee involved, and costly for the ATO to pursue.

Before July 2014, the main — and major — financial penalty for a SMSF trustee involved the ATO deeming a super fund as non-complying. If a super fund was deemed non-complying, the super fund lost nearly half of its assets and earnings in penalty tax. Alternatively, the ATO could (and still can) disqualify you as a SMSF trustee, or force you to fix a breach of the super rules, or take you to court to impose hefty civil or criminal penalties. The 'big stick' nature of these types of penalties often meant the ATO opted for the softer educative approach.

Since 1 July 2014, the ATO can impose three new types of penalty:

- ✔ **Administrative penalty:** A financial penalty.
- ✔ **Rectification direction:** An order to fix something that you caused by breaking the super rules.
- ✔ **Education direction:** An order to undertake an approved course to re-educate yourself about the super laws.

The introduction of a range of financial penalties for misbehaving SMSF trustees, and new enforcement powers for the ATO, means that you are much more likely to be exposed to unfriendly ATO attention than at any time in the past.

Copping an administrative penalty

Although the strong-arm penalties (non-complying fund, disqualification and criminal penalties) are still available in the ATO arsenal, since 1 July 2014 the ATO can also impose an array of financial penalties for naughty SMSF trustee behaviour. An *administrative penalty,* which is a financial penalty, can range from $1,700 (for failing to sign and store the SMSF trustee declaration) to $10,200 (for lending money to fund members).

Table 11-1 lists some of the ATO's administrative penalties, which took effect from 1 July 2014. At the time of writing, a penalty unit is worth $170, which means a fine of 10 penalty units (for example, for failing to sign and store the SMSF trustee declaration) works out to be a fine of $1700.

If your super fund breaches the super rules and the ATO imposes an administrative penalty, the fine must be paid by you personally; you cannot dip into the cash sitting in your SMSF.

You can find the full list of administrative penalties set out in *Schedule 2 of the Tax and Superannuation Laws Amendment (2014 Measures No 1) Act.*

Table 11-1	Examples of SMSF Administrative Penalties	
Breach	*Penalty Units*	*Dollar Value of Penalty*
Failing to keep SMSF money and other assets separate from personal assets	20	$3,400
Failing to properly prepare accounts and statements	10	$1,700
Lending to members or relatives of members	60	$10,200
Breaking the borrowing rules (see Chapter 16)	60	$10,200
Failing to keep copies of minutes of trustee meetings	10	$1,700
Breaking the in-house asset rules (see Chapter 15)	60	$10,200

Source: Adapted from Schedule 2 of the Tax and Superannuation Laws Amendment (2014 Measures No 1) Act.

ATO's seven deadly sins of DIY super

Year in, year out, the ATO reports similar black spots in SMSF trustee behaviour. I like to call these black spots the 'DIY super deadly sins', reflecting the ATO's evangelical devotion to hunting down trustees committing such acts. And these sins are

- **Illegally accessing super.** As trustee of your SMSF, you're subject to strict rules about when you can pay your benefit early. You can't get your super until you reach a certain age and retire, or satisfy another condition of release (see Chapter 19). If you break this rule, then you risk losing one-half of your super benefits in financial penalties. On average, each year, the ATO removes about 400 SMSFs from the Super Fund Lookup search facility (for details about this SMSF list, refer to Step 8 in Chapter 7).

- **Breaching the sole purpose test (SPT).** Staying true to the SPT is one of the ten commandments of DIY super. For example, some trustees have invested in golf club memberships with playing rights — and, also, just so happen to be keen golfers. I illustrate the plight of golfers later in this chapter in the section, 'Thou Shalt Comply with the Sole Purpose Test'.

- **Failing to lodge a SMSF tax return, or lodging late.** You can expect no forgiveness for this heinous act because the ATO uses the information in your fund's tax return to monitor compliance, super contributions and income tax obligations (for details about ATO reporting requirements, see Chapter 12). Naughty trustees can be fined several thousand dollars per transgression, or even be jailed.

- **Breaking the in-house asset rule.** Briefly, you can have no more than 5 per cent of your fund's total investments, including leases of fund assets, with related parties, such as a fund member or a fund member's relative. These investments (or loans or leases) are known as *in-house assets*. I explain in-house assets, and the limited exceptions to this rule, in Chapter 15.

- **Lending money to members.** Don't even think about it. (For the reasons why, see Chapter 15.)

- **Mixing personal assets with fund assets.** As a trustee, you must keep the assets of the fund separate from your own money and, if you run a business, separate from your business assets. (I explain this rule in Chapter 15.)

- **Failing to document ownership of SMSF assets.** This sin (also covered in Chapter 15) is often the cause for mixing personal assets with fund assets (refer to the preceding sin).

The seven deadly sins make an intimidating list for budding (and experienced) SMSF trustees but, even so, you can still taste the forbidden fruit in your SMSF. I explain some of these legal temptations in Part IV.

Forcing you to lift your super game

Remember that a rectification direction involves the ATO ordering a SMSF trustee to rectify a specific breach in a specified way within a specified period of time. As a SMSF trustee, if you fail to act on the rectification direction, you'll automatically be hit with a fine of $1,700, and the failure is viewed as a serious offence.

The ATO can also give you an education direction, which requires you to undertake a specific training course within a specified time period. You must also provide the ATO with evidence of completion of the course, such as a certificate. For good measure, you will then be required to sign, or re-sign the SMSF trustee declaration to confirm that you understand your trustee obligations. If you fail to undertake the education course, you can be hit with a penalty of $850 (for trustee obligations, refer to Chapters 8 and 9). The penalty imposed for failing to act on the education direction must be paid from your personal savings rather than from yourSMSF coffers.

According to the ATO, the free, approved course you must undertake when you receive an education direction is generally one of four options. The first course is jointly administered by the two major accounting organisations, CPA Australia and Chartered Accountants Australia and New Zealand. A further two courses are run by the SMSF Professionals' Association of Australia (SPAA) and SMSF Wisdom, respectively. The alternative is that you will be ordered to attend a free SMSF trustee webinar run by the ATO. But why wait for an education direction from the ATO to undertake some helpful trustee education? You can check out the course run by the accounting bodies by visiting www.smsftrustee .com, the SPAA course by visiting www.spaa.asn.au, and the SMSF Wisdom course at http://smsfwisdom.com.au/. You can complete the online course and then print your attainment certificate. Note that if you choose to sit the test, and then later you are hit with an education direction, then you must sit the test again.

Thou Shalt Comply with the Sole Purpose Test

The purpose of running a SMSF is to provide retirement benefits for the fund's members. Sounds obvious, don't you think?

Superannuation is about saving for your retirement but, due to the incredibly attractive tax concessions associated with super, some Australians are tempted to enjoy some of the super benefits before retirement. They want — and smile about — the tax concessions such as tax-deductible super contributions and 15 per cent tax on fund earnings, and tax-exempt earnings in pension phase (for details about super tax, see Chapters 13 and 18), but they also want a pre-retirement benefit from that pile of money accumulating in their super accounts.

The sole purpose test (SPT) is designed to stop opportunistic individuals from using their super benefits for current-day benefits. Briefly, the SPT means you must maintain your SMSF for at least one core purpose, namely, payment of benefits on or after retirement. A core purpose is also considered to be providing benefit payments when a fund member reaches the age of 65, or when a member dies.

Provided that you're maintaining a fund for a core purpose, your fund can also pay benefits for ancillary purposes without breaching the SPT, such as in the event of a member's ill health, or as death benefits to dependants of a retired fund member. I explain the definition of the SPT in more detail in Chapter 9.

Doing your SPT homework

In the SMSF trustee declaration that new trustees must sign (refer to Chapter 9), you declare that you 'understand it is [your] responsibility to ensure the fund is maintained for the purpose of providing benefits to the members upon their retirement (or attainment of a certain age), or their beneficiaries if a member dies'. When signing the declaration, you also declare that '[you] understand that [you] should regularly evaluate whether the fund continues to be the appropriate vehicle to meet this purpose'.

The SPT has always been a headache for the regulators because most funds can generally show that a fund's investments have a primary link with providing retirement benefits. The ATO in its publication *Running a self-managed superannuation fund* (NAT 11032), explains that one of the main ways to determine whether a breach has occurred is to examine the character and purpose of the fund's investments. If you enjoy a direct or indirect benefit before retirement from your SMSF's investment — that is, more than an incidental or insignificant benefit — your fund is probably breaching the SPT.

Example: According to the ATO, a SMSF can invest in holiday apartments via a property syndicate, and SMSF trustees can stay in the apartments at market rent (and may receive an upgrade) without breaching the sole purpose test. A SMSF can invest in a residential property in a beachside town, but SMSF trustees *can't* rent the house for holidays or permanent use.

Clear as mud? Exactly. The SPT is one of the more difficult areas for regulators because the test is vague — meaning you can have two super funds with a similar set of circumstances, and one fund is found to have breached the SPT, while the other is found to be operating within the SPT. The most common breaches of the SPT are

✔ Investments that offer a pre-retirement benefit

✔ Financial assistance or a pre-retirement benefit provided to a fund member or other party, to the financial detriment of the SMSF

The ATO has issued a SMSF ruling (SMSFR 2008/2) that explains the application of the SPT, and the types of circumstances that fall within, and fall outside, the SPT. Although the ruling arguably triggers more questions than answers due to the difficulty in pinning down the meaning of the SPT, the ruling does provide some useful guidance for SMSF trustees considering complicated arrangements for their SMSF. I detail these circumstances in the the two sections that follow.

Failing the SPT

According to the ATO, factors that would lean towards a conclusion that a SMSF is not complying with the SPT are

✔ The trustee specifically negotiated an additional pre-retirement (that is, current-day) benefit, in addition to the underlying investment.

✔ The existence of a specific pre-retirement benefit has influenced the trustee to choose one investment over another.

✔ The benefit provided by the SMSF to a member or related party is at a cost or financial detriment to the fund.

✔ A pattern of events indicate that a material benefit isn't consistent with the SPT.

Complying with SPT

According to the ATO, factors that would lean towards a conclusion that a SMSF is complying with the SPT are

✔ The benefit is an inherent or unavoidable part of other activities that comply with the SPT.

✔ The benefit is remote or isolated or insignificant when assessed against the fund activities that comply with the SPT.

✔ The SMSF provides the benefit on a commercial basis, and at no cost or financial detriment to the SMSF.

✔ Activities are consistent with the covenants set out in Section 52 of the SIS Act (refer to the copy of the SMSF trustee declaration in Chapter 9, and check out the section titled 'Trustee duties' in the declaration).

✔ Investments and activities are consistent with the fund's investment strategy (see Chapters 14 and 15 for tips on how to properly consider and formulate your fund's investment strategy).

Citing some examples of SPT

The ATO's SMSF ruling (SMSFR 2008/2) provides examples to help SMSF trustees understand how the ATO applies the SPT to particular scenarios.

Scenarios that the SMSFR 2008/2 ruling covers include

✔ **Deliberately choosing an investment with non-retirement benefit.** Your fund breaches the SPT if you actively choose a fund investment because it offers a current-day benefit, at the expense of, rather than complementary to, long-term retirement benefits.

✔ **Investing in golf memberships.** A SMSF may own a golf membership provided it assigns the membership rights to another party at market value, although this scenario isn't the case if two individual SMSFs swap membership rights with a member from each fund.

✔ **Investing in holiday apartments.** A right to be upgraded to a higher standard property, which may be attached to an interest in a holiday apartment complex, is within SPT, but free accommodation isn't within SPT. I discuss investing in property within your SMSF in Chapter 17.

Although not included in SMSFR 2008/2, the ATO has publicly stated that it's monitoring promoters who advertise SMSF conferences in overseas destinations, especially where the conference has minimal content relating to SMSF education and training. Be careful when the advertisement suggests that you can claim the full cost of travel, accommodation and meals via your SMSF when attending these workshops.

Chapter 12

Act Like You're the Boss — Reporting

*I*magine this: Two Australian Taxation Office (ATO) representatives knock on your door and ask to see your super fund's financial reports, member accounts and other fund records. Can you help them? Do you know what fund records you ought to be keeping?

One of the representatives then drops into the conversation that you provided incorrect tax file numbers (TFNs) for your fund's members in the SMSF's last annual return, and that your return was lodged late. Do you know when (and what) your fund is supposed to report to the ATO? Do you know enough about your fund's activities to challenge, or confirm, the ATO's comments? Although, in the first instance, an ATO representative is more likely to phone you or your accountant/adviser or auditor to ask these types of questions, you can expect a face-to-face meeting at some stage if you don't successfully manage your SMSF's obligations.

In this chapter, I focus on the **R** (that is, reporting) in your DIY super CART obligations — remember, CART is my acronym for **C**ompliance, **A**dministration, **R**eporting and **T**ax management. I take you through your recording and reporting responsibilities, and the important task of appointing your SMSF's auditor — after all, you're the boss, when running a SMSF. I also provide a handy record-keeping checklist to help your fund keep on the right side of the super laws.

Raising the Bar on Record-Keeping

The ATO has flagged that poor and inadequate record-keeping (including misreporting in annual returns), and late lodgement of annual returns are common problems with SMSFs, and that SMSF trustees need to raise their standards when record-keeping and when reporting to the ATO. The threat of an ATO review or financial penalty is likely to be sufficient motivation to ensure your fund's reports and other records are in order.

Instead of treating the reporting task as purely a compliance requirement, you can approach the challenge as the boss and owner of your super fund. Maintaining accurate records and lodging annual returns on time is simply good management practice. Regularly tracking how your fund is faring throughout the year can help you make better investment decisions and make the most of any tax planning for your fund (see Chapters 13 and 18), and personally (with regard to making super contributions; refer to Chapter 4).

Properly recording, and storing, your fund's documents and reports can also reduce the chances of you losing important documents, or making mistakes with member accounts (including your own member account), particularly when paying benefits, or when reporting benefit payments or super contributions (or TFNs) to the ATO.

SMSF Reporting (and Record-Keeping) in a Nutshell

SMSF trustees are required to undertake the following tasks:

- ✔ Sign and store important documents. For example, you must keep minutes of trustee meetings and decisions for at least ten years.
- ✔ Maintain accurate fund records, including accounting records.
- ✔ Properly record investment transactions and ownership of assets (for details about the rules relating to documenting ownership of investments, see Chapter 15).
- ✔ Record benefit components and comply with benefit payment standards (see Part V in this book).
- ✔ Create financial and tax reports.
- ✔ Report to members. You must keep paper or electronic copies of member reports for at least ten years.

✔ Appoint an approved SMSF auditor, and provide the auditor with the necessary documents to conduct the fund audit.

✔ Lodge annual returns, on or before the due date, and keep copies of lodged annual returns for at least five years.

Generally speaking, a fund's financial records must be kept for at least five years, and a fund's non-financial records, such as trustee minutes, must be kept for at least ten years. Table 12-1 summarises the main documents that your SMSF must retain, including the length of time that you must keep the records. I also include a chapter reference column so that, if you want, you can quickly find more information on each item.

If you don't want to be hands-on with your fund's reporting or record-keeping, you can delegate this task (but not the responsibility) to a service provider. I discuss your outsourcing options in Chapter 10.

Table 12-1	Record-Keeping Checklist	
Administrative Records	*Store for ...*	*Chapter Reference*
Trust deed and deed amendments	Life of fund, plus 10 years	6 & 7
Registration documents (ABN, TFN and GST)	Life of fund, plus 10 years	7
Minutes of trustee meetings and decisions	At least 10 years	7
Written consents to act as trustee	As long as trustee, plus 10 years	7 & 8
Trustee declarations	As long as trustee, plus 10 years	9
Record of change in fund trustees	At least 10 years	8
Investment strategy	Life of fund, plus 10 years	15
Death benefit nominations (DBNs)	As long as member, plus 10 years	24
Notice of fund compliance (ATO sends this after lodgement of first year's return)	Life of fund, plus 10 years	12
Letter of engagement for approved auditor	Duration of appointment, plus 10 years	12

(continued)

Table 12-1 *(continued)*

Financial and Tax Records	Store for ...	Chapter Reference
Letter of engagement and service contract for professional administrator/accountant	Duration of appointment, plus 10 years	10
Accounting records	At least 5 years	12
Annual operating statement (profit & loss)	At least 5 years	12
Statement of financial position (balance sheet)	At least 5 years	12
Records used to prepare annual returns and accounts	Depends on records, but at least 5 years, usually longer	12
Annual returns	At least 5 years	12
Records that explain your fund's assessable income and deductible expenses	At least 5 years, and possibly longer	12, 13 & 18
Documents showing ownership of assets	Life of fund, or at least 10 years after disposing of asset	15
Bank account statements	At least 5 years	7, 15 & 22
Records to show contributions, rollovers and payments to members	At least 5 years, and possibly longer	4 & Part V
Record of each member's account	As long as member, and then at least 10 years	4, 7, 13, 21 & 22
Record of each member's TFN	As long as member, and then at least 5 years	4
PAYG payment summaries	At least 5 years	12, 19, 21 & 22
PAYG withholding payment summary	At least 5 years	12, 18, 21 & 22
Actuarial certificate	At least 5 years	21 & 22

Source: List of administrative and financial records adapted and expanded from table appearing on page 23 of ATO publication 'Setting up a self-managed super fund' (NAT 71923). The author has included storage time frames and chapter references.

Delivering Accurate Accounting and Financial Reporting

As trustee of your SMSF, you must keep accurate financial records — which can be kept electronically — for each year of income. You can set up and manage your fund accounts yourself.

Alternatively, you can appoint your accountant to help you set up systems to make record-keeping a pleasant experience, or your accountant (or another service provider — refer to Chapter 10) can manage your accounts on your behalf.

Your accounting obligations include keeping accurate accounting records that are easy to read, and that explain the transactions and financial position of your fund. You must also prepare two annual statements:

- ✔ *Operating statement* — also known as *profit and loss statement*, showing all transactions, expenses and earnings for the year.
- ✔ *Statement of financial position* — also known as the *balance sheet*, which shows your fund's financial position.

Most service providers, including accountants, use specialist SMSF software to produce a fund's financial accounts and other reports necessary for an approved auditor to review the fund, and for the fund to lodge its annual return each year. You can get an idea of the types of SMSF software available by doing a search for **SMSF software** on the internet.

In most cases, a SMSF operates on a *cash basis* for accounting purposes. Cash basis means that you record a transaction when the fund receives the money (or actually pays out money) rather than on an *accruals basis* (when the entitlement arises or when the fund receives an invoice).

Keeping the 'Taxman' Happy — Tax Records

You may be relieved to discover that the 'taxman' (that is, the ATO) is an easy organisation to please. The taxman's good cheer shines upon you if your SMSF follows the super rules, maintains proper records, pays the appropriate taxes and lodges its annual returns on time. I discuss lodging your fund's annual return in the next section.

The ATO is particularly interested in your income tax record-keeping, such as documentation relating to fund deductions, transactions involving purchases or sales of assets, any capital gains tax liability and any fund losses. In the ATO's publication *Self-managed superannuation fund annual return instructions* (NAT 71606), the ATO lists additional records that your SMSF must keep if your existing fund records don't contain the information specified in the return instructions. These include

✔ Notices and elections such as the notice required when a member claims a tax deduction for a super contribution (for more information about this notice, refer to Chapter 4)

✔ Documents containing details of any estimate, determination or calculation made while preparing the tax return, together with details of the basis and method used in arriving at the amounts reported in the tax return

✔ A statement describing and listing the fund's accounting systems and records, such as the chart of accounts that are kept manually and electronically

If the ATO does choose to take a closer look at your SMSF — that is, conducts a tax audit or a *specific issue audit* (reviews one aspect of your fund's operations over a single financial year, or multiple years) — you can expect the ATO officials to request even more information, such as:

✔ All documents (including worksheets) that explain your fund's transactions

✔ Fund records that show all assets are in the name of the trustee of the fund

✔ Records of private company dividends, trust distributions from related trusts (if any) or other non-arm's length income

✔ Records of all foreign source income and calculation of foreign tax credits (if any)

✔ Copy of life insurance policies (if any)

Lodging SMSF Annual Returns

Each year, your SMSF must lodge a return with the ATO on or before the due lodgement date. The annual return is designed to report income tax, report member contributions, and provide the ATO with key information about your compliance with the super and tax laws.

When lodging your fund's return, you also must pay the annual supervisory levy of $259. If your SMSF is newly established, then your fund must pay two years of the ATO levy with your first SMSF annual return, totalling $518.

The ATO produces an annual publication to assist SMSF trustees when completing the annual return. You can access the publication *Self-managed superannuation fund annual return instructions* (NAT 71606) by visiting the ATO website (www.ato.gov.au) and clicking on Super⇨Self-Managed Super Funds⇨Lodge your annual return, then clicking on 'instructions' within the text at the end of the page.

Your fund's financial accounts and records must be audited each year by a registered approved SMSF auditor who is appointed by the trustees. Your fund's audit must be conducted *before* your fund's annual return lodgement date, because you can't lodge your SMSF annual return until the fund's audit is completed. I explain the rules relating to your fund's audit and appointing approved SMSF auditors in the section 'Auditing Your SMSF Auditor', later in the chapter.

Ticking off by lodgement date

Any newly established SMSF must lodge the fund's first annual return by 28 February, following the financial year ending 30 June, when using a tax agent. A newly established SMSF planning to prepare its own first SMSF annual return must lodge by 31 October following the financial year ending 30 June.

If your SMSF has been in existence for more than one financial year, and you prepare your fund's annual return without the assistance of a tax agent, your lodgement date is usually 28 February, following the financial year-end. If your SMSF appoints a tax agent, then your fund must lodge the fund's annual return in line with the ATO's lodgement program, which can be as late as the following May, for the financial year ending 30 June.

To avoid administrative penalties, you must lodge your fund's annual return by the due lodgement date.

Combining tax and regulatory information

Your fund's SMSF annual return isn't just a tax return. The ATO also asks you very important compliance questions that you must answer, covering areas such as whether your SMSF:

✔ Meets the definition of 'Australian superannuation fund' and remains eligible for tax concessions. (For an explanation of an Australian superannuation fund, refer to Chapter 8.)

✔ Paid an income stream to one or more fund members, and whether the fund has paid pension account members the minimum benefit payment during the financial year (for information about these super pension payments, see Chapter 21).

Member contributions information

You must report all contributions that your fund receives from members during the financial year, in the SMSF annual return. You also must report benefits transferred from other super fund accounts into your SMSF.

The ATO uses the contributions data for the following purposes:

✔ Calculate the co-contribution entitlement (if any)

✔ Check whether a fund member has exceeded the contributions cap

✔ Monitor whether employers are meeting Superannuation Guarantee (SG) obligations

For more information on co-contributions, contributions caps and SG obligations, refer to Chapter 4.

Auditing Your SMSF Auditor

The *Superannuation Industry (Supervision) Act 1993* (SIS Act — super's statutory bible) requires that trustees of a SMSF must appoint an 'approved SMSF auditor' in each income year to audit the fund's operations, and that the auditor must provide the trustees with an audit report in the approved form.

The appointed auditor must conduct two audits — a financial audit and a compliance audit — on your SMSF, at the end of each year. A financial audit reviews the financial operation of the fund, including accounting records and transactions. The financial audit independently verifies that your accounts are accurate. A compliance audit reviews whether your SMSF complied with the super laws throughout the year — independently verifying that your fund is squeaky clean in terms of your fund's super CART obligations, including compliance with super's special investment rules (for more information about investment rules, see Chapter 15).

Only a registered approved SMSF auditor can conduct these audits — that is, the auditor is registered by ASIC and holds a unique SMSF auditor number (SAN), as I describe in Chapter 5 and in more detail in the following section. Furthermore, the auditor's appointment must be formalised with a letter of engagement, signed by the auditor and the fund's trustees.

According to the ATO, there are just over 7,000 approved auditors in Australia, and these busy people audit more than half a million SMSFs. Notably, about 3,000 of these approved auditors audit fewer than 20 SMSFs each, which leaves around 4,000 approved auditors reviewing more than 400,000 SMSFs.

Ticking four items on your auditor checklist

Appointing an approved SMSF auditor should be more than an afterthought when the end of the financial year is approaching. An approved SMSF auditor is also expected to be the ATO's eyes and ears. Use the following SMSF auditor checklist to help make sure your fund, and your fund's auditor, meets the ATO's requirements:

- ✔ **Ensure auditor independence:** Ask a potential approved SMSF auditor if she satisfies the independence requirements. The industry associations that auditors belong to require an auditor to be independent of a SMSF's operations. The ATO's view is that a lack of independence is likely to be a factor contributing to a poorer quality audit, particularly where the appointed auditor is also the accountant involved in the day-to-day management of the SMSF, or responsible for maintaining the accounts and preparing the fund's financial reports (see the sidebar 'Is your SMSF auditor wearing too many hats?').

- ✔ **Check SMSF auditor number on ASIC register of approved auditors:** The SAN also needs to be included in your fund's SMSF annual return.

- ✔ **Appoint your SMSF auditor no later than 45 days before your fund's annual return must be lodged:** You must appoint your fund's auditor no later than 45 days before the date by which the auditor must give an audit report — or, at least 46 days before you lodge your super fund's annual return with the ATO.

- ✔ **Expect receipt of approved form:** Expect your SMSF auditor to provide you with an audit report using the approved form. The approved form that your SMSF auditor must use is called the *Self-managed superannuation fund independent auditor's report* (NAT 11466).

Receiving a reprimand from the auditor

Your fund's approved SMSF auditor must provide the trustees with an audit report and a management letter (which outlines the audit findings) before the due lodgement date for your fund's return. If the auditor is of the view that your fund breaches the superannuation laws or that the financial position of your SMSF may be unsatisfactory, he must notify the fund's trustees upon forming this opinion.

In many cases, your fund's auditor is compelled to report the breach also to the ATO; for example, when the super fund fails to meet the definition of a SMSF (refer to Chapters 1 and 8), or when SMSF trustees lend money to fund members or relatives of fund members (see Chapter 15).

New SMSFs need to be particularly vigilant about the super rules. If your SMSF blots the super rules copybook in the first 15 months of operation (from date of fund establishment), your SMSF-approved auditor must report your bad behaviour to the ATO using an Auditor Contravention Report (ACR), if the value of the single breach of the rules is greater than $2,000. Your fund's auditor must report the breach even when the breach is minor from a compliance point of view. If your SMSF has been around for longer than 15 months, your approved SMSF auditor may still report a breach of the super rules to the ATO using the ACR, but he must follow strict guidelines before doing so.

Is your SMSF auditor wearing too many hats?

Is your SMSF auditor independent? Your SMSF auditor must be independent — that is, free from bias, personal interest and association. Your auditor also must be *seen* to be independent.

According to the ATO, if a SMSF auditor intends to remain independent, then he or she should not accept an audit engagement where the SMSF auditor:

✔ Is a trustee or director of corporate trustee of the SMSF

✔ Is a relative or close associate of an individual or corporate trustee of the SMSF

✔ Has personally prepared the fund accounts and statements for the SMSF being audited

In accordance with the SIS regulations, the *Self-managed superannuation fund independent auditor's report* (NAT 11466) now includes a specific statement that the auditor has complied with auditor independence requirements.

Chapter 13

It's Always Tax Time

*Y*ou can save for your retirement any way you like, but a superannuation fund is the most popular retirement vehicle in Australia because you receive financial rewards — in the form of tax breaks — for locking your savings away.

In some sections of the Australian community you find individuals who believe that superannuation is just for 'high-flyers' with large incomes, who can reduce the amount of income tax they pay by making super contributions. The largesse continues when the high-flyers retire — tax-free super for over-60s and tax-free earnings on super fund assets. Such opinions serve only to make lazy headlines and encourage the spread of misinformation. Certainly, the more money you have, the more chances you have of taking advantage of super's tax breaks, but you don't need to be earning lots of money to gain tax benefits from super.

By reading this chapter, you can get a working understanding of how tax affects your self-managed super fund (SMSF) and your individual member benefits. I explain how your super contributions are taxed (if at all), what level of tax applies to your super fund earnings when you're accumulating super savings, and also the tax treatment of your SMSF earnings when you start taking a pension. I save the best news for last: The promise of tax-free super benefits on or after the age of 60. As much as possible, I talk tax in plain English but, on occasion, I delve into more technical detail. Don't worry, I alert you with the Technical Stuff icon when I do.

The tax on super fund earnings in accumulation phase is 15 per cent. The tax on concessional (such as salary sacrifice and tax-deductible) super contributions is also 15 per cent for most Australians, although it jumps to 30 per cent tax on super contributions for those Australians earning more than $300,000 a year. If an individual earns more than $18,200 a year (for the 2014–15 financial year, or earns more than $20,542 after allowing for the Low Income Tax Offset), superannuation can be a tax-effective option because your rate of personal income tax moves into the 19 per cent bracket after your income exceeds $18,200, while the super contributions tax remains at 15 per cent. Your marginal tax rate increases to 32.5 per cent after your income exceeds $37,000, while the super tax again remains at 15 per cent on super fund earnings, and concessional (before-tax) contributions. (If you're aged 65 or over, you may pay less income tax, or even no income tax, at these income levels.) While I'm not sure about your views, I don't think a person earning more than $18,200 or $20,542 a year (for the 2014–15 year) is an income high-flyer.

According to the ATO, around 128,000 Australians will pay a lot more tax on super contributions than the rest of the population. Since 1 July 2012 (the start of the 2012–13 year financial year), if you earn more than $300,000 a year (including rental property items and some other tax-related items), you can expect to pay 30 per cent tax on concessional super contributions, which is double the usual rate of 15 per cent tax. Concessional contributions include your employer's Superannuation Guarantee (SG) contributions, any salary sacrifice contributions you decide to make, and other employer contributions (for more information on contributions, refer to Chapter 4). The tax on super fund earnings, however, remains at 15 per cent for all Australians.

As a SMSF trustee, you must meet your tax obligations, such as keeping records and lodging tax returns (refer to Chapter 12), and satisfying contribution rules, but there's a very good reason for complying with such rules — you pay less tax!

Unlocking the Door to a Tax-Free Future

A superannuation account is effectively a long-term investment account with generous tax incentives designed to provide you with a benefit when you retire. The superannuation tax system is complicated, but complicated taxes don't eliminate the fact that your super contributions, and your super account, receive *concessional tax treatment* — you pay a rate of tax on your super that is less than what most individuals ordinarily pay on employment income, or on investment earnings, they receive during the year.

Super can be positively fascinating when you're faced with the prospect of saving yourself thousands of dollars in tax. In retirement, the deal on super gets even better — your SMSF pension account's earnings are exempt from tax, and any benefits paid out of your SMSF, as a lump sum or pension, are tax-free income when paid to fund members aged 60 or over (subject to satisfying a condition of release — see Chapter 19).

Here's the short course in super taxes. Your SMSF collects tax on behalf of the taxman at four stages:

- **Contributions:** When you, or your employer, make tax-deductible (concessional, and also known as before-tax) contributions to your SMSF, the taxman takes 15 per cent of the super contribution, and this tax is known as contributions tax. However, if you earn less than $37,000 a year, you may be entitled to a refund of the 15 per cent contributions tax (I explain who is eligible for the refund in Chapter 4). For those Australians who have an adjusted taxable income of more than $300,000 a year, the taxman will also put his hand out for an additional 15 per cent tax (known as *Division 293 tax*) on your super contributions after you lodge both your fund's annual return, and your personal tax return for the year.

- **Earnings:** When your SMSF earns income (that is, investment earnings) while your super account accumulates savings, and before you start a super pension, your SMSF pays 15 per cent tax on those earnings. Fund earnings on super pension assets are exempt from earnings tax.

- **Benefit payments:** When you receive a superannuation benefit before the age of 60 from your SMSF, tax may be payable on your benefit payment. If you're also a member of certain public sector funds (for details about these funds, refer to Chapter 2), you may pay tax on your non-SMSF super pension benefit, even after the age of 60, if your pension benefit is considered to come from an untaxed source (I explain the tax treatment of untaxed benefits, which generally relate to older public service super schemes, on my website, SuperGuide at www.superguide.com.au).

- **Death benefits:** After you die, tax may be payable if your super benefits are paid to an individual who is considered a non-dependant under the tax laws. A *non-dependant*, under the tax laws, is typically an independent adult child. I explain death benefits and taxes in Chapter 24.

Table 13-1 presents a summary of the main super taxes applicable to your SMSF.

Table 13-1	Possible Taxes Affecting Your SMSF	
Tax	*Tax Rates*	*What Part of Your Super Is Taxed?*
Contributions Tax*		
Contributions Tax	15%	Tax applies to any concessional (before-tax) superannuation contributions. Likely refund of this tax for those earning less than $37,000 (refer to Chapter 4).
Division 293 Tax	15%	Additional tax applies to any concessional contributions paid by those with an adjusted taxable income of more than $300,000 a year.
Earnings Taxes** (in Accumulation Phase)		
Investment Income Tax	15%	Tax on investment earnings of fund. No earnings tax payable when account is in pension phase.
Capital Gains Tax (CGT)	15% (effective rate of 10% after CGT discount)	Tax on capital gains in your fund. Effective tax rate of 10% for gains on assets held for more than 12 months. No tax payable on capital gains in pension phase.
Non-Arm's Length Income	47%	Income derived from a source that is not on a commercial arm's-length basis. Tax also payable on this income in pension phase.
Benefit Payment Taxes: Aged Under 60		
Lump Sums	0% to 20% plus Medicare levy	Tax payable on 'taxable component'.[†] If reached preservation age (currently 55), then tax payable only on benefits above low rate cap,[‡] and then tax rate is 15% plus Medicare levy. If under preservation age, total benefit is subject to tax rate of 20% plus Medicare levy.
Pensions	Marginal tax rate (MTR) plus Medicare levy with 15% pension offset for over-55s	Income sourced from 'taxable component'[†] counted as part of taxable income, so subject to MTR. If under preservation age (currently age 55), then no 15% pension offset.
Benefit Payment Taxes: Aged 60 and Over		
Lump Sums	0%	Tax-free payment.
Pensions	0%	Tax-free income payments.

Tax	Tax Rates	What Part of Your Super Is Taxed?
Death Benefits Taxes		
Lump Sums	0% to 30%	Tax-free to 'dependants under the tax laws'. Tax-free component is still tax-free even when paid to 'non-dependants under tax laws'. Any tax payable is 15% on taxable component, and life insurance proceeds can be subject to 30% benefits tax.
Pensions	Depends on age of deceased member, and benefit recipient	Pensions can be payable to certain dependants only. Tax payable when both deceased and recipient under the age of 60.

Notes:

1. Benefits from an untaxed source aren't included in this table, although in relation to SMSFs, such benefits aren't relevant unless a benefit includes a life insurance payout, which is paid to a non-dependant (see Chapter 24). An untaxed source is a super fund that hasn't paid tax on employer super contributions and super fund earnings. Typically, pension benefits from an untaxed source are paid from some public sector super funds, and more tax is payable when such benefits are paid. I explain benefits from an untaxed source on my website, SuperGuide (www.superguide.com.au).

2. Although super benefits receive special tax treatment, super benefits received under the age of 60 count towards personal assessable income, which means your other income combined with your super payments could push you into a higher tax bracket for non-super income. Seek tax advice from your accountant.

* Contributions are included in a super fund's assessable income, which is subject to earnings tax of 15 per cent. In relation to contributions, this tax is commonly known as 'contributions tax'.

** No earnings tax payable on earnings from pension assets, that is, assets financing a pension/income stream.

† Superannuation benefits can be made up of two components — taxable component and tax-free component. Tax-free component is always tax-free and taxable component is taxed depending on size of benefit and age of fund member. Depending on the level of taxable income, the Medicare levy (a levy imposed on taxpayers to fund the public health system) is likely to be payable.

‡ Taxable component of a lump sum is tax-free up to the low rate cap of $185,000 (for 2014–15 year) for benefits from taxed source (a SMSF is a taxed source). Depending on level of taxable income, the Medicare levy is likely to be payable.

Source: Data compiled from information available on the ATO website (www.ato.gov.au). Table created, and analysis provided, by Trish Power.

Only complying superannuation funds receive the concessional tax rates applicable to super funds (as shown in Table 13-1). (***Remember:*** A complying super fund operates within the superannuation and tax laws and acts in accordance with the rules of the fund; that is, in accordance with your fund's trust deed.) If your fund becomes a non-complying fund, your fund's trustee must pay the top marginal rate of tax on the total assets of your fund, *less* any non-concessional (after-tax) superannuation contributions, *plus* the top marginal tax rate on fund earnings. Since 1 July 2014, the top marginal tax rate is 47 per cent. From 1 July 2017, the top tax rate reverts to 45 per cent, when the federal government removes the temporary budget repair levy of 2 per cent on high-income earners, and certain other taxpayers, including non-complying super funds. In Chapter 11, I explain what you need to do (and what not to do!) to ensure your SMSF continues to be a complying fund.

If you're making decisions about your savings or retirement strategies with significant tax implications, or considering financial transactions with tax consequences, I suggest you seek expert tax advice from an accountant and registered tax agent. Each person's tax situation is unique and talking to an expert means obtaining the most up-to-date advice pertaining to your circumstances. (For help finding a taxation expert, refer to Chapter 5).

If your SMSF has access to an accountant/tax agent, you don't need to be a tax expert to run your own SMSF or to manage your tax strategies. Even so, keeping informed of what's happening in the super tax area is reasonably straightforward. I discuss the tax basics in this chapter, and in Chapter 18, and in Part V of this book. If, however, you want to find out more about the super taxes beyond this book, a starting point is the ATO website (www.ato.gov.au/super).

Reducing Income Tax the Super Way

Contributing to your super fund can be the most tax-effective way to save for your retirement. Your fund's earnings are taxed at 15 per cent, and you can make contributions from your pre-tax salary. If you're mainly self-employed or if you're not an employee, you can ordinarily receive a tax deduction for your super contributions.

Australia has different marginal rates of tax (nil to 47 per cent plus Medicare levy) for different levels of personal income to ensure Australians have a minimum tax-free income while paying a higher rate of tax on higher levels of income. You can make the most of superannuation by making

✔ Concessional contributions, also known as *before-tax contributions*, under a salary sacrifice arrangement (which I explain in Chapter 4).

✔ Concessional contributions that are claimed as a deduction in an individual's tax return. Personal *tax-deductible contributions* are available if you're self-employed, or not employed, or you receive only a small proportion of your income from an employer.

✔ Non-concessional contributions, also known as *after-tax contributions*.

I explain the rules you must satisfy to make such super contributions in Chapter 4, and I provide more detailed information on popular super contribution strategies on my website, SuperGuide (www.superguide.com.au).

As a SMSF fund member, if you fail to provide your personal tax file number to your SMSF, or if you exceed your contributions caps, you or your super benefit may be subject to penalty tax. I also explain your non-concessional and concessional contributions caps and your options when you exceed those caps in Chapter 4.

If you run your own business, you may be eligible for some generous tax concessions, known as *small business entity concessions*, on any profit from the sale of your business. The policy behind these exemptions is to recognise that many self-employed people choose to build up the value of their business as a way of providing for their retirement, instead of regularly contributing to a super fund. I explain the concessions, and the exemptions available in the sidebar 'Retiring your tax-friendly business profits', later in the chapter.

Copping Contributions Tax

Superannuation contributions can be divided neatly into two types — concessional and non-concessional (refer to Chapter 4). Only concessional (before-tax) contributions — when you or your employer makes tax-deductible contributions — are hit with a contributions tax of 15 per cent (plus an additional 15 per cent tax if you earn more than $300,000 a year).

Employer contributions, including salary-sacrificed and Superannuation Guarantee contributions, are subject to contributions tax. If you're not an employee or otherwise eligible, any contributions for which you successfully claim a tax deduction are also subject to the contributions tax. For the privilege of claiming a tax deduction the government takes 15 cents contributions tax, via your SMSF, from every dollar of your contributions, leaving 85 per cent of each contribution for your fund to invest. If your adjusted taxable income is more than $300,000 as an individual, then your concessional contributions are hit with an additional 15 per cent tax after you lodge your personal tax return, taking the total tax haul on your concessional contributions to 30 per cent.

Believe it or not, 15 per cent tax (or 30 per cent tax for high-income earners) paid by your SMSF is generally better tax-wise than pocketing the money as regular income where you may personally pay tax of up to 47 per cent of each dollar plus 2 per cent Medicare levy. For the 2014–15 financial year, if your taxable income is more than $180,000 a year, you pay 47 per cent income tax plus Medicare levy, or 37 cents in the dollar plus Medicare levy (if your taxable income is between $80,000 and $180,000), or 32.5 cents in the dollar plus Medicare levy (if your taxable income is more than $37,000 but less than $80,000). Depending on your income, your top marginal tax rate can even be 0 per cent (when taxable income is under $18,200), or 19 per cent (if taxable income is more than $18,200 but less than $37,000). *Taxable income* is assessable income less any tax deductions (and assessable income is gross income included in an income tax return before any deductions are allowed).

Officially, the term 'contributions tax' doesn't exist. Concessional contributions are treated as assessable income within a super fund, and that assessable income is subject to an earnings tax of 15 per cent. In relation to contributions, this tax is commonly known as 'contributions tax'. I explain the reason for this silliness later in the chapter, in the section 'Including contributions as earnings'. Note that the additional 15 per cent tax on concessional contributions made by high-income earners is known as Division 293 tax, which is deducted once an individual lodges his personal income tax return.

Earnings Tax in Accumulation Phase

Your SMSF is a taxpayer just like you and pays tax on any income the fund earns in accumulation phase throughout the year. Your fund, however, pays a much lower rate of tax on earnings — 15 per cent — than most Australians pay when they earn income (refer to the previous section 'Copping Contributions Tax').

Super funds also get a special tax deal on any capital gains they make when working out the fund's income tax bill. A capital gain occurs when your fund makes a profit on the sale of an asset.

You may pay a higher rate of tax on part of your SMSF's income if your fund receives income from a non-arm's length source, such as private company dividends. I explain the tax treatment of this type of special income in Chapter 18.

Including contributions as earnings

Your super fund's assessable income, including your fund's investment income, but less deductions, is taxed at 15 per cent.

Your fund's assessable income includes any concessional contributions (such as employer contributions or tax-deductible contributions) made to the fund during the year. Obviously, treating contributions as income is a nonsense, but this nonsense enables your super fund to reduce any tax payable on investments or contributions by using 'franking credits', which can offset any tax payable on your fund's income.

Franking credits arise from 'franked dividends'. *Franked dividends* are dividends earned on company shares where 30 per cent company income tax has already been paid on the income. The pre-paid tax is known as *franking credits*, which you can then use to offset your fund's tax bill. The federal government plans to reduce company tax to 28.5 per cent from 1 July 2015 (subject to legislation), which will in turn reduce franking credits. I explain how your SMSF can take advantage of franking credits, and the impact of the proposed company tax changes, in Chapter 18.

Discounting capital gains

Any 'capital gain' that your super fund receives when it disposes of an asset for a profit becomes part of your fund's assessable income. A *capital gain* arises when your fund makes a profit on the sale of an asset. Ordinarily, your fund's assessable income less deductions (that is, your fund's taxable income), is subject to an income tax of 15 per cent but, in relation to capital gains, your super fund can take advantage of the *capital gains tax (CGT) discount* when it sells an asset that it has held for more than 12 months.

Under the CGT discount rules, only two-thirds of the capital gain is included in the fund's assessable income, when the asset is held for more than 12 months. This advantageous rule means that the tax rate is effectively 10 per cent — that is, two-thirds of the fund's concessional income tax rate of 15 per cent. I explain what happens with your fund's capital gains in more detail in Chapter 18.

Any capital gains on the sale of assets held for less than 12 months are subject to 15 per cent tax. Such gains aren't eligible for the 33.33 per cent CGT discount.

Tax-Exempt Earnings in Pension Phase

Besides enjoying tax-free income in retirement (see the section 'Paying Tax-Free Benefits to Over-60s', later in the chapter), a compelling argument for taking an 'income stream' in retirement is that the earnings on assets financing your income stream are exempt from tax. An *income stream* is a series of payments, and is more commonly known as a *pension*. (I explain the exciting things that happen when you start paying super benefits from your SMSF in Part V of the book.)

Think about this tax advantage: You receive tax-free income from your SMSF pension, and your tax-free income is sourced from assets that are invested in a tax-exempt environment. In comparison, if you invest your savings outside the super environment, the earnings on your savings are subject to income tax, and any income you earn is taxed at your marginal tax rate, although you may be eligible for special tax offsets if you're aged 65 or over.

Your super fund's earnings in pension phase are considered exempt income, which means such income isn't subject to earnings tax, but nor can your fund claim expenses incurred while earning that income. The situation becomes more complex when you have members continuing to contribute to the SMSF, while some, or all, of the members are also receiving a pension from the fund in the same financial year. If the trustees of your SMSF expect that your fund is going to be accepting contributions and paying out pensions, I suggest you talk to your accountant or SMSF adviser about your fund's tax management well before your fund commences any pensions. I explain the issues you need to think about when contributing while also taking a pension in Chapter 22.

Franking credits (refer to the section 'Including contributions as earnings' earlier in this chapter) sourced from franked dividends paid by Australian companies can be very valuable for SMSFs in reducing the amount of tax that a SMSF must pay. If your SMSF is in pension phase, you can even claim a tax refund representing your fund's franking credits! I explain the tax magic of franked dividends in Chapter 18.

Paying Tax-Free Benefits to Over-60s

In Australia, the country's decision makers have waved a legislative wand and decided that retiring in Australia can mean never again paying income tax. If you're aged 60 or over and retired, you can receive super benefits from your SMSF tax-free — as a lump sum or as an income stream. You can enjoy this tax-free nirvana as a member of most larger funds, too. (I explain the tax treatment of super benefits received before the age of 60 in Chapter 19.)

Not only can you enjoy tax-free super income from the age of 60, but you can gain a second benefit from the super tax rules when you earn non-super income while also receiving a SMSF pension or taking a lump sum. Your SMSF lump sum or pension isn't counted as income for income tax purposes, which means that this income isn't included in your tax return.

What this tax-free super world means is that when you earn non-super income, you can take advantage of the income tax-free threshold of $18,200 (for the 2014–15 year), and various low income tax offsets. For example, you can receive $100,000 income from your SMSF, and $20,542 (for the 2014–15 year) from part-time work and pay no tax. If you're aged 65 or over, you can earn even more non-super income and pay no tax.

I explain the tax rules on super in retirement, both before and after the age 60, in Part V of this book. I cover the non-super tax rules and their relationship with super on my website, SuperGuide (www.superguide .com.au).

Tax-free super has always been a feature of Australia's retirement system but, before July 2007, you usually had to hire advisers and get involved in creative gymnastics to make it happen — not unlike what you have to do to secure tax-free income when you retire before the age of 60. If you do withdraw any of your super before the age of 60 (or you retire before you turn 60), the taxable component of your benefit payments are usually subject to tax. I explain the tax payable if you retire (or withdraw super benefits for other reasons) before the age of 60, in Chapter 19.

Retiring your tax-friendly business profits

If you run your own business, you may be able to access some generous exemptions and discounts on CGT, known as *small business entity concessions*. These include

- **15-year exemption:** As a business owner, when you sell active business assets that you've held continuously for 15 years or more, you can ignore capital gains for tax purposes, subject to owning less than $6 million in net assets (excluding your home and super). You must be aged 55 years or older, and be retiring, or be permanently incapacitated. This exemption is known as the 15-year exemption. If you've held your assets for fewer than 15 years, you can take advantage of the other CGT discounts and exemptions.

- **50 per cent CGT concession:** If your business is not set up as a company, you can reduce by 50 per cent a capital gain on the sale of an asset held for at least 12 months. This concession isn't available to companies.

- **50 per cent active asset reduction:** The reduction for active assets can be applied to a capital gain that has already been halved by the 50 per cent CGT concession (refer to the previous point), which means just 25 per cent of a capital gain is possibly subject to tax. If set up as a company, then 50 per cent of total capital gain is potentially subject to tax.

- **CGT retirement exemption:** The small business CGT retirement exemption can apply to the remaining 25 per cent of the capital gain potentially eliminating the capital gain, or remaining 50 per cent (if your business is set up as a company). You can use this retirement exemption until you reach your lifetime maximum of $500,000,

provided the monies are used for retirement purposes. If your spouse is a joint owner of the business, as a couple you have two lifetime limits totalling $1 million. If you dispose of any business assets and claim the CGT retirement exemption before you reach the age of 55, you must roll over the amount, known as a *capital gains tax exempt component*, until you retire. If you sell the asset after the age of 55 and you retire, you can choose to take the tax-free capital gain as cash. If you roll over the money, the component is preserved until you retire from the workforce, or meet another condition of release (see Chapter 19 for more information on accessing your super benefits).

- **Rollover exemption:** You can defer any CGT payable on any capital gain from the sale of a business asset provided you purchase another active business asset with the proceeds of the sale.

Get advice if you run a business and want to take advantage of any CGT exemptions or discounts. The CGT concessions have complex rules and are subject to eligibility criteria. Remember, the exemptions interact with other CGT rules and your accountant (refer to Chapter 5) is the best person to work out the most appropriate option for you and your business.

Note: You may be eligible for a lifetime limit of $1.355 million (for the 2014–15 year) for non-concessional (after-tax) contributions you choose to make from the proceeds of the disposal of qualifying small business assets. This limit is in addition to the annual non-concessional contribution limit of $180,000, or the bring-forward cap of $540,000 for anyone under age 65 (for the 2014–15 year).

Part IV
Investing Your DIY Super Money

Five Must-Dos When Drafting a SMSF Investment Strategy

- **Return:** As SMSF trustee, when drafting and regularly reviewing your SMSF's investment strategy, you need to consider the likely return from an investment, and whether such an investment is consistent with your SMSF's investment objectives.

- **Risk:** You can't focus solely on the likely return of an investment —your fund's investment strategy must require you to consider the risk involved in making an investment.

- **Diversification:** You must consider whether your fund assets need to be diversified across a spread of asset classes, such as cash, shares and property, and whether your fund assets also need to be diversified across a spread of specific investments.

- **Cashflow needs:** You need to ensure that the cashflow needs of your SMSF are not compromised when deciding on your overall investment strategy. Typical cash flow requirements of a SMSF include paying fund expenses and super taxes, and if a SMSF is in pension phase, paying out regular super pension payments.

- **Insurance cover for SMSF members:** When drafting the SMSF's investment strategy, and when reviewing the strategy at least annually, you also need to decide if the fund should take out insurance cover for one or more of its members.

Visit www.dummies.com/extras/diysuperau for an article (free!) about investing your DIY super money.

In this part ...

✔ Take a short course on the world of investing, including the balancing act between risk and return, and the importance of diversification.

✔ Understand the special investment rules that apply to SMSF investing, including the importance of drafting and regularly reviewing a SMSF investment strategy.

✔ Appreciate that borrowing within a SMSF is only permitted in limited circumstances.

✔ Explore the possibilities of investing in property via your SMSF.

✔ Consider the tax implications of your SMSF investment decisions while accumulating super, and when drawing down on a super pension.

Chapter 14

Exploring the World of
Super Investing

*I*nvesting your self-managed super fund (SMSF) savings is the serious end
of your retirement planning. Deciding where, and what, you're going to
invest in can be exhilarating, hair-raising, mundane, depressing and deeply
satisfying — all at the same time!

When investing for the long term you need to keep one eye on what's
happening today, and one eye on the future — and I mean both the
long-term and medium-term future. The economic malaise that hits the
investment markets during a market downturn eventually passes, and a
robust investment portfolio needs to survive to thrive another day.

In this chapter, I provide a snapshot of one of the worst-case scenarios in
investing, and I ask you the important question about your ability to invest
your super monies. I spend some time discussing risk and its relationship
with investment returns, and I explain the main asset classes that your SMSF
can choose to invest in. I also provide a comparison of investing directly
versus investing via managed funds versus wraps — an important decision
when running your own fund.

Investing is a huge subject, and four or five chapters can't do the topic
justice. I recommend you read this chapter to gauge your level of
investment knowledge — even if you consider yourself an experienced

investor — before turning to the rest of the investment chapters in this part. In these chapters I concentrate on the special investment issues and rules that are unique to SMSFs, and how such rules work in practice.

When investing via a SMSF, you must follow special investment rules including drafting and regularly reviewing your fund's investment strategy. You also must be mindful of the specific investment restrictions that apply to SMSF investing.

Getting Ready for the Investment Roller-Coaster

Australia, like the rest of the world, can expect to have property booms and busts, volatile sharemarkets, economic downturns and upturns, and company collapses. Unfortunately, during 2008 and 2009, the world experienced more property busts, sharemarket meltdowns and economic downturns than at any other time since the early 1930s. Okay, during 1990 and 1991, unemployment figures and the general Australian economy were also horrendous; and, while I'm at it, you may want to throw in the credit squeeze of 1961, if you suffered through that time, and the 1987 stockmarket crash.

During 2008, Australia's sharemarket dropped nearly 40 per cent, while some major Australian companies disintegrated. The federal government guaranteed bank deposits to ward off massive cash withdrawals by panicked depositors. Many Australian listed property trusts (now called Australian Real Estate Investment Trusts — A-REITs) and unlisted property schemes were forced to freeze redemptions (withdrawals) by investors holding units in the property schemes — unit holders who wanted to move cash out of the debt-ridden property trusts, and into the safe haven of government-guaranteed bank deposits. The property schemes froze withdrawals to prevent forced asset sales and, in so doing, attempted to protect the value of the property assets held by the scheme, and to protect the long-term interests of investors. (I explain REITs and unlisted property schemes in Chapter 17.)

During 2009, most major companies announced earnings downgrades, and more and more companies announced job losses, while personal bankruptcies were on the rise, triggered by burgeoning credit card debt and unemployment.

You can look towards the US economy and the European economies for the seeds of doom that descended upon Australia during 2008 and 2009. The economic crisis that beset the world's economies is called the Global Financial Crisis (GFC), although Europe and the United States call the GFC the *Great Recession.*

If you've watched television or read the daily newspapers over the past half dozen years, then you're probably sick of hearing about the GFC, and wondering why I'm writing about an economic situation that imploded in 2008 and 2009 more than six years on. Why also am I opening the first chapter on investing in this book with doom and gloom?

As an investor, the GFC holds valuable lessons for all investors, including SMSF trustees. Further, at the time of writing this book in late 2014, the Australian sharemarket had not yet returned to the levels it reached before the GFC savaged investment markets during 2008 and 2009. As a consequence, many SMSF investors (and large super funds) are still working through the fallout from the GFC, the greatest market collapse since the Great Depression hit the world in the 1930s. I hold strong views on why so many investors were hit hard by the GFC, and you may be surprised by what I have to say in the sidebar 'Four lessons from the G-F-C (Grab For Cash)', later in the chapter.

I haven't yet met an investor who didn't lose some money during 2008 and 2009, but the investors who are in the strongest position post-GFC are those investors, including SMSFs, who conducted due diligence on their investment strategy and investments throughout 2008 and 2009, and in the years since the GFC. I explain the steps involved in drafting, implementing and reviewing an investment strategy for your SMSF in Chapter 15.

How Steep Is Your Investment Learning Curve?

Contrary to popular opinion, your SMSF is an investor, not an investment. Many Australians, including journalists and commentators, confuse the underlying investments of a super fund (such as shares or property) with the investment vehicle; that is, the super fund.

Commentators often observe that super is a 'good' or a 'bad' investment, which means they don't understand how super works. If you're purchasing shares directly, for example, through a stockbroker, you don't call yourself an investment — you're the investor. Likewise, when your super fund is purchasing shares through a stockbroker, your fund isn't the investment even though your SMSF oversees an investment portfolio.

Running your own SMSF gives you control over how your superannuation money is invested. Taking on such a challenge can be exciting but the question to ask yourself is: 'Am I an experienced investor?'

Some experts don't share my view that novice investors and SMSFs don't mix. Certain DIY super providers claim your SMSF is the perfect place to improve your knowledge of investing. Ah, but the use of the word 'improve' is integral because it assumes you have a basic understanding of investing. You need to ask yourself: Do I have a working knowledge of asset classes, risk and return and the advantages of diversification?

 If you know absolutely nothing about investing, my view is that running a SMSF isn't the place to begin your investment education. Stick with the fund you're already in or choose a fund that gives you lots of investment choice, instead of jeopardising your retirement savings with beginner investment decisions. (For information on choosing a fund and investment choice, see my SuperGuide website at `www.superguide.com.au`.)

 If you're serious about being responsible for investing your super monies, then I strongly suggest you read as widely as possible. Follow the financial news in the daily papers and on television. Critically assess all information that you come across and identify who is providing this information. Even if you consider yourself an experienced investor, read through all of Part IV to help you determine your level of SMSF investment knowledge. Then, I recommend you read ASIC's guide to investing, 'Investing between the flags' (visit `www.moneysmart.gov.au` and download a copy). If reading this chapter, the other Part IV chapters, and the ASIC investing booklet confirms what you already know about investing and you have the time to devote to your SMSF, then you're probably a candidate for investing your own superannuation monies.

 Even when you appoint a financial adviser (refer to Chapter 5) to assist you in selecting your fund's investments, you need to fully understand what investments and products the adviser is recommending for your super fund. Later in this chapter, I share a scary investment story where some SMSF trustees and investors relied on financial advice that claimed a highly risky investment was as 'safe as houses' (see the sidebar 'Westpoint woes').

Four lessons from the G-F-C (Grab For Cash)

I was in Europe when the Global Financial Crisis (GFC) officially hit in October 2008 (although investment markets had been falling dramatically since late 2007). The impact of the GFC saw the United Kingdom bail out its major banks. Ireland came to a standstill, becoming the first country in the world to guarantee bank deposits in response to the secondary 'crisis of confidence' in the banking system. Spain was also grappling with struggling banks, while Iceland simply imploded with calls from the Icelandic community demanding 'women only' to take over the running of the country and its male-dominated financial system.

Even with the drama escalating in Europe, most of the GFC action (and reaction to the GFC) was happening across the Atlantic Ocean in the United States. Billions of dollars were handed out by the US government to major financial organisations. Many more bail-outs followed in the next 18 months.

The world's credit squeeze was exacerbated by the massive arrogance (and sometimes fraud) of bankers, investment bankers and hedge fund managers, and the undue influence they had over the US government's decision makers leading up to the GFC. The world's media was also fooled by the so-called market experts who had vested interests in propping up markets on unsustainable debt for as long as possible.

Merely months earlier, in 2007, in Australia most sharemarket pundits and commentators were predicting the economic boom was going to go on forever (or at least the next 30 years) because of China's need for resources. I wasn't one of these individuals and nor were a handful of other commentators. For much of 2007, I was writing articles reminding SMSF trustees and other investors to reset their investment strategies for changing times and to review the riskiness of investment portfolios against possible economic shocks.

No-one likes an individual who pronounces: 'I told you so' and I certainly can't claim the mantle of soothsayer. I didn't expect world markets to collapse and I was surprised by the severity of the GFC as much as anybody.

Many months before the investment markets started deteriorating from late 2007, however, I was nervous about the state of the US economy and particularly its crumbling property market. I fully understood that the unravelling of the US economy, when it happened, was not going to be pretty.

I was tracking this development for several months before the US property market imploded, courtesy of an excellent Australian journalist, the late David Hirst, who wrote a column for the Melbourne *Age* and other publications, exploring the underlying rot of the US economy and the neglect by Wall Street.

The origins of the GFC were linked to the proliferation of *sub-prime house mortgages* (loans with ridiculously low interest rates to people who couldn't afford the loans longer term) in the US residential property market. During the mid-2000s, the sub-prime loans were about to mature into regular home loans with market rates of interest. Most of the individuals subject to these loans would be unable to afford the higher loan repayments when the market rates of interest kicked in. And that's what happened!

What compounded the problem in the US is that, unlike Australia, an individual in the United States can effectively walk away from

(continued)

(continued)

a home loan (and his home) with no recourse to other assets the individual may own, except for the nasty long-term black mark on the former home-owner's credit rating.

To be honest, I hadn't had much faith in the US economy since the major US banks and investment banks bailed out the hedge fund Long Term Capital Management in late 1998, with the magnanimous nod from the US Federal Reserve. The 1998 bailout was to prevent a catastrophic domino effect on the US sharemarket and debt markets (sound familiar?).

More remarkably, while the US property market was unravelling during 2007, fund managers in Australia continued to flog financial products, known as *collateralised debt obligations* (CDOs), representing these packaged sub-prime loans and other debts, to Australia's superannuation funds and to local councils. Many individuals in the financial industry, entrusted with responsibility to look after the interests of investors, and super fund members, failed to mitigate losses from falling markets and dud sub-prime investments.

In my view, the four main lessons that can be learnt from the GFC debacle are:

✔ Prudent fund managers, super funds and individual investors must heed all of the market information available, instead of just the information that the market wants to hear.

✔ Experts aren't always right, and sometimes they're just plain wrong. More precisely, investments experts are never infallible and can even be gullible, just like individual investors.

✔ The future is impossible to predict accurately, and the only defence against the future's uncertainty is to spread your risk.

✔ If you're willing to take greater risks, be sure you understand the financial consequences — that is, ask what's the worst thing that can happen?

Understanding the Basic Ingredients of Super Investing

Have you noticed that people are always happy to tell you the good news stories of investing but not the bad news stories, unless the story relates to someone else? Human nature is a funny thing, and the world of investing certainly isn't immune from the psychology of human behaviour. If people are making big money on a particular type of investment, eventually everyone hears about it and every man and his dog is climbing over each other to get in on the act before the price collapses. I call this behaviour speculating rather than investing.

Investing, on the other hand, is the act of purchasing an asset or an interest in an asset, with the intention of getting a financial return. Regardless of how complicated an investment may be, the purpose of any investment is to produce a return on your money, either immediately or at a later time.

Don't forget about risk and return

What are the chances that you can lose your super money on an investment? This question can be viewed as a fairly accurate definition of risk. For example, before 2008, if retirees and other investors knew that it was possible to lose 40 per cent of their money in less than 12 months on a diversified share portfolio, then I very much doubt that super funds, including SMSFs, would have held so much super money in Australian shares and international shares. Such a dramatic event can happen again, but the likelihood of such a huge fall recurring in the next few years is considered unlikely — but, remember, it is a risk, so it's not impossible.

Risk is usually associated with loss and can translate into the loss of cold hard cash or loss of lifestyle or even loss of opportunity. A mild form of risk is the possibility of earning a return lower than expected on an investment. An extreme and very devastating form of risk is the chance of losing part or all of your original investment — that is, negative earnings and loss of capital.

What then are the chances that your investment can boost your super savings? This second question flips the concept of risk upside down, and helps you focus on the main game of your SMSF: Investing your fund's superannuation money to provide the largest retirement benefit possible, or to reach a target retirement balance, by taking a level of risk that your fund members are willing to tolerate.

An easy way to think about risk responsibly is to think of R-I-S-K as an acronym — **R**easonable **I**nvestment **S**trategies with a **K**icker.

Investing for the long tomorrow

In the past 15 years or so, superannuation fund returns have been spectacularly good and also spectacularly bad. Do you remember the dire predictions that double-digit returns for super funds were an event of the past and not to expect them again, after dismal super fund returns in 2002 and 2003? Surprise, surprise. The financial years 2004, 2005, 2006 and 2007 were bumper years for super returns, mainly due to the roaring performance of the Australian sharemarket. And then the sharemarket turned in December 2007, and the GFC hit Australia in late 2008 — ouch!

If you had any of your super money in international shares in the early 2000s, you were probably wondering if that section of the market was ever going to turn around. By 2006 and 2007, international shares were delivering stronger returns, until the GFC hit world sharemarkets, eradicating the recent gains.

On average, large super fund returns have been positive for the 2009–10, 2010–11, 2011–12, 2012–13 and 2013–14 financial years, but delivered losses for the 2007–08 and 2008–09 financial years.

Post-GFC, investment markets have rebounded in recent years, with the Australian sharemarket delivering double-digit returns for the 2013 (21.9 per cent) and 2014 (17.3 per cent) financial years, according to superannuation rating company Chant West.

The moral of this brief tale is that the long-term investment return is what matters to you when you have your money locked away for your retirement in 15, 20 or 30 years' time. A super fund may deliver 20 per cent one year, and negative 10 per cent the next year, but when you average those returns over the two years, the fund's average annual return is 5 per cent — not great but not dire. But two years still isn't long enough to truly assess the long-term performance of a fund. I explain how to benchmark your SMSF's investment performance in Chapter 15.

The longer the time frame you have to invest, the more risk you can tolerate because your portfolio has time to recover from any market volatility. Over the long-term, the traditional investments that have delivered the highest long-term returns have been shares and property. These asset classes have greater volatility (although direct property investment has much lower volatility than listed property), which means returns can go up and down within a very short time, but they also deliver the greatest returns. The GFC, however, has spooked millions of investors, which means that many investors remain tentative about riskier assets. For the latest performance statistics for superannuation funds and the different asset classes, visit my website, SuperGuide (www.superguide.com.au).

Appreciating Asset Classes Leads to Investment Success

The most effective way to manage risk is by diversifying your investments — spreading your risk over different types of *assets*, different countries and different industries. An asset can be any item of economic value but, when it comes to investing, you're ordinarily talking about *financial assets*, which are divided into broad categories called *asset classes* — cash, fixed interest, shares, property and alternative investments. I list the long-term returns

SMSF investment: Three most popular asset classes

Each quarter, the ATO releases SMSF statistics derived from annual return data. Some of the more interesting data outlines the investments that SMSF trustees choose, and how much SMSF money is invested in the different asset types.

Year in and year out, these three most popular asset classes for SMSF trustees are: Australian shares, cash and property. As at June 2014, the three main asset categories represented 77 per cent of all SMSF investments. On average, SMSF trustees invest one-third of their SMSF money directly in listed Australian shares (32.7 per cent), 29 per cent in cash and term deposits, and 15.6 per cent in direct property, according to June 2014 statistics, released in September 2014 by the ATO. SMSF money is also invested indirectly in Australian shares and property via managed funds and public trusts.

In 2004, three asset classes represented two-thirds (66 per cent) of all SMSF money, with 31 per cent held in Australian shares, 23 per cent held in cash and term deposits (and debt securities) and 12 per cent in direct property.

Over the ten-year period, from 2004 to 2014, the proportion of SMSF money invested in direct property has increased by roughly four percentage points, from 12 per cent in 2004 to 15.6 per cent in 2014.

International investments aren't a big focus for SMSF trustees, with less than one half of 1 per cent of SMSF money invested directly in overseas markets; and a small allocation to overseas managed investments. Presumably, SMSF trustees have some overseas exposure via other managed funds investment (roughly 5 per cent of SMSF money is invested in managed funds, and another 12.8 per cent is invested in a mix of asset classes via public trusts and other trusts).

For more information on where SMSF trustees invest their super money, visit the ATO website (www.ato.gov.au) or my website, SuperGuide (www.superguide.com.au).

Source: Adapted extract from article 'SMSF investment: Three most popular asset classes, and the rest (updated)', originally published on consumer website, www.superguide.com.au. Copyright Trish Power. Reproduced with permission.

associated with the main asset classes and asset sub-classes on my website, SuperGuide (www.superguide.com.au).

If you want to find out about the specifics of what makes a good investment, you may want to chat to your adviser or do your own research. In any case, the most cost-effective way of using your adviser is to do your own research first so you can ask the right questions. You can visit numerous websites (see Appendix B for some starting points) that provide you with useful background information as well as specific information on different investments.

Cool as cash

Cash is a low-risk investment that delivers a positive return every year. When other assets such as shares and property aren't doing too well, you often hear market commentators predicting a 'flight to cash'. Examples of cash include bank accounts, online high-interest bank accounts, cash management accounts, and term deposits with terms of six months or less.

The danger that hovers around relying too much on cash as an asset class is that inflation can erode the value of your investment. For example, if you're earning 3 per cent on your term deposit but inflation is 3 per cent, then your real return is zero per cent.

Fuzzy fixed interest

Fixed interest investments can include longer-term (more than six months) bank term deposits and bonds. *Bonds* are relatively low risk and are in some ways like term deposits and, in other ways, like loans. You give (lend) money to a bank, company or government and, in return, it promises to pay you a certain amount at set periods and repay you the original amount after an agreed period of time. The big difference, however, between term deposits and bonds is that bondholders can trade the bonds (that is, buy or sell them), before they're due to be repaid. Bond trading is ordinarily the domain of financial experts, and can involve international bonds as well.

The category of fixed interest can sometimes be a bit fuzzy, because it can also include debentures, preference shares, bond funds and mortgage funds. Companies issue *debentures* to raise capital for projects, and the amount handed over by the investor is effectively treated as a company debt. *Preference shares* of a company are also known as *hybrid securities*, and pay a set dividend that has preference over the payment of ordinary dividends on other company shares. Preference shareholders also rank in front of ordinary shareholders if the company collapses. *Bond funds* are simply managed funds that give the retail investor access to specific types of bonds, or a wider choice of bonds, and bond trading. A *mortgage fund* is a pooled investment arrangement, like a managed fund, that lends money to third parties in exchange for a mortgage on a house, office, factory or any other form of real estate.

Since the GFC hit in 2008, investors have been in search of a fixed interest investment that doesn't implode at the first sign of an economic downturn. Government bonds are the least risky (depending on the stability of the country involved), while the security of company bonds and preference shares depends on the financial health of the underlying company. Different bonds, and different preference shares, and different debentures have different risk ratings, which means your fund needs to choose carefully when making a decision to invest in more sophisticated fixed interest investments.

Betting on bricks and mortar — property

Property is a broad asset class encompassing residential property, individual shops, individual offices, car parks, office buildings, factories, shopping centres and other developments. As a SMSF trustee, you can either invest in these investments directly, or indirectly via A-REITs, managed funds and unlisted property schemes. Income on these investments is via rent and via potential capital gains when properties are sold.

The upside of property investing is that you receive a regular income in the form of rent, and hopefully you make a profit when you sell the investment. The downside of property as an asset class, particularly when investing directly, is you usually need a big chunk of money to purchase this type of asset, and that it may take some time to sell the investment. I explain property investing and SMSFs in more detail in Chapter 17.

Sailing in on shares

By purchasing company *shares*, you're buying a share of a company that entitles you to a share of the profits in the form of dividends and the benefit of any increase in the share price because of the strong performance of the company. You also share the impact of any drop in share price, if you sell your shares at that time. You can invest in Australian or international shares.

Purchasing Australian shares that pay dividends can also give your SMSF access to franked dividends that entitle you to franking credits, which can partially or fully offset the tax payable on your fund earnings. To understand the benefits of franked dividends and franking credits, especially when taking an income stream from your SMSF, see Chapter 18.

Australia is a mere 2 per cent of the world sharemarket, yet most Australians who invest directly don't go near the international sharemarkets. I don't blame them because as an individual it can be difficult to get up-to-date and thorough information on overseas stocks. In addition, a falling or rising Australian dollar can wipe out any returns you may receive on overseas assets, unless you hedge (that is, use strategies to offset the impact of changes in the dollar) your portfolio for this possibility.

Investing a percentage of your DIY super monies in a managed fund that invests in international markets can be a practical and prudent way to access the other 98 per cent of the world sharemarkets. I compare investing directly in shares with investing via managed funds later in the chapter, in the section 'Take Your Pick: Investing Directly, Using Managed Funds or Wraps'.

Alert to alternative investments

In the search for greater returns, large super funds now regularly invest in *alternative investments* that are basically subsets of the major asset classes or different investment styles. Examples of these investment categories include:

- ✔ **Infrastructure:** *Infrastructure investment* is effectively a subset of property, because the investments relate to building bridges, toll roads, hospitals and even pipelines.

- ✔ **Hedge funds:** Your fund may choose to invest in a *hedge fund* or *absolute return fund*, which invests in the same underlying assets that your fund does, but uses derivatives and different investment styles to what a regular investor uses. (A *derivative* is a financial asset or liability whose value is linked to an underlying asset such as shares.). Ordinarily, managers of a hedge fund promise positive returns — regardless of whether the industry benchmarks are returning a negative performance — while minimising the volatility of the fund portfolio. In short, exposing your SMSF to new investment techniques is best executed via a managed fund, but choose wisely because most hedge funds haven't lived up to their lofty promises.

- ✔ **Private equity:** Big superannuation funds are now investing in promising companies that aren't yet listed on any sharemarket. This type of investing is called *private equity investment* — an investment that can be risky but, likewise, the rewards can be huge if the super funds back the right companies. As an individual investor (such as a SMSF), you usually need to invest via a managed fund to access private equity investment.

- ✔ **Collectibles:** These include coins, artwork and antique convertibles. If you plan to invest in collectibles you need to be prepared to satisfy strict storage and insurance requirements (for more info on these requirements, see the ATO website – www.ato.gov.au/super).

Take Your Pick: Investing Directly, Using Managed Funds or Wraps

Most people who choose to run their own funds do so because they want control over where their super money is invested. Self-managed super funds offer a lot more flexibility than larger super funds, and also more flexibility than most super wraps in regards to what types of investments you can invest in (such as buying real estate directly) and purchasing collectibles (such as works of art and wine). A wrap service separately identifies your investment in each master trust or each managed fund you invest in via the wrap, and gives you a consolidated report of all of your transactions.

As soon as you decide you can and want to set up your own fund (for info about this first step, refer to Chapters 1 and 7), you can decide whether you invest your DIY super monies directly or use managed funds (typically via a master trust), or by investing in managed funds using a wrap service within your SMSF. A *managed fund* is an investment vehicle that pools the money of a large number of investors into a single fund with a common investment strategy. A *master trust* is a similar concept to a managed fund but invests the pooled money into one or more underlying investment vehicles.

In a nutshell, when investing your SMSF monies you have the following options:

- ✔ Invest your super money directly into shares, real estate, fixed interest, cash and other assets.
- ✔ Use master trusts/managed funds to invest your money.
- ✔ Use a combination of direct investing and managed funds/master trusts.
- ✔ Use a wrap to administer and invest your money.

Your decision on whether to invest directly or rely on fund managers to do your fund's investing usually depends on how much time you can devote to your super investments, how competent you are at investing, and your willingness to operate within the investment rules that relate to super funds. I discuss the special investment rules applicable to SMSFs in Chapter 15.

Master trusts/managed funds can be an appropriate way to invest some of your fund's assets when you want to invest in an asset class that you don't know much about (such as commercial property), or for which you can't access up-to-date information (such as international shares), or when you don't have sufficient resources to achieve sufficient diversification (such as private equity or infrastructure investments). However, I question the merits (and cost) of running your own fund if you're going to invest all of your super money in managed funds, particularly if all of your super money is going to be invested and administered via a wrap service.

Westpoint woes

Four thousand investors, and almost one-half of them SMSF trustees, initially lost nearly $400 million in the collapse of Westpoint and its related companies. Westpoint was a Perth-based apartment development company, but the group also raised funds from the 'mum and dad' market to build the apartments.

Although not all Westpoint investors used an adviser, Westpoint raised most funds via arrangements with commission-based advisers (refer to Chapter 5), or via implicit endorsement from reputable service providers. In return for a whopping commission of 10 per cent, advisers flogged Westpoint products that supposedly delivered a 'triple guaranteed' return of 12 per cent. The guarantee associated with the investment product was provided by a Westpoint company, which of course meant the guarantee was worthless.

In fact, the return of 12 per cent wasn't paid from profits from the sale of apartments but from new money coming into Westpoint from investors seeking a conservative investment. The investors had invested their money in a high-risk mezzanine-style finance arrangement, rather than a conservative 'safe as houses' investment.

Most mezzanine arrangements are secured by a second mortgage, which means that if the company defaults on your interest payment or fails to return your original capital, you must sell the property to get your money. That's usually fairly tricky because the crowd who hold the first mortgage have first bite — and don't expect many crumbs left over. In the case of Westpoint, I understand that investors didn't even have their investment secured against a second mortgage.

Westpoint eventually became just a cleverly marketed 'Ponzi scheme'. Ponzi schemes pop up constantly to catch the naive investor, and sometimes they even trick the more experienced investors — for example, New Yorker Bernie Madoff stole billions of dollars from some of the most experienced investors in the world with his non-existent hedge fund, Ascot Partners.

A Ponzi scheme, named after a 1920s American conman Charles Ponzi, usually has two key features: It claims to have no or little risk, and promises high returns. In the early days of this type of scheme, investors are indeed getting the high returns promised because the money isn't coming from successful investments but from new investors handing over their money. Eventually, the money stops flowing and the last investors to enter the scheme are always the hardest hit, while the earlier investors lose their original investments. Some forms of this scam are known as pyramid schemes.

Both Westpoint and Bernie Madoff are important reminders for all investors: When checking the merits of an investment, don't rely on the lure of high returns or the comforting words of the product promoter.

Note: Over several years, the financial regulator ASIC pursued several parties involved with the Westpoint companies. ASIC was able to secure compensation representing around 40 cents in the dollar for investors from the original $388 million lost in the Westpoint products.

Chapter 15

Super's Special Investment Rules

*O*ne of the advantages of running your own super fund is that your retirement plans are integrated into your working life and personal life. Any decent adviser guiding you on the merits of a SMSF takes into account your business and family commitments, your existing investments inside and outside of superannuation, and your level of income and potential tax bill.

In this chapter, I explain the steps involved in drafting and implementing your fund's investment strategy (or strategies). In particular, I take you through the process of identifying your DIY super fund's investment objectives and the process of working out what asset classes your fund is going to invest in. I also explain the unique investment rules that apply to super funds, in particular, SMSFs.

SMSF Investing for Two Stages

When investing your super monies, you need to be mindful that your SMSF can have two stages — an accumulation phase and a pension phase — or a combination of both. The *accumulation phase* of your SMSF super fund is when you're amassing a superannuation investment portfolio in the anticipation of funding your retirement at some point in the future. If you're the only member (or other fund members are also in accumulation phase), apart from taxes and running costs, usually no assets or money are being withdrawn from your SMSF.

The *pension phase* of a super fund is when your SMSF is paying you an income stream (or a pension), on your retirement or on reaching a certain age. If you have ceased contributing to your fund then you're now relying only on investment returns from your superannuation balance to help fund your retirement. Any earnings on super investments that are funding an income stream are tax-exempt in the fund. I discuss taxes on investment earnings in Chapters 13 and 18, and taxes on retirement incomes in Chapters 13, 18 and 19. (For more information on running a SMSF pension, see Chapters 21 and 22.)

Depending on the age of each fund member, and whether they've retired, different members may have different investment strategies. You can have one or more members in accumulation phase and one or more members in pension phase in the one SMSF, or even have up to four members in both accumulation and pension phases concurrently.

Remembering the Three Musts ...

As trustee of your SMSF, you're responsible for investing your fund's assets and monitoring the performance of those assets. Investing via your superannuation fund is markedly different from investing outside of super, because you must

✔ **Follow your fund's trust deed.** You receive your powers as trustee from what is set out in your fund's trust deed (refer to Chapter 7). You can invest in a particular asset only if your fund's trust deed expressly permits such an investment: For example, if your trust deed doesn't permit you to invest in collectibles (such as antique cars or wine), you can't invest in that type of asset, unless you change your trust deed.

✔ **Follow your fund's investment strategy.** As trustee, you must invest in accordance with your fund's investment strategy. If you formulate a strategy that states you must diversify the fund's investments into fixed interest, property and shares and you invest only in property, this means you're not following your fund's investment strategy, which is, of course, a no-no, and you may be subject to penalties. You must also regularly review your super fund's investment strategy. I discuss your fund's investment strategy in the next section.

✔ **Not break any investment rules.** Under superannuation laws, you're subject to special investment rules that are intended to minimise the chances of your superannuation assets being exposed to undue risk or being used to benefit members before they retire. I discuss these rules, later in this chapter, in the section 'Walking the Investment Tightrope'.

Consider seeking expert advice (refer to Chapter 5) and/or do some comprehensive research when drafting your investment strategy, selecting your investments and monitoring your investments. The largest super funds in Australia regularly seek expert investment advice, particularly on new ways of investing and when exploring new types of investments or emerging investment markets.

Wait! Set Your Fund's Investment Strategy

Every super fund is legally required to have an investment strategy. An *investment strategy* identifies financial goals (investment objectives) for the fund, and helps determine the fund members' tolerance for risk and the investment time horizon for each member.

Your fund's investment strategy is the key to your fund's success. This means that you need to get your strategy right and be prepared to review the strategy regularly.

Your SMSF's investment strategy, by law, must take into account the whole of your fund's circumstances, including

- **Risk and return:** The risk of making any investment and the likely return on that investment, taking into account your fund's investment objectives and expected cashflow requirements.

- **Diversification:** The composition of your fund's investments as a whole and whether you've considered the appropriate spread of risk across industry sectors, asset classes and countries. If you choose to invest in a single asset class or a single asset, make sure you document that you considered the risk of taking this action, and check that your trust deed permits such an investment.

- **Liquidity and ability to discharge your fund's liabilities:** The ability of your fund to pay taxes, expenses and benefits when they're due for payment. Investing 100 per cent of your fund's assets in one investment may mean you don't have enough cash to cover your SMSF's expenses (refer to Chapter 6), or to pay benefits (see Part V in this book).

- **Insurance needs of fund members:** An assessment of whether the SMSF trustees should hold a contract of insurance that provides insurance cover for one or more fund members.

Formulating, implementing and regularly reviewing your SMSF's investment strategy involves

✔ Drafting your fund's investment objectives.

✔ Assessing whether your SMSF should take out insurance cover for one or more of your fund members.

✔ Determining your fund's asset allocation.

✔ Selecting and monitoring specific assets.

✔ Regularly reviewing your fund's investment strategy, including your fund's asset allocation.

Here's an added incentive for you to focus on your investment strategy: The ATO is hunting down those SMSFs that don't have an investment strategy in place, and may hit you with an administrative penalty of $3,400 if you fail to draft and implement your fund's investment strategy. If you intentionally or recklessly fail to develop your SMSF's investment strategy, the fine could end up being a whopping $17,000. In extreme circumstances, your fund can even be deemed to be non-complying, which means you're liable to pay the top rate of income tax on the taxable income of your fund, and the top rate of income (refer to Chapter 9) on the assets (less non-concessional contributions) of your fund.

Identifying your goals — your DIY super fund's investment objectives

The first step in formulating your investment strategy is to decide how well you want your fund to perform: Your desired investment outcome or the investment objective for your fund. The objective of your fund is likely to be linked to how much money you believe you need to fund your retirement (for info on funding the lifestyle you want, refer to Chapter 3), the number of years until retirement and the level of contributions you intend to make.

Any objective(s) you decide on also needs to be measurable. Many funds draft their fund's investment objectives using industry benchmarks or a desired return in percentage terms. Examples of fund investment objectives include the following:

✔ To deliver an average annual rate of return exceeding any CPI increase by 4 per cent over 5-year periods. (The CPI, or *Consumer Price Index*, tracks the rate of inflation.)

✔ To deliver an annual average 'real rate of return' of 5 per cent over 7-year periods. A *real rate of return* means the fund's return after taking into account the effects of inflation.

✔ To deliver an annual real rate of return of 7 per cent over 7-year periods by maximising the use of dividend franking credits (see Chapter 18 for an explanation of franked dividends) to reduce any tax on fund earnings.

Assessing the insurance needs of your SMSF members

In late 2012, the federal government changed the super rules to force SMSF trustees to consider the insurance needs of fund members when formulating and reviewing a SMSF investment strategy. The requirement to consider whether the trustees of a SMSF should hold a contract of insurance that provides cover for fund members does not, however, require SMSF trustees to actually take out insurance cover for fund members.

As a SMSF trustee, you will need to keep documentary evidence that you have considered the issue of insurance for fund members. According to the explanatory memorandum accompanying the legislation introducing this change, trustees can provide this evidence by documenting decisions in the SMSF's investment strategy or documenting the decisions in the minutes of trustee meetings held during the income year. For information on the types of insurance that SMSF trustees can purchase for SMSF members, see Chapter 24.

Getting into position — your DIY super fund's asset allocation

What asset class combination do you need to meet your fund's long-term investment goals or objectives?

The secret to long-term investment success is getting the right asset allocation for your DIY super fund. Asset allocation is an extension of diversification. Whereas diversification is spreading your risk by investing across a broad range of assets, *asset allocation* is the process to determine *how much* you allocate to each asset class — for example, the percentage of your portfolio to be invested in growth assets such as shares and property.

Understanding your *risk tolerance* (your ability to cope with the ups and downs in investment returns and potential losses), and the risk tolerance of any other members of your SMSF, can ensure that your fund's asset allocation reflects your long-term objectives and the level of risk you're willing to take to get there. You can't totally eliminate risk and, generally, the lower the risk the lower the return.

Ideally, retirees running a SMSF pension, should hold about two years' worth of income in cash within a SMSF to minimise the risk of forced asset sales to pay for everyday bills, and other living costs, or to meet minimum pension payments requirements (for details about SMSF pensions and minimum payments, see Chapter 21). However, if you have many years until retirement, and you have a high tolerance for risk, then the trustees of your SMSF may choose to hold minimal levels of cash.

Table 15-1 compares the broad risk (volatility), return, tax effectiveness and investment time frames for the main asset classes.

Table 15-1	**Comparing Risk and Return of Asset Classes**				
Measure	*Cash*	*Fixed Interest*	*Australian Shares*	*Property*	*International Assets*
Investment time frame (years)	1+	3–5+	5+	5–7+	5–7+
Importance to long-term returns	Small	Medium	High	High	High
Role in portfolio	Liquidity	Income Stability	Exposure to underlying economic growth	Inflation hedge Income producer	Exposure to underlying global economic growth
Likely return	Low–medium	Medium	Medium–high	High	High
Likely return over 5-year period	Low (CPI plus 2.5%)	Low (CPI plus 2.5%)	Medium–high (CPI plus 4%)	Medium–high (CPI plus 4%)	High (CPI plus 4.5%)
Type of return	Income taxable	Income taxable	Franked income Capital gain	Income Capital gain	Income Capital gain
Likely risk (volatility)	None–low	Low	Medium–high	Medium–high	High

Measure	Cash	Fixed Interest	Australian Shares	Property	International Assets
Tax effective	No	No	Yes[*]	Yes[*]	No
Good for	Liquidity	Income Capital stability	Capital growth Income	Income Inflation hedge	Growth
Bad for	Growth Wealth accumulation	Wealth accumulation	Stability	Liquidity	Stability Liquidity

No tax on growth of investment until sold. Share income (dividends) provides franking credits (see Chapter 18).

Source: Adapted from table from pages 96–97 of You Don't Have to be Rich to Become Wealthy, *by Trish Power, Ian Murdoch and Jamie Nemtsas (Wrightbooks). Reproduced with permission of Trish Power, Ian Murdoch and Jamie Nemtsas. (This book is no longer in print.)*

Ready, set, go! Selecting, and monitoring, specific investments

As mentioned in Chapter 14, the majority of SMSFs invest only in traditional investments such as cash, fixed interest, shares and direct property. If you keep your fund's investments simple, you require less effort to keep within the special investment rules that apply to super funds. On the other hand, if you choose to take advantage of the more innovative opportunities available within SMSFs, you need to know about and be certain that you follow the super rules.

Your SMSF can invest in any asset, provided that

- ✔ **The primary purpose of investing in a particular asset is to maximise your fund member's retirement benefits.** This is known as meeting the sole purpose test. I discuss this test later in the chapter, and at length in Chapters 9 and 11.

- ✔ **Your trust deed permits the investment.** In other words, your trust deed states the types of investments permitted by your fund, and the investment you have selected falls within one of these types of investments.

- ✔ **The investment fits within super's investment rules**. If your fund invests in non-traditional assets such as collectibles (for example, works of art), or invests in or with related parties, then you better be sure that you fully understand DIY super's special investment rules. I discuss these special rules later in the chapter in 'Walking the Investment Tightrope'.

As trustee of your own fund, you can invest in anything that you consider fits within your fund's investment strategy — gold, real estate, artwork, the rights to songs, shares, term deposits, private equity, property trusts. (For more information on property and SMSFs, see Chapter 17.)

You can also invest in options and warrants, which are derivatives of shares. Derivatives are linked to an underlying asset and, in the case of options and warrants, usually give you the right to purchase or sell a share or other asset at an agreed price at some time in the future. If your SMSF invests in derivatives, your fund may need a *derivative risk statement* — a statement that your fund's trustees prepare explaining your SMSF's risk management policies when using derivatives.

Understanding how the large super funds invest members' super savings can help you create a robust SMSF investment portfolio, and provide a performance comparison for your fund. On my website, SuperGuide (www.superguide.com.au), I explain the main investment options available in large funds and the risks associated with the different investment portfolios. In Chapter 14, I also discuss some of the issues you need to consider when developing an investment strategy and investing.

Reviewing your fund's investment strategy and asset allocation

You must regularly review your fund's investment strategy, which you should typically undertake at least every 12 months. A sensible approach is to also review your fund's investment strategy whenever your fund or a fund member has a significant event, such as admission of new members, a member retiring or divorcing, or when one or more of your fund's investments is delivering less-than-expected returns. For example, you may choose to review your super fund's long-term investment objectives if one or more of your SMSF members are close to retirement.

You can review your fund's asset allocation, and decide whether the proportion of your SMSF's money invested to each asset class is appropriate. You can also review your fund's investments, and your fund's insurance cover for members (if any), to ensure the investments and insurance are still appropriate and consistent with your fund's strategy.

Benchmarking Your DIY Super Returns

When reviewing your fund's investment strategy, it is likely you will be reviewing your fund's investment performance. A rough guide to benchmarking your SMSF's investment return is to take into account the current industry thinking on an achievable long-term return. The current view is that a super fund offering a 'balanced option' should be able to deliver an average long-term return of around 7 per cent a year after fees and taxes. A *balanced option* usually has 70 per cent or more of the portfolio's assets invested in growth assets such as shares, property and alternative investments.

 If averages and typical allocations don't reflect your fund's spread of investments, and you want to work out a benchmark for your DIY super fund's asset allocation, then, by all means, you can use 'Trish's tried and true guide' to identify a tailored performance benchmark for your SMSF, as follows:

1. **Identify all categories of assets held within your fund.**

2. **Value all asset holdings (as at 30 June, or another chosen date).**

3. **Calculate return on each asset class within the fund.**

4. **Determine what percentage of total assets are held in each asset class.**

5. **Calculate total return after fees and taxes (and don't forget to include tax benefits of franking credits for any Australian shares), based on asset allocation.**

    For example, if 50 per cent of assets are held in Australian shares, then 50 per cent of your fund's return on this asset class is going to count towards your fund's weighted total return.

6. **Using industry benchmarks, calculate benchmark return based on asset allocation of your fund.**

    That is, repeat Steps 4 and 5 but using benchmark returns rather than your fund's returns. (I explain benchmark returns in more detail later in this section.)

7. **Compare your fund's returns with the benchmark returns.**

Alternatively, if you use trading software for investing, you may be able to do these benchmarking calculations with a click of a button — hopefully. Some readers create Excel spreadsheets that automatically provide this information after loading the asset class returns, and asset class benchmark returns, into their fund's Excel file.

Most large super funds list the benchmark indices that they use, and what that benchmark return is, for a set period. You can also use these benchmark indices for your fund, which means you're benchmarking your fund in the same way that the large funds do (for a sample of some benchmark indices, go to my SuperGuide at www.superguide.com.au). If your SMSF money is invested in a pocket of the market (for example, in small company shares), then you may want to use a specific benchmark, such as S&P/ASX Small Ordinaries Index.

Three rating companies that comprehensively cover the superannuation industry produce excellent data that provides benchmark indices for investments within super funds, and returns for these indices for set periods. Note that the benchmark indices are based on large super funds, but that's not a bad comparison, considering that's where your super money would be if you weren't in a SMSF. You can access this information by visiting one of the following sites:

- **Chant West:** Visit www.chantwest.com.au, select 'Quick links' and click on 'Super Fund Returns' and 'Pension Fund Returns'.

- **Selecting Super:** Go to www.selectingsuper.com.au, click on 'Performance Tables for Super and Retirement Funds' and then click on 'Benchmark indices'.

- **Super Ratings:** Visit www.superratings.com.au then follow the links to the benchmark you're after.

Walking the Investment Tightrope

Any investments you make as trustee of your self-managed super fund must stay on the right side of super's investment restrictions, which are intended to ensure that your super savings are invested for your eventual retirement, and that your personal assets are kept separate from your fund's assets.

The easiest way to stay on top of super's special investment rules is to re-read the SMSF declaration that you must sign when you're appointed a trustee. (For a copy of the declaration, turn back to Chapter 9.) In the SMSF declaration you declare that you understand the following:

- It is your responsibility to ensure the fund is maintained for the purpose of providing benefits to members (sole purpose test)

- By law you must:
  - Prepare, implement and regularly review an investment strategy (refer to the section 'Wait! Set Your Fund's Investment Strategy' earlier in the chapter)
  - Ensure that your money and other assets are kept separate from your SMSF's assets
  - Take appropriate action to protect the ownership of fund assets

✔ You are prohibited from:

- Lending money, or providing other forms of financial assistance, to fund members or relatives of fund members

- Purchasing assets from fund members or related parties, unless those assets are listed securities or are classed as 'business real property', or are managed funds (for more info on this exception, see the section 'Purchasing assets from members or relatives' later in this chapter)

- Borrowing money on behalf of the fund, except in limited circumstances

- Having more than 5 per cent of the fund's total assets as loans to, or investments in, related parties of the fund, or having more than 5 per cent of assets subject to a lease arrangement between the trustee and a member or related party (the in-house asset rule)

- Entering into investments on behalf of your SMSF that are not made on a commercial basis; that is, any investment must be made on an arm's-length basis.

You must take super's special investment rules seriously, because the ATO certainly does. In Chapter 11, I identify what I describe as the ATO's seven deadly sins — the perennial black spots in SMSF trustee behaviour. Five of those deadly sins appear in the preceding list. If you commit such sins or break any other investment rules, you or your fund could be hit with hefty penalties. I explain SMSF penalties in Chapters 9 and 11.

Your fund can't directly borrow money, except in two specific instances. Also, your fund may be able to borrow money indirectly in limited circumstances. I explain a SMSF's 'borrowing' opportunities in Chapter 16.

Meeting the sole purpose test

As trustee of your fund, you must ensure that your fund meets the sole purpose test (SPT) when investing — any investments your fund makes must be for the primary purpose of funding your retirement instead of providing current-day benefits. Plain-vanilla assets, such as shares, investment properties and term deposits that aren't connected to any of your fund's members or relatives or business partners, meet the SPT requirements.

For more information on why the SPT is the underlying moral basis for superannuation trustee behaviour, refer to Chapter 9. And for all the details on compliance, skip back to Chapter 11.

Assets that are connected in some way to fund members or relatives or business partners, or are considered to be unusual or 'exotic' assets — such as motor vehicles, racing yachts and antiques — may still meet the SPT, but they're usually subject to greater scrutiny. And if you enjoy a direct or indirect benefit before retirement from one or more of your SMSF's investments, then you need to ensure that your fund still meets the SPT.

Special rules apply to collectibles. For example, if you hold artwork, antiques or other collectibles within your SMSF, then you must store these investments according to strict guidelines. The assets must also be properly insured and independently valued. The storage requirement was introduced to prevent SMSF trustees enjoying the collectibles as a current-day benefit. Trustees of SMSFs holding collectibles and personal use assets since 30 June 2011, or before that date, have until 30 June 2016 to comply with the storage, insurance and valuation requirements.

Keeping fund assets separate

You wear a very distinctive cap when you take on the role of SMSF trustee — you act on behalf of fund members, including yourself. Legally, your role as a SMSF trustee is different from your role as fund member, which means you must manage your SMSF separately from your personal and business affairs.

The ATO is very clear on this point: You must keep your fund's assets, including bank accounts and supporting financial records, separate from your personal and business assets.

Ensuring assets are in the fund's name

Investing as trustee of your SMSF is similar to investing in your own name except that you must ensure any assets you buy on behalf of your fund (and fund members) are held in your name 'as trustee' of the fund. An exception to this rule is generally applied when a SMSF owns real estate, which is explained later in this chapter. If you have a corporate trustee, the investment must be purchased and held in the name of the trustee company 'as trustee'.

You must protect the ownership of fund assets, which means that you need to ensure the fund's trustees are registered as owners of all assets. Such evidence can protect the fund's assets from personal creditors mistaking fund assets as personal assets. For example, a shareholding simply in the name of, say, **Geoff and Sue Norton**, is not sufficient as evidence of ownership of SMSF assets.

If investing in property, depending on the state in which you live, the local property rules may not permit you to use the name of the fund on title documents, but require the name(s) of the trustee(s). In such circumstances, you need to clearly identify fund ownership by using a declaration of trust or another type of legal instrument. For more information on SMSFs and property investments, see Chapter 17.

Lending money to members — don't!

Don't even think about slipping a few thousand dollars to a fund member to tide them over hard times. As trustee, you can't lend your super fund's money, or provide any other form of financial assistance, to a member or member's relative. A relative is defined to mean a parent, grandparent, brother, sister, uncle, aunt, nephew, niece, lineal descendant, or adopted child of the member, or of the member's spouse (including same-sex spouse). A relative also includes a spouse (including same-sex spouse) of the member, or the spouse (including same-sex spouse) of any of the member's relatives as set out in the previous sentence.

According to the ATO, using SMSF assets to give *financial assistance* means providing any assistance that improves the financial position of a person directly or indirectly, including any loans. Remember, you can't lend money to any relatives of members either. If you lend money to a member or relative of a member you can be subject to a hefty financial penalty (for details about these fines, refer to Chapters 9 and 11).

Purchasing assets from members or relatives

Under section 66 of the *Superannuation Industry (Supervision) Act 1993* (SIS Act), you can't purchase assets (or transfer assets as a super contribution — refer to Chapter 4) from fund members or related parties, except when the asset falls within certain categories, including:

- ✔ **Listed security:** A *listed security* can be shares, units, bonds, interests in managed investment schemes and other securities listed for quotation on an *approved stock exchange* or licensed market. In Australia, the approved exchanges are: the Australian Securities Exchange, the Bendigo Stock Exchange and the National Stock Exchange of Australia. You can also transfer international shares listed on more than 120 exchanges around the world, including London, Hong Kong and New York exchanges. You can find the complete list of approved exchanges on the ATO website.

- ✔ **Managed funds:** The managed fund must be a widely held unit trust, typically a retail or wholesale managed fund where 75 per cent of income and capital entitlements are controlled by more than 20 unrelated unit holders. *Note:* Not all fund manager systems can cope with transfers of managed fund accounts, which means you need to double-check that they intend to transfer the account, rather than sell the units in your name and re-issue them in the fund's name, thereby costing you transaction fees and potentially other costs.

- ✔ **Business real property:** This relates to land and buildings used wholly and exclusively in a business, and can include offices, shops, factories and even farms. A SMSF can purchase business real property from a member as an investment, and can then even lease the property back to the same fund member. This generous exemption doesn't apply to residential property. For more info on investing in business real property, see Chapter 17.

- ✔ **In-house assets valued at less than 5 per cent of fund assets:** These are investments in, or loans to, or leasing arrangements with, related parties. I explain in-house assets in more detail in the section 'Investing too close to home', later in the chapter.

If your SMSF is considering purchasing assets from fund members, then chat to a SMSF expert about your proposal, and take a closer look at Section 66 of the SIS Act. Any assets owned by fund members that don't fall within the exceptions listed in Section 66 can't be bought by your SMSF, or transferred to the fund as a contribution.

The transfer of an asset is a change of ownership that triggers the capital gains tax (CGT) rules for the individual transferring the asset into the fund. I explain transferring assets as super contributions (in specie contributions), as well as the implications of CGT when making in specie contributions, in Chapter 4.

When transferring a personal asset into a SMSF, the asset must be valued at market value at the time of transfer. For example, a listed shareholding is valued at the share price on the day of transfer, while a managed fund investment is valued at the unit price on the day of transfer. Any valuation should be based on objective and substantiated data. According to the ATO, the SMSF trustees should consider using a qualified valuer when the value of the asset represents a significant chunk of the fund's assets, or when the nature of the asset indicates that the valuation is likely to be complex or difficult.

No direct borrowing of money

Your fund can't directly borrow money, except in two instances.

- ✔ If you need cash to pay a member's benefit, you can borrow money. Any loan term must be no longer than 90 days and the loan amount must be less than 10 per cent of your fund's assets.
- ✔ You can borrow money for up to seven days to settle a share transaction. I explain these rules in Chapter 16.

Your fund can also use a limited recourse borrowing arrangement to borrow money. If you do some research, or chat to a financial adviser, you can discover plenty of strategies that enable you to use gearing (borrowing) in relation to DIY super fund investments without your fund directly borrowing money. You can invest in managed funds that borrow money (*geared managed funds*), or heaven forbid . . . have a punt on contracts for difference (CFDs). I explain limited recourse borrowing arrangements, and some of the other 'borrowing' opportunities in Chapter 16.

Investing too close to home

You must be extra careful when investing in assets that are linked with fund members or relatives of fund members.

Remember that in general terms, your SMSF can't invest in, or lend money to, or lease a fund asset to, a fund member or a relative of a fund member, or your business partner or her spouse or children. These investments, or loans or leases, are known as *in-house assets* (IHA). Investments in unit trusts and companies that are related to your fund members are also caught by the in-house asset rule.

To be precise, you can invest in an IHA, but the total value of all IHAs must be less than 5 per cent of the value of your fund's total assets. For example, if a fund owns a residential property and leases it to a fund member, the total value of the property would count as an IHA. According to the ATO, if the value of the property is less than 5 per cent of the fund's total assets, the investment is within the in-house asset rules and, presumably, allowed. But wait! Before you try this at home, such an arrangement is highly likely to breach the sole purpose test (refer to the section 'Meeting the sole purpose test', earlier in the chapter, and Chapter 17).

Leasing an office or factory from your super fund for your use in your personal business is excluded from having to meet the IHA rule (and the sole purpose test). You may be able to take advantage of other exclusions; but I suggest you talk to your adviser first before dabbling in IHAs.

Keeping your investments at arm's length

Any investment or any other transaction you make as trustee of your SMSF must be on an *arm's-length basis*. In other words, the sale or purchase of any asset must be on commercial terms, not at mates' rates. For example, if your business is leasing an office from your super fund (see Chapter 17 for more information on this scenario), you must pay a market rate of rent and have a formal lease arrangement.

The ATO makes a lot of noise about investigating transactions where a relationship exists between the trustee and other party to the transaction — to ensure the transaction is on commercial terms. If your investment or transaction isn't at arm's length, you can be subject to a hefty financial penalty.

Chapter 16

Borrowing and DIY Super

*U*sing borrowed money to invest is a popular way to accelerate wealth accumulation. Borrowing to invest is also known as *gearing* and involves an individual borrowing money to buy an income-producing asset. The income earned from the geared asset is then used to cover the expenses in purchasing and maintaining the asset, including repaying the loan. If the costs of investing, including interest payments, are greater than the income earned on the asset, individual taxpayers can then offset other income with the loss on the geared investment.

Borrowing to invest is a higher-risk strategy that relies on the investment returns or tax benefits associated with such a strategy outweighing the interest costs. Any loan that you take out still has to be repaid, which means the returns and tax benefits on that geared investment would at least have to deliver the costs of borrowing money to make the strategy worthwhile.

When borrowing to invest, the assets that you invest in are usually used as security for the loan, which means the bank has an interest in the investment. If you can't repay your loan, then the bank can claim the property or shareholding, and can potentially demand more money from you if the sale of the asset delivers less money than the amount borrowed.

Using borrowed money to invest within your self-managed super fund (SMSF) is more complicated and a lot more restrictive than using gearing to purchase investments outside of the SMSF environment, In this chapter, I explain the 'no borrowing' rule applicable to SMSFs, and the three specific exceptions to this ban on borrowing. I also take you through nine 'borrowing' scenarios, and share the ATO's view on whether the scenarios stay on the right side of the super rules.

Any gearing decision must be appropriate for fund members. You need to consider whether a borrowing-to-invest strategy takes into account the risk and return of the underlying investment, the risk profile of your SMSF members, your fund's cashflow demands and whether your fund is sufficiently diversified. A major advantage of gearing is the ability to invest in more investments, or in an asset that is worth a greater amount of money, because you have more money to invest. Taking such an aggressive approach can increase your investment earnings if the value of your investment portfolio increases. A distinct drawback of gearing, however, is that using such a strategy can dramatically increase your losses when the value of the investment portfolio falls.

No Borrowing is the General Rule

So, are SMSFs permitted to borrow money when investing, or to borrow money for any other reason? Well . . . the general answer is no, but in the following section I outline the three special circumstances where loans are allowed when they satisfy certain conditions.

The general restriction on borrowing is designed to reduce the risk to retirement incomes from super funds gearing their assets. The biggest risk of traditional gearing is that when you're unable to repay a loan, the lender can generally reclaim the asset and sell the asset from under you. Even worse, if such traditional borrowing were permitted by super funds, the lender may have further claims on other fund assets. Perhaps the government should have introduced a similar rule to protect Australians from some of those gung-ho companies that collapsed due to excessive use of debt during the GFC of 2008 and 2009 (for more information on the GFC fallout, refer to Chapter 14).

Subsection 67(1) of the *Superannuation Industry (Supervision) Act 1993* (SIS Act) bans a SMSF trustee from borrowing money or maintaining an existing borrowing. However, just because someone gives your super fund money, doesn't make that transfer of cash a 'borrowing'. According to the ATO, a *borrowing* is an arrangement that exhibits these two characteristics:

- ✔ A temporary transfer of money from one party (lender) to another (borrower).
- ✔ An obligation or intention to repay the money to the lender.

Transactions that aren't considered borrowings include a super fund receiving super contributions, or the practice of reimbursing a third party for payment of fund expenses, or accepting the normal business payment terms of service providers (such as, pay within 30 days) when the fund incurs expenses.

If your fund enters a margin lending arrangement to buy shares, or takes out a bank overdraft to pay for an investment, be aware that your SMSF is breaking the 'no borrowing' rules. I explain the ATO's view on these and other typical borrowing scenarios in the section 'ATO's Call: Nine Borrowing Scenarios', later in the chapter.

Understanding the Three Special Borrowing Exceptions

Although borrowing is ordinarily prohibited under section 67(1) of the SIS Act, there are three main exceptions to this general prohibition allowed by section 67 and section 67A of the SIS Act. Borrowings that are permitted under the super rules include

- ✔ A loan to meet a liability to pay a fund member's benefits.
- ✔ A short-term loan to cover settlement of a securities transaction, for example, a share purchase.
- ✔ An arrangement or structure that enables the purchase of an asset using certain limited recourse borrowing arrangements (LRBA). I provide the details about LRBAs in the section 'Purchasing an asset using a limited recourse borrowing arrangement', later in this chapter.

Borrowing to cover benefit payments

A loan to meet a benefit payment liability must satisfy strict conditions. A SMSF can borrow to finance a benefit payment to a fund member if the

- ✔ Fund member's benefit payment is required by law, or by the fund's trust deed
- ✔ SMSF trustee can't pay the benefit unless the fund can borrow money
- ✔ Loan is for no more than 90 days
- ✔ Total loan is for no more than 10 per cent of the value of the SMSF's assets

Borrowing to cover settlement of a share transaction

A SMSF can borrow money to finalise the settlement of a share purchase, or other type of securities transaction (see subsection 67(3) of SIS Act), if it meets three conditions. A super fund trustee can only borrow money to settle a share purchase if

- ✔ At the time the investment was made, it was likely that the borrowing would not be needed.
- ✔ The period of the loan is no more than seven days.
- ✔ The total amount borrowed doesn't exceed 10 per cent of the fund's assets.

A possible scenario where this exception may apply, perhaps, is if a delay occurs at the bank in clearing a super contribution deposited to the fund's bank account, and the fund was relying on that contribution to settle on a share transaction. Another scenario may be where a delay occurs in the payment of an earnings distribution from a fund investment, and that income was intended to finance another investment purchase.

The super laws also permit the Tax Commissioner to make written determinations exempting certain share purchase borrowings that may not fit within the strict conditions outlined in the preceding list. Such determinations, however, are rare. For more information on the ATO's activities in this area, contact the ATO on 13 10 20, or chat with your adviser.

Purchasing an asset using a limited recourse borrowing arrangement

A SMSF can borrow money indirectly using a *limited recourse borrowing arrangement* (*LRBA*). The key element of a LRBA is that any recourse the lender has under the LRBA against the SMSF trustee is limited to the single fund asset purchased using the LRBA.

Purchasing an SMSF asset using a LRBA is becoming increasingly popular with SMSF trustees hoping to gear an investment portfolio without breaking super's 'no borrowing' rules. Even so, at the time of writing, the amount of SMSF money involved in LRBAs is statistically insignificant — less than 2 per cent of all SMSF money is invested in assets using LRBAs.

Before September 2007, there were limited opportunities to use borrowed monies to purchase a SMSF asset, such as listed shares or a business-related property. In September 2007, the borrowing rules for SMSFs were relaxed and then finetuned in July 2010. However, the specific borrowing arrangements permitted to be used by SMSFs are still subject to very strict conditions.

Cutting through the novelty factor

Not everyone in the superannuation industry supports the use of gearing within super funds. Some experts believe that gearing places super savings at too much risk, while others argue that if SMSF trustees can invest in geared managed funds and highly geared listed companies, then using LRBAs is also legitimate.

A bigger issue for SMSF trustees is ensuring that a gearing decision is consistent with the investment strategy of the fund, and that the fund's trust deed permits such arrangements. Using a LRBA to help your SMSF purchase an investment has significant financial implications. As a SMSF trustee, some of the questions you need to ask include:

✔ Is borrowing to invest an appropriate investment for my SMSF, taking into account the risk and return of the underlying investment?

✔ Have I considered the risk profile of the SMSF members?

✔ Will my SMSF be able to meet all of the fund's financial commitments, including loan repayments?

Meeting the LRBA rules

A SMSF can use a LRBA to invest in any asset that a SMSF can invest in directly, such as Australian or overseas shares, property, managed funds or even a collectible. For example, a SMSF trustee can't purchase a residential investment property owned by a fund member under a LRBA arrangement because a residential property owned by a fund member can't be purchased by a SMSF. If the residential property is bought from an unrelated party, however, then the SMSF can use a LRBA to purchase the residential property.

Unlike a residential property, a business-related property, such as an office or warehouse, can be bought from related parties. For information on investing in property via your SMSF, and using LRBAs for property investments, check out Chapter 17.

If your SMSF decides to use a LRBA to purchase an asset, then the arrangement you use must meet the following conditions:

✔ The borrowed monies are used to purchase a single asset, or a collection of identical assets, with the same market value, treated as a single asset — for example, a parcel of shares for a single listed company.

- Your fund cannot use the LRBA monies to 'improve' a purchased asset. Note that renovating an older property does not equate to improving the property in certain circumstances (see Chapter 17 for info on why renovating a property may be okay under LRBA rules, but improving one isn't).

- You and the other SMSF trustees receive the beneficial interest in the purchased asset, but the legal ownership of the asset is held in trust; what's known as the *holding trust*.

- You and the other SMSF trustees have the right to acquire the legal ownership of the asset by making one or more payments.

- Any recourse that the LRBA lender has under the LRBA against you as a SMSF trustee is limited to the single fund asset (including rights to income). Remember that limited recourse means that the maximum your fund can lose is the original capital investment: Your fund can't lose more than the original amount invested (including amount borrowed). The lender (product provider) only has recourse to the asset in question when your fund defaults on the loan, rather than recourse to other fund assets.

- A LRBA lender can demand an individual to provide a personal guarantee for the LRBA, but against personal assets.

- You can only replace the asset subject to the LRBA in limited circumstances; alternatively, you must take out a new LRBA.

Do your sums

My view of limited recourse borrowing arrangements within SMSFs is that just because you can, doesn't mean that you should. Expect to read a lot of hype and hoopla about gearing within SMSFs; for some property promoters it's as if the act of gearing is an investment in itself.

One of my reservations about some of the SMSF borrowing products on the market is that investing in this way is expensive, so you need to do your sums to work out the net benefit of such an investment approach. Don't get distracted by the complicated structure of these products.

You need to ask: Is the expected return on the underlying investment going to exceed the annual interest costs, any management charges, and any additional establishment and add-on costs that the product promoter is going to charge? If you also believe that the underlying investment is consistent with your fund's investment strategy, then this type of investment, using a LRBA to help finance the investment, can have a place in a SMSF's investment portfolio.

ATO's Call: Nine Borrowing Scenarios

The ATO has produced some useful guidance for SMSF trustees on what the regulator considers to be a 'borrowing' in its SMSF Ruling: SMSFR 2009/2 (*Self Managed Superannuation Funds: the meaning of 'borrow money' or 'maintain an existing borrowing of money' for the purposes of section 67 of the Superannuation Industry (Supervision) Act 1993*). I know, this ruling's title is long-winded; that's why I've put it in brackets.

Paragraphs 58 to 98 of the ATO ruling on borrowing provide examples of different financing arrangements and outlines in some detail whether such arrangements are considered borrowings (and treated as a breach), or comply with the 'no borrowing' rule (and considered within the super rules).

Here's a summary of the ATO's views on the main types of financing arrangements:

- ✔ **Borrowing money from members — a breach.** Borrowing money from fund members isn't permitted and breaches the 'no borrowing' rule, unless one of the exceptions applies (for an outline on these, see 'Understanding the Three Special Borrowing Exceptions', earlier in the chapter).

- ✔ **Contracts for difference (CFD) — depends.** A *CFD* is a high-risk, highly leveraged financial derivative. If trustees of a SMSF invest in CFDs, then the trustees must make additional payments when a loss occurs from movements in the price of the underlying assets. The requirement to pay a deposit and meet margin calls isn't a borrowing because no money has been temporarily transferred to the SMSF trustees under the CFD arrangement. Not all CFD arrangements are okay, however. I explain the ATO's position on CFDs in more detail in the sidebar 'CFDs — created for danger'.

- ✔ **Deferred repayment of amount paid on behalf of SMSF — a breach.** Say a SMSF doesn't have enough money to purchase an asset, so a fund member uses personal money to pay for the asset, which is then held in the fund's name; the SMSF trustees agree to repay the fund member at an agreed time in the future. This arrangement is a borrowing because of the temporary transfer of money with an obligation to repay, and is in breach unless an exception applies (for the special circumstances where borrowing is permitted, refer to the section 'Understanding the Three Special Borrowing Exceptions', earlier in the chapter). If no obligation to repay exists, the payment from the member could be treated as a contribution.

✔ **Instalment purchase agreement — within the super rules.** SMSF trustees purchase an asset from an owner of the asset who agrees that SMSF trustees can receive immediate use of the asset if they pay for the asset in ten equal instalments over a period of time. Title passes on final payment. This arrangement isn't a borrowing because the investment is simply paid for via instalments: There is no transfer of money. If such an arrangement did involve the SMSF borrowing money, then the SMSF may be able to take advantage of the LRBA exception. (For more info on LRBAs, refer to 'Purchasing an asset using a limited recourse borrowing arrangement', earlier in the chapter.)

✔ **Making a super contribution — within the super rules.** Trustees of a SMSF want to buy an asset on behalf of the fund. The fund doesn't have enough money to purchase the asset, so the fund members each make super contributions to the fund. The trustees can now buy the asset outright. The member contributions satisfy the contribution rules (refer to Chapter 4) and aren't considered borrowings, which means the fund isn't in breach of the 'no borrowing' rule.

✔ **Margin lending — a breach.** What if SMSF trustees maintain a margin lending account, which has a cash and loan component? In this scenario each drawdown of the account involves a borrowing, and each drawdown is a separate breach of the 'no borrowing' rule.

✔ **Payments made on behalf of SMSF — within the super rules.** The bill for the preparation and lodgement of the SMSF's tax return is paid by the SMSF's employer sponsor; that is, the employer making super contributions on behalf of the SMSF member or members. Instead of reimbursing the employer, the SMSF trustees agree that the employer's obligation to pay super contributions will be reduced. Paying the fund's bill isn't a borrowing because there is no obligation to repay borrowing. The amount paid by the employer sponsor is counted as employer super contributions.

✔ **Reimbursement of payments made on behalf of SMSF — within the super rules.** A fund member pays the fund accountant's bill out of personal money on behalf of the SMSF. The member is reimbursed by the SMSF. The payment isn't a borrowing because there wasn't a temporary transfer of money, and the member was immediately reimbursed.

✔ **Taking out a bank overdraft — a breach.** Say a SMSF trustee writes a cheque and insufficient funds are in the bank account to cover the full value of the cheque. The bank account becomes overdrawn. This overdraft is a borrowing and in breach of the 'no borrowing' rule, unless an exception applies (for a reminder of what's allowed, refer to 'Understanding the Three Special Borrowing Exceptions', earlier in the chapter).

CFDs — created for danger

If you're a regular reader of the money sections in the daily or business newspapers, you would have seen the countless advertisements promoting contracts for difference or CFDs. They seem so simple — make 100 per cent return in a week, or turn $10,000 into $1.6 million in three months. The promises go on and on. Promoters of CFD trading seminars really don't know if you're going to make this type of money and, of course, the chances are high that you won't — but why should anyone let sound investment principles get in the way of a 'get rich quick' dream?

CFDs aren't for learner investors and CFDs are most certainly not a long-term investment. CFDs are a trading product. What the advertisements don't tell you is that you're dealing with a risky short-term investment that can wipe out your investment in a day — or perhaps not, if the market swings in the right direction.

When you purchase a CFD, you're purchasing a contract, which means the actual investment is a contractual arrangement. CFDs operate on the basis that you pay a deposit on a company shareholding (usually between 5 per cent and 40 per cent) and the CFD provider finances the rest, for which you pay interest daily. As an investor holding a typical CFD, you receive the gain on any increase in share price and any dividends due. If the price drops, the investor (you) pays the difference to the CFD provider. If the price drops dramatically, you can be exposed to a lot more liability than the initial deposit paid. You can also hold a short CFD position; that is, you can bet that a price is going to fall.

According to the ATO, CFDs are a legitimate investment for SMSFs under certain circumstances. A SMSF can't use fund assets as security for the CFD. The super regulations ban trustees from giving a charge over, or in relation to, an asset of the fund.

A SMSF can, however, pay cash into a CFD bank account as collateral for any margin payments on the contract. *Note:* The operation of the CFD bank account and the obligation to pay deposits and margins doesn't create a charge over any assets of the fund.

Confused? Talk with your adviser or the ATO before proceeding with CFD transactions within a SMSF. But before talking to your adviser, check out ASIC's publication, *Thinking of Trading Contracts for Difference (CFDs)?*, which you can download from ASIC's MoneySmart website (www.moneysmart.gov.au).

Chapter 17

Investing in Property

*P*roperty seems to be the poor cousin to shares when you read about investing in the newspapers. For every one property analyst quoted in business pages of papers, there are usually a dozen or more share analysts discussing the sharemarket. Despite this lack of media coverage or, perhaps because of it, property continues to be a popular option for Australian investors, and is becoming increasingly popular with SMSF trustees.

Property as an asset class is a broad term that can describe ownership of a home, an office building, a shopping centre, a car park, a factory or even a farm. Investors can choose to buy property directly, or invest in property indirectly via listed investment vehicles and managed funds.

 The choice of property investments available to SMSFs is similar to the options available outside of superannuation, except that some special rules, peculiar to super, apply and these influence the type of property you choose to buy within the SMSF structure. The application of these special rules, including a major exception to the 'no borrowing' rules, warrants a separate chapter on property investing.

In this chapter, I outline the main types of property investments that investors consider. I discuss the general restrictions on SMSFs buying property from related parties, and the exemptions that apply to business-related property. I also discuss the limited borrowing options available to SMSFs when property investing — in particular, purchasing property using a limited recourse borrowing arrangement (LRBA).

The Short Story on SMSF Property Investing

Property as an investment class can be divided into three main categories:

✔ **Residential:** Houses and flats

✔ **Commercial and industrial:** Shops, offices and factories

✔ **Indirect property investments:** Unlisted and listed investment vehicles

A SMSF can invest directly in all types of property — residential, commercial and industrial. A SMSF can also invest in property indirectly, typically via listed and unlisted property investment vehicles. In the following sections I explain how a SMSF can invest in each of these types of property investments.

Investors seek returns from property investments in two ways: Capital gains when the property increases in value, and rental income from tenants of the property. Property is considered a growth asset by many investors because of the potential capital gains; although, due to the rental income received, some investors rely on property as an income-producing asset.

If you're planning to purchase a property within your SMSF, do your research. You can find countless books on property investing that can assist your SMSF decision making. However, you must also follow the super rules, which ensures, inter alia, that a SMSF investment is made to help build a retirement benefit for a fund member, rather than for other non-retirement purposes.

Here are the main issues that you need to consider when purchasing property within your SMSF:

✔ The investment must be consistent with your fund's investment strategy, taking into account the investment's risk and return, and your fund's diversification requirements. (Refer to Chapter 15 for a detailed discussion on drafting a SMSF investment strategy.)

✔ You can't borrow money within a SMSF (refer to Chapter 16), except in special circumstances (see the section 'Pumped-Up Property Plans — LRBAs', later in the chapter).

✔ You or your family, or your business partner, can't use the SMSF-owned property unless your fund has purchased business-related real estate (see the section 'Special Opportunities for Business-Related Property', later in the chapter).

✔ You need to maintain a ready source of cash to pay your fund's ongoing administration costs, taxes and possible payment of any benefits.

Investing directly in property

A major limitation when investing in direct property is that you need to have a lot of money to buy a single asset. Also, if you need to sell the asset at short notice, then you may have to take a lower price to ensure a quick sale.

Investing in direct property within a SMSF is often not a practical option because most SMSFs don't have large enough account balances to buy a property outright, especially if a fund needs to hold cash to pay expenses (for info about SMSF costs, refer to Chapter 6) or to pay pensions to members (see Chapters 21 and 22). Another barrier to property investing within a SMSF is that a SMSF can't take out a regular mortgage over a fund asset, which means a super fund has to buy a property outright or use more sophisticated means of borrowing in order to purchase the asset for the SMSF.

I explain the special borrowing rules applicable to SMSFs in Chapter 16, and how these rules apply to property investing in the section 'Pumped-Up Property Plans — LRBAs', later in the chapter.

Note that any property your fund purchases must be in the name of your SMSF, or in the name of the individuals as trustee of your fund. If the laws of your state don't permit property to be held in this way (which is often the case when your fund has individual trustees rather than a corporate trustee — refer to Chapter 8), a legal instrument (such as a declaration of trust), recognising the fund's interest is usually necessary.

Indirect property investing

You can obtain exposure to property within your SMSF without buying an asset directly, and without setting up complicated borrowing arrangements. To do so, you place SMSF money in investment products that hire professionals to invest in a range of property investments. An advantage of investing in property via investment vehicles is that you gain exposure to a broader range of property investments than if you invested the same amount of money directly. During the GFC of 2008 and 2009, however, this sector performed poorly.

Typically, a SMSF trustee can invest indirectly in property using:

✔ **Australian Real Estate Investment Trusts (A-REITs):** Formerly known as a listed property trust (LPT), an A-REIT is an investment vehicle listed on the Australian Securities Exchange (ASX). An A-REIT invests directly in property, usually industrial (factories), retail (shops and shopping complexes) and/or commercial (offices) property. Investors can purchase units in the trust via the ASX. The major drawback with A-REITs is that if you're investing in property to diversify from holding shares, A-REITS ordinarily rise and fall in line with sharemarket sentiment. During the GFC of 2008 and 2009, many A-REITS suffered savage falls in unit prices because of the general collapse in the sharemarket and as a result of the massive levels of debt that many A-REITs were holding due to ambitious property purchases. More recently, A-REITs have delivered stellar returns for the 2013 and 2014 financial years. I cover the risk and returns associated with listed property investments and other assets in Chapter 15.

✔ **Property managed funds:** You can consider investing in a managed fund that invests in A-REITs, or a managed fund that invests directly in property. Using a managed fund that invests only in property can give your SMSF portfolio exposure to international and/or Australian direct property, while retaining liquidity over your cash. Australian retail investors, including SMSF investors, usually invest in global REITs via a managed fund or master trust. Most managed funds allow you to redeem your cash when you request the withdrawal of your investment.

✔ **Unlisted property schemes (UPSs):** UPSs were previously known as unlisted property trusts, and are slightly different to property managed funds, although the differences are becoming more blurred. Neither UPSs nor property managed funds are listed on the ASX, but UPSs usually have stricter withdrawal conditions. Some UPSs don't allow you to withdraw your investment until the trust ends, while many others have a 12-month minimum notice period. During 2008 and 2009, many UPSs cut income distributions and froze withdrawals.

Mortgage funds aren't the same as property managed funds. *Property managed funds* pool investors' money and invest in property assets. In comparison, a mortgage fund invests in residential and commercial mortgages rather than actual property assets. During 2008 and 2009, many mortgage funds also froze redemptions (withdrawals).

ASIC has produced an excellent publication that provides an introduction to unlisted property schemes (called 'Investing in unlisted property schemes? Independent guide for investors about unlisted property schemes'). You can download a copy of the PDF from ASIC's consumer website, MoneySmart (www.moneysmart.gov.au), or you can phone ASIC on 1300 300 630 and request a paper copy.

What's All the Fuss about Residential Property?

One of the frequently asked DIY super investment questions on my website (www.superguide.com.au) is: Can my SMSF buy a residential property?

The answer is yes, if it's purchased from an unrelated third party. A SMSF can invest in residential property such as a house, flat or townhouse. If the property fits within the fund's investment strategy, and the SMSF has the money to buy the property and cover buying costs, including stamp duty, the fund can then proceed with the purchase.

Another popular DIY super question is: Can my SMSF buy a residential property that I own outside my fund?

The answer is no. A SMSF can't purchase residential property from a SMSF member or other related party (refer to Chapter 15).

Next question: Can I stay in the property that my SMSF owns?

Usually the answer is 'no'. Residential property, including holiday homes, can be acceptable SMSF investments, provided you (or your family) don't use them.

In most cases, if you use your SMSF property investments, you breach the sole purpose test (refer to Chapters 9 and 11). The ATO then considers the primary purpose of the investment isn't for your retirement but for your pre-retirement enjoyment. Also, you potentially fail the in-house asset rule (for more info about this rule, refer to Chapter 15 and the sidebar 'What Katy did: Holiday house or business premises?'). Of course, there can be exceptions, and the ATO is amenable to the following scenario: A SMSF can invest in holiday apartments via a property syndicate and SMSF trustees can stay in the apartments at market rent (and may receive an upgrade) without breaching the sole purpose test.

What Katy did: Holiday house or business premises?

Katy has run her own business for several years and recently set up a SMSF with her husband, Ken. They have total fund assets of $750,000 after transferring super balances from other funds.

Katy is keen to buy a holiday apartment in northern New South Wales, valued at $250,000. Ken thinks it's a great investment for their SMSF and he daydreams about using the apartment for a couple of weeks each year when the apartment isn't booked for holiday rental.

They meet with their adviser to talk about the property. The adviser has an apartment in the same region and, taking into account his client's SMSF investment strategy (refer to Chapter 15), the adviser thinks the property is an excellent investment. He warns them, however, that the holidays they're planning for themselves in the apartment aren't going to happen, even if they pay market rent.

Ken, disappointed with this advice, suggests that maybe his brother or Katy's sisters can rent the apartment in the slow times, if Katy and Ken can't. Ken's brother is a related party so the adviser's answer is no.

Under the super rules, if Katy or Ken rent the beach house owned by the fund, the investment becomes an in-house asset (IHA). An asset of a SMSF that is subject to a lease between the trustee of the fund and a fund member is an IHA, and SMSFs can have no more than 5 per cent of fund assets as IHAs (refer to Chapter 15). As soon as

a lease arrangement is in place, the total value of the asset is taken into account for IHA purposes, for the length of the lease. The apartment works out to be 33 per cent of the fund's assets, which clearly exceeds the IHA limit of 5 per cent. If Katy and Ken's fund exceeds this 5 per cent limit, as trustees, they may be liable to penalties. The use of the property by fund members is also highly likely to breach the sole purpose test.

In short, Katy and Ken, as SMSF trustees, can still invest in the holiday apartment but they can't use the apartment.

Deciding not to invest in the NSW holiday apartment, Katy and Ken chat with their adviser about another property opportunity on the horizon. The office that Katy leases for her business has come up for sale and the owners want $600,000. Katy and Ken were considering buying the property and leasing it back to Katy's business from their SMSF, but after the discussions around the holiday home, Ken is going cold on the idea.

Katy and Ken's adviser explains that SMSFs receive an exemption for such leases, even though a lease between a SMSF and a fund member would normally be an in-house asset, in this case representing 80 per cent of the fund's $750,000 in fund assets.

In short, Katy and Ken can rent the office from their SMSF because SMSFs receive special treatment when it relates to leases of business real estate.

Special Opportunities for Business-Related Property

The opportunity to make investments in business-related real property, owned by fund members, is one area where SMSFs beat any other type of superannuation fund, especially for those running their own businesses.

You can invest up to 100 per cent of your SMSF's assets in business real property, such as a shop, office, a factory or even a farm. *Business real property* is used wholly or exclusively for business purposes. You can also lease the property back to your business without breaking any rules. Your SMSF can even buy an office or factory or other business real property from a member of your fund and not break any rules. Too good to be true? This kind of investment is indeed a possibility.

Your SMSF can invest in business real property that you use in your business or even a relative's business. For example, your super fund can buy an office that your business then leases from your SMSF at a commercial rate of rent. The advantage of this arrangement is that any rent on your office is directed towards your retirement savings.

You do, however, have to consider whether such a major single investment reflects your fund's investment strategy, and provides your fund with sufficient diversification and liquidity (refer to Chapter 15 for a detailed explanation of what to consider when drafting your fund's investment strategy).

The phrase 'for business purposes' includes primary production businesses. A SMSF can even invest in a farm owned by fund members or other related parties. The farm must be a commercial operation — it can't be primarily a domestic residence or hobby operation. Even if a farm includes a private residence, a farm can satisfy the business real property definition, provided no more than two hectares of land, including the dwelling, is used for private or domestic purposes.

The ATO has produced a SMSF ruling explaining what business real property means, including when an activity is a business, and when such a business is seen to attach to a property. The ruling (SMSFR 2009/1, called *Self-Managed Superannuation Funds: business real property for the purposes of the Superannuation Industry (Supervision) Act 1993*) includes helpful scenarios to illustrate the application of this special exemption for SMSFs.

You can also make in specie (non-cash) contributions into your super fund in the form of business real property, subject to your contributions cap (for more info on super contributions, including in specie contributions, refer to Chapter 4), and/or your small business retirement exemptions (refer to Chapter 13).

If you're considering contributing business real property to your SMSF, then the best strategy is to talk to an adviser about the possible capital gains tax implications and the potential stamp duty costs and other tax consequences.

In most cases, a SMSF doesn't have to register for *GST* (the goods and services tax). GST is a 10 per cent tax on most goods and services. If your fund is considering purchasing, or currently owns, business real property, however, you may decide to register your fund for GST in order to claim back GST credits. Your fund is required to register for GST if the GST turnover exceeds $75,000 a year. Most investment income and transactions don't count towards GST turnover, but rental income from a business-related property is counted towards the GST threshold. You can find more information about GST and your SMSF on the ATO website (www.ato.gov.au), or chat with your fund's adviser/accountant (refer to Chapter 5) about any GST implications.

Pumped-Up Property Plans — LRBAs

Super funds aren't permitted to use traditional loans (except for two exceptions relating to share settlements and benefit payments; for info on these two borrowing exceptions, refer to Chapter 16). However, a SMSF is permitted to borrow when investing in direct property using a limited recourse borrowing arrangement (LRBA). Why? Because any recourse the lender has under the LRBA against the SMSF trustee is limited to the single fund asset purchased using the LRBA.

In one paragraph, here's how a LRBA works. The SMSF doesn't take out a direct loan; rather, it enters a contract to pay instalments for an underlying asset. The borrowing within the geared product is used to buy an asset held on trust by the provider. The SMSF trustee receives the beneficial interest and a right to purchase the underlying asset. The fund doesn't secure any existing fund assets to invest via the LRBA — the only asset at risk is the underlying asset linked to the LRBA, which means the product generally charges some form of loan insurance in case you default on the loan. The loan is then repaid by the SMSF making instalment payments.

The green light on LRBAs means that SMSF trustees can now access property assets using funding that may not have been legal, or viable, before the LRBA option became available.

LRBAs aren't the only 'borrowing' option for SMSFs. A SMSF may be able to purchase a property financed in part using personal borrowings. A trustee of a SMSF can use a joint venture to invest in property with fund members. The investment is purchased through a unit trust structure. The fund member can use personal borrowings, provided the assets of the SMSF aren't secured against the debt. Usually, such an arrangement involves borrowing against a non-super investment property and using the cash to purchase the joint venture investment.

If you're a SMSF trustee and considering investing in property using any form of borrowing, including structures that utilise personal borrowings, seek advice before you proceed. Ask your fund's accountant or other advisers who know and understand SMSF rules.

Ignoring hype about LRBA magic pills

You're likely to hear a lot of puff from commentators about limited recourse borrowing arrangements. Despite the hype, a LRBA isn't a magic pill that miraculously delivers you a stupendous property investment. The LRBA is simply that — an arrangement, rather than an investment. You (or the product promoter offering the LRBA) have to select a suitable property investment for your fund. The LRBA then enables that investment to take place.

For example, you may be able to access a LRBA that enables your SMSF to invest in residential property, provided you have 25 per cent of the purchase price, plus enough cash to cover buying costs, including stamp duty. Another product on the market allows a SMSF to buy commercial property, provided the SMSF can cover 45 per cent of the purchase price plus buying costs.

Purchasing property (or any type of asset permitted by the super rules) by using a LRBA is a legitimate option for SMSF investors, but such an investment approach involves borrowing (or gearing, as outlined in Chapter 16). When property values are rising, geared products enable to you to accumulate wealth at a much faster rate because you have access to the returns on more assets. In falling markets, however, your losses are also greater when you borrow to invest.

What matters when investing — whether you use borrowed money or not — is the quality of the underlying property investment. You also need to be mindful of the costs of such an arrangement. As a SMSF trustee, you need to ask yourself whether the expected returns on the investment justify the costs of the LRBA. These LRBA products aren't necessarily cheap, and you may discover you're being charged several levels of fees, depending on whether you borrow money from a related party (such as a fund member) or a commercial provider. In addition to an interest cost for the loan, you may also pay a 2 to 3 per cent protection fee in case your fund defaults on the loan, and potentially management fees if the product promoter manages the SMSF's property.

In the scenario described in the preceding paragraph, assuming a 5 or 6 per cent base interest rate on the loan, the SMSF property investment, financed via a LRBA, must deliver a return of at least 8 or 9 per cent a year to justify the costs.

Passing six LRBA tests

Some promoters of LRBAs infer that these products are just like taking out a home loan and repaying the loan over time. You need to fully understand that this 'borrowing' caper isn't a regular arrangement, and can be relatively expensive to set up (refer to the previous section) and to maintain over time. Your LRBA must also meet special conditions.

According to the ATO, if your super fund chooses to use a LRBA, the arrangement must satisfy the following conditions:

✔ The fund uses the borrowed monies to purchase a single asset, or a collection of identical assets that have the same market value.

✔ The fund can't use the LRBA monies to 'improve' a purchased asset. I explain what the ATO means by 'improve' in the next section.

✔ The SMSF trustees receive the beneficial interest in the purchased asset, but the legal ownership of the asset is held on trust (the holding trust).

✔ The SMSF trustees have the right to acquire the legal ownership of the asset by making one or more payments.

✔ Any recourse that the lender (or other party) has under the LRBA against the SMSF trustees is limited to the single fund asset (including rights to income). Lenders can legally demand an individual to provide a guarantee against personal assets.

✔ Replacing the asset subject to the LRBA is possible in very specific ways — for example, where a company undertakes a share split or unit split, or via a company takeover or merger. *Note*: If cash is received as part of the share split or company takeover, then the replacement asset doesn't satisfy the pre-existing LRBA conditions.

You can find more information on LRBAs, such as the dangers of personal guarantees for SMSF arrangements, in an ATO publication called *Limited recourse borrowing arrangements by self-managed superannuation funds — questions and answers* (NAT 70793). Download the publication from the ATO website (www.ato.gov.au) or obtain a copy by phoning the ATO on 13 10 20.

Understanding the LRBA difference between repairing and improving

In May 2012, the ATO published a final ruling explaining some key concepts used in the LRBA rules. The ruling, SMSFR 2012/1 (*Self-managed superannuation funds: limited recourse borrowing arrangements — application of key concepts*), deals mainly with property investment and LRBAs, and clarifies the difference between renovating and improving a property.

The key message from the ATO ruling is that when using a LRBA, you can maintain or repair a property but you can't improve it, and the ruling explains the difference between renovating and improving. Note also, that you can improve a property purchased using a LRBA, but you can't use borrowed money to finance the improvement.

Specifically, SMSFR 2012/1 states that it's okay to use borrowed money from an existing LRBA to maintain or repair the property subject to the LRBA, but you can't use LRBA money to improve the property. According to the SMSFR 2012/1 ruling, these key words have the following meanings:

- **Maintaining:** Ordinarily means work done to prevent defects, damage or deterioration of an asset, or in anticipation of future defects, damage or deterioration, provided that the work merely ensures the continued functioning of the asset in its present state.

- **Repairing:** Ordinarily means remedying or making good defects in, damage to, or deterioration of an asset, and contemplates the continued existence of the asset. A repair is usually occasional and partial, restoring the function of the asset without changing its character. Repairing may include restoration to its former appearance, form state or condition.

- **Improving:** Ordinarily means significant alteration to the state or function of the asset for the better; for example, substantial alterations, or the addition of further features.

SMSFR 2012/1 also takes you through several scenarios and provides guidance on whether the work is a repair or improvement, depending on the circumstances. I advise any SMSF trustee considering purchasing an older property to read this ruling, or discuss this ruling with their SMSF adviser (refer to Chapter 5). You can download a copy of SMSFR 2012/1 from the ATO website (www.ato.gov.au).

Chapter 18

Investing and Super Tax

*M*any people huff and puff about the number of taxes imposed on superannuation and how confusing it all is. However, in terms of super tax incentives, most Australians are on a fairly good wicket.

The superannuation tax system is more complicated than it needs to be, but complicated taxes don't eliminate the fact that super is one of the most tax-effective retirement vehicles available. I'm not, however, going to gloss over the reality. Tax is a necessary evil in a civilised society and, historically, superannuation has been hit with the evil tax stick more times than many other investment vehicles.

In this chapter, you get a working understanding of how your super fund's investments are taxed while you're accumulating super savings for retirement, and what tax consequences are in store for your fund's investments when you start a superannuation pension. Although the tax rules when investing your SMSF money can be complex, I also explain the extra-special tax deal your fund enjoys when it receives franked dividends from holding Australian shares. As much as possible, I talk tax in plain English, but on occasion I slip into detail to ensure you have the information you need to understand the super taxes that affect your fund's investment earnings.

Educating Yourself about Earnings Tax

Your super fund is a taxpayer, just like you. During accumulation phase — when you haven't started a super pension with your superannuation account — your SMSF pays tax on any income (less expenses) the SMSF earns throughout the year. Your fund, however, pays a much lower rate on earnings than most Australians pay when they earn income.

Accounting for 15 per cent earnings tax

Your super fund's assessable income, including your fund's investment income, is taxed at 15 per cent. The investment income tax of 15 per cent also applies to capital gains. Any capital gain that your super fund receives when it disposes of an asset for a profit also becomes part of your fund's assessable income. I explain the tax treatment of capital gains, and the special treatment of certain capital gains, later in the chapter, in the section 'Coping with Capital Gains Tax'. Table 18-1 outlines the tax rates applicable to SMSF investment earnings (during accumulation phase).

During pension phase — the period during which a super account pays a superannuation pension — the earnings on your SMSF assets financing superannuation pensions (known as 'exempt current pension income'), are exempt from tax. I explain the tax status of the earnings on your SMSF pension account, more specifically exempt current pension income, in the section 'Eliminating Earnings Tax in Pension Phase', later in this chapter.

Your fund's assessable income includes your concessional contributions (including any employer contributions). Treating contributions as income is unusual but such treatment means that your SMSF can reduce your super fund's tax bill by reducing any tax payable on investments or contributions by using franking credits. Franking credits arise from franked dividends, which are company shares where tax has already been paid on the income. I explain the benefits of franking credits for SMSFs in the section, 'Making Tax Magic with Franked Dividends', later in the chapter. I explain the contribution rules in Chapter 4, and the taxes applicable to contributions in more detail in Chapter 13.

Accepting a higher tax bill for related-party income

If your SMSF receives income from a non-arm's length source — that is, income such as private company dividends or non-arm's length trust distributions — then you can expect this income to be hit with a much higher level of tax. This type of income is known as *non-arm's length income*.

If you have been running your SMSF for a long time, you may know this type of income by its previous name — *special income.*

In the SMSF return that your fund must complete each year (refer to Chapter 12), the page itemising your SMSF's assessable income includes a separate section for net non-arm's length income (if any), which includes any deductions linked to that non-arm's length income. Any assessable income other than net non-arm's length income is the low tax component, which is the balance of your super fund's income, and is taxed at the concessional rate of 15 per cent (as shown in Table 18-1). In the past, the low tax component was called the standard component. You pay tax on the non-arm's length income at the highest marginal tax rate (47 per cent, as shown in Table 18-1). If your fund expects to receive such income, I strongly suggest you chat to your adviser/accountant about the tax implications for your fund.

Although earnings on SMSF assets financing a super pension are generally tax-exempt, non-arm's length income is taxable even when your super account is in pension phase. I explain the tax treatment of investment earnings on pension assets in the next section 'Eliminating Earnings Tax in Pension Phase' later in this chapter.

Table 18-1	Earning Taxes Affecting Your SMSF in Accumulation Phase	
Tax	*Tax Rates*	*What Part of Your Super is Taxed?*
Investment income tax[*]	15%	Tax on investment earnings of fund. No earnings tax is payable when account is in pension phase.
Capital gains tax (CGT)	15% (effective rate of 10% after CGT discount)	Tax on capital gains in your fund. Effective tax rate of 10% for gains on assets held for more than 12 months. No tax is payable on capital gains in pension phase.
Non-arm's length income	47%	Income derived from a source that is not on a commercial arm's-length basis. Tax also payable on this income in pension phase.

[*] *Contributions are included in a super fund's assessable income, which is subject to earnings tax of 15 per cent. In relation to contributions, this tax is commonly known as 'contributions tax'.*
Note: No investment income tax is payable on earnings from pension assets — that is, assets financing a pension/income stream.

Super: A child of the tax revolution

Four years changed the world of superannuation tax forever — 1983, 1988, 1990 and 2007. Before 1983, superannuation was a simple concept where only 5 per cent of any super payout was included in your assessable income. The downside was that not many people had super in those days unless they worked in the public sector or were a senior office worker.

In 1983, the Labor government of the day announced that from 1 July 1983, a higher level of tax of 30 per cent applied to any lump sum retirement payment. This new tax didn't apply to any benefits accrued before 1 July 1983, which meant that any benefit representing service before 1 July 1983 was known as your pre-July 1983 component and only 5 per cent of that component was included in your assessable income.

In 1988, the federal government fiddled with super taxes in two ways. The government slapped a 15 per cent tax on super fund earnings, which were previously exempt from tax. The government also legislated for the effective pre-payment of your benefits tax, bringing forward half of the 30 per cent tax paid on super benefits (introduced in 1983) and attaching it to any before-tax contributions (now called concessional contributions, refer to Chapter 4). What this meant for super fund members was that before-tax contributions were now taxed at 15 per cent when they reached the fund, and the benefits tax was reduced to 15 per cent, give or take a few exceptions.

In 1990, the federal government reformed the reasonable benefits rules (RBLs) — any concessionally taxed benefits you received from super funds or your employers over your lifetime were recorded and the accumulated total couldn't exceed a limit known as your RBL. The government then simplified these limits in 1994 introducing flat dollar limits for lump sums, which were indexed annually in line with increases in average weekly earnings.

In 2007, the super system was turned on its head. The federal government abolished RBLs, and you can now expect tax-free retirement benefits when you take your benefits on or after the age of 60, with the exception of payments from some government super funds. Further, for those under the age of 60, the tax rules are simpler than they were before July 2007. If you take your super benefits before the age of 60, your superannuation benefits are now split into two components — taxable and tax-free — rather than the eight components that applied previously. I discuss the tax rules applicable to super benefit payments in Chapters 13 and 19.

Eliminating Earnings Tax in Pension Phase

One of the more financially exciting aspects of using a super fund for your retirement plans is that when you start a superannuation pension, the earnings on assets financing your super pension are exempt from tax.

The tax-exempt treatment of earnings on pension assets applies whether you're a member of a large fund, a small APRA fund or a SMSF.

The tax-exempt status of your pension earnings is in addition to the tax-free pension payments you can expect to receive from your SMSF on or after the age of 60 (refer to Chapter 19).

The money, or capital, that you use to finance your SMSF superannuation pension is usually invested in a similar way to how your super benefit is invested while you're accumulating super savings, with some exceptions. Investment earnings on this pension capital are exempt from tax because the money is being used to finance your pension, which means more money is working towards funding your retirement. In comparison, if you invest your savings outside the super environment, the earnings on your savings are subject to income tax.

The official term for investment earnings that are derived from pension assets is *exempt current pension income* (*ECPI*). For your SMSF to be able to claim ECPI, your fund must ensure that all necessary steps have been taken, including:

✔ All SMSF assets supporting the pension have been revalued at market value, as at the start of each financial year (1 July).

✔ Minimum pension amounts have been paid to the member or members (see Chapter 21 for info on how to run a SMSF pension).

✔ If the SMSF is also running one or more super accounts in accumulation phase, the SMSF has obtained an actuarial certificate to identify the ECPI, unless the pension assets are segregated from the accumulation phase assets (see Chapter 22 for info on unsegregated assets and actuarial certificates).

Any expenses you incur when running a SMSF account in pension phase cannot be claimed in your SMSF tax return. If an expense relates to both accumulation and pension phase, the deduction can be apportioned against assessable income related to the accumulation phase.

If you choose to, you can leave your super account in accumulation phase indefinitely — you're not forced to take a lump sum or start a super pension. By choosing such a strategy, however, your super account's fund earnings on assets in accumulation phase continue to be subject to 15 per cent investment income tax.

Making Tax Magic with Franked Dividends

Investing in shares can deliver income in the form of dividends, and capital growth when the share price increases (see earlier chapters in this Part for information on investing within your SMSF). Purchasing Australian shares that pay dividends may give your SMSF access to franked dividends, which are dividends where tax has already been paid on the income.

The pre-paid tax, currently 30 per cent on company income, is known as franking credits, which means you can offset the tax payable by your fund by taking advantage of the franking credits. If no tax is payable by your fund (for example, your SMSF is in pension phase) you can even claim a tax refund when your SMSF is entitled to franking credits.

If you want your fund to be entitled to franking credits, your SMSF must hold a company's shares for at least 45 days, excluding the day of purchase and the day of sale.

Reducing tax during accumulation phase

Franking credits can be effective in reducing or eliminating the tax payable on:

- ✔ Your super fund's earnings, including any capital gains tax (CGT) you may have to pay (see the section 'Coping with Capital Gains Tax' later in the chapter)
- ✔ The tax your fund pays on concessional (before-tax) contributions

The pre-paid tax of 30 per cent attached to franking credits clearly exceeds the 15 per cent tax to be paid on a fund's investment earnings, which means your fund can use the excess franking credits to reduce the final tax bill payable on other assessable income. **Note**: The federal government is planning to reduce the company tax rate to 28.5 per cent from 1 July 2015 and then impose a 1.5 per cent levy on the largest 3200 Australian companies to fund a paid parental leave (PPL) scheme, subject to legislation. The implications of this proposed drop in company tax is that SMSF share investors will receive reduced franking credits, which will mean more tax payable during accumulation phase. The PPL levy is not considered company tax, which means it does not attract franking credits.

If you run a SMSF, you can more easily take advantage of franking credits than if you're a member of a larger super fund. The reporting systems of most large super funds, unless they offer a specific direct investing Australian share option, aren't designed to allocate company dividends and associated franking credits to individual super accounts.

Not all Australian shares pay franked dividends, and even shares that are franked may not be fully franked. In some cases, particularly where a company has significant overseas income or has suffered company losses, a dividend may be unfranked, or just a portion of the dividend is franked, which means that the dividend is partly franked. In this situation, your fund can claim a tax credit for the portion of the dividend that is franked.

The share listings in the business section of most daily newspapers indicate which companies pay franked dividends, partly franked dividends or unfranked dividends.

Receiving tax refunds during pension phase

Franking credits are very valuable for SMSFs in pension phase because your fund is receiving tax-exempt fund earnings, which means your fund is in a zero-tax environment. What happens then to franking credits in such an environment? You can claim a tax refund representing your fund's franking credits!

After completing and lodging your fund's tax return (refer to Chapter 12), you can expect a tax refund from the ATO. Oh, and the tax refund belongs to your fund, and must be deposited into your fund's bank account.

Coping with Capital Gains Tax

During accumulation phase, a capital gain that your super fund receives when it disposes of an asset for a profit becomes part of your fund's assessable income. Your fund's assessable income less deductions is taxable income, and your fund pays tax on this income. A capital gain arises when your fund makes a profit on the sale of an asset.

Super funds get a special tax deal on any capital gains they make when working out the fund's income tax bill, depending on how long your

SMSF has owned the asset. Capital gains earned by your SMSF during the accumulation phase are treated the following way for tax purposes:

- ✔ **Assets held for longer than 12 months:** Although SMSF investment earnings are subject to 15 per cent tax, when a capital gain is involved and the asset sold has been owned by the fund for longer than 12 months, then only two-thirds of the gain counts towards your SMSF's assessable income. The 33.33 per cent reduction in capital gain for tax purposes is known as the capital gains tax (CGT) discount. The effective tax rate for capital gains on assets owned for longer than 12 months is 10 per cent, rather than the usual 15 per cent.

- ✔ **Assets sold within 12 months of purchase:** If you hold a SMSF asset for less than 12 months, any capital gain on the sale is taxed at 15 per cent; no CGT discount applies.

Your fund's net capital gain is included in your SMSF's assessable income. The *net capital gain* is calculated as follows: Your fund's total gain for the year *less* total capital losses for the year (including unapplied capital losses from previous financial years) less the CGT discount. A capital loss cannot be claimed against non-capital income, such as dividend income or interest or rental income. A capital loss can only be offset against a capital gain.

During pension phase, any capital gains your SMSF receives are exempt from earnings tax. If your fund suffers a capital loss on a pension asset, then you can only offset this loss against capital gains from the sale of pension assets.

If your SMSF has assets that it acquired before 21 September 1999, any capital gains on disposal may be subject to the frozen indexation valuation method. Also, if your super fund purchased any existing fund assets before June 1988, then a trip to an accountant may also be in order, because such assets are treated differently for CGT purposes.

Part V

Paying Super Benefits from Your Fund

Five Questions to Ask Before Retiring

- **At what age should I retire?** Before retiring you need to consider your health, your finances — including access to super — and the tax implications of any decisions, and your lifestyle plans for your retirement.

- **How much money is enough?** The amount of money you need for retirement will depend on the age you retire, how long you expect to live, how you invest your retirement savings and whether you're eligible for a full or part Age Pension.

- **How long can I expect to live?** The earlier you retire, the longer you can expect your retirement phase to be. A person's average life expectancy at the age they choose to retire is a reasonable benchmark for retirement planning, but allow for the possibility that you may live longer than average, or even die earlier than expected.

- **When can I access my super benefits?** If your retirement plans are heavily dependent on accessing your super benefits, then retiring before you reach preservation age (at least age 55) is probably not a good idea.

- **When can I claim the Age Pension (if at all)?** If you're eligible for the Age Pension, you can expect that you'll need a lower amount of personal savings for your retirement, but note that the Age Pension is only available later in life.

Check out www.dummies.com/extras/diysuperau for more info about paying super benefits from your fund.

In this part ...

- ✔ Understand the tax and super implications of retiring before age 60, or working beyond age 60, including the impact on your SMSF.

- ✔ Appreciate the relationship between your super benefits and your potential Age Pension entitlements.

- ✔ Follow the special rules when running a SMSF pension, including calculating pension components and following the minimum pension payment rules.

- ✔ Consider the special requirements when contributing to a SMSF while also running a pension from the same SMSF.

- ✔ Appreciate the superannuation (and SMSF) implications if your marriage or de facto relationship breaks down.

- ✔ Plan for how your family can benefit from your super benefits if you die, including insurance options and working out what happens to your SMSF.

Chapter 19

Retiring is Just the Beginning

*R*etirement is a magical word that can evoke images of sunny days, relaxed travelling, long walks and spending quality time with family and friends — at least, that's what I hope my own retirement is going to be like. On the other hand, the prospect of retirement can also trigger fear-filled thoughts about managing money, stressing over investment markets and wondering whether your money is going to last your entire retirement. (To evaluate your tolerance for investment risk, refer to Chapters 14 and 15; to see whether you can make your retirement money last, refer to Chapter 3.)

If you run your own super fund, you have the added responsibility of controlling your retirement income. For many self-managed super fund (SMSF) trustees, this stage can be the most exciting phase of running a SMSF, while for others the prospect of having to manage and monitor one's own retirement portfolio isn't the type of retirement 'job' they had in mind.

Even before you embark on your retirement journey, however, you have significant decisions to make, such as the timing of your retirement, whether to keep all your savings in the super system, your possible tax bill, whether you plan to continue working and/or making super contributions, and your eligibility (if any) for the Age Pension.

In this chapter I touch on all of these issues, including the implications of retiring before the age of 60, and why most Australians can't cash their super before the age of 55. I explain how your benefit is taxed and why taking a pension can deliver you a tax-friendlier, and sometimes tax-free, retirement before the tax-free age of 60. I also explain the rules that apply when accessing your tax-free super benefits on or after the age of 60.

This chapter provides an overview of the superannuation rules in retirement, whereas Chapters 21 and 22 deal specifically with SMSF pensions. Chapter 22 mainly deals with some of the issues SMSF trustees face when running (or restarting) a SMSF pension while continuing to contribute to super. I also delve into the general retirement rules, in particular the tax rules in retirement, on my website, SuperGuide (www.superguide.com.au).

Navigating Your Retirement Road

Only you know the answer to the question: When is the right time to retire?

You may be hoping to leave your job on your designated retirement day and never have to work for a living again. Or, you may be one of the growing number of Australians who plan to gradually leave the workforce by taking up a part-time role or even beginning a new career. Whatever grand exit from the workforce that you're planning, you need to work out what sources of income you plan to have in retirement, including what you're going to do with your super.

Regardless of whether you run a SMSF or rely on a professionally managed super fund (refer to Chapter 2) to look after your retirement savings, you can never really turn off from the job of looking after your retirement income. The horror investment years of 2008 and 2009, the precarious world economies of 2010, 2011 and 2012, and the global political volatility of 2013 and 2014, prove that investors, particularly those who rely solely on the earnings from investments to live, must be vigilant about who's looking after their money (refer to Chapters 2 and 5) and how those savings are invested (refer to Part IV of this book).

Taking terminology to task

One of the first steps in the retirement-planning process is to get your head around the terminology associated with retirement. Why does dealing with superannuation and retirement reveal so many strange and wonderful terms? The answer is: Because so many people are interested in the subject, including the government; and, of course, the financial world can't help tinkering with popular subjects.

Getting some of the retirement terminology out of the way makes for a handy checklist:

- A *superannuation lump sum* is a lump sum payment from a superannuation fund.

- An *income stream* is a series of regular payments over time, just like being paid wages or a salary.

- A *superannuation income stream* is virtually identical to a plain-vanilla income stream, except the income is paid from a super fund, usually during your retirement.

- A *pension* is the popular term for an income stream payable from a superannuation fund. If you belong to a corporate or public sector fund (refer to Chapter 2), your fund may automatically pay you a pension when you retire. Or, more likely, if you belong to an industry or retail super fund (refer to Chapter 2), you have to make the decision to purchase a pension from your existing fund, or from a different pension provider. You also have to make an active decision to start a SMSF pension (see Chapter 21).

- An *annuity* is an income stream that looks the same as a pension but is payable by a life insurance company rather than a super fund.

- A *transition-to-retirement pension* (I call it a *TRIP*) is a non-commutable pension that enables you to access part of your super benefits each year before you retire (but only after you reach your preservation age — see the section 'Preserving Your Super Fortune', later in the chapter). *Non-commutable* means that you can't convert the preserved component of the pension into a lump sum payment. In the case of a TRIP, however, you can convert your pension into a lump sum once you retire or reach the age of 65. I explain how a TRIP works in Chapters 21 and 22.

Preparing for R day

As you come to grips with retirement terminology, you can begin to consider what your retirement is going to look like. Your retirement is likely to be a lot more relaxing if you do some planning, and appreciate the issues behind your superannuation payout:

- **Ensure your money lasts.** Taking your entire super as a lump sum may be tempting, especially if you're planning a luxury ocean cruise or you want to buy a retirement holiday home, or you have some other retirement-dream purchase in mind. The burning question is: Are you going to blow the lot or invest the money outside of super? If your super is your only source of income, and you fritter your lump sum, you may find yourself relying solely on the federal government Age Pension (see Chapter 20, and for information on how much money is enough for retirement, refer to Chapter 3).

✔ **Check you can access your super.** Most Australians aren't permitted to withdraw a super benefit before at least the age of 55, except in exceptional circumstances. The restriction on accessing super benefits is known as preservation. Ordinarily you must reach your preservation age and retire, to access super benefits. Your preservation age is age 55, if born before July 1960, or age 60 for anyone born after June 1964, and age 56, 57, 58 or 59 for anyone born between those dates (see the section 'Gaining access to your super benefits', later in this chapter). If you joined a superannuation fund before 1 July 1999, however, you may hold some super benefits that you can cash before you reach your preservation age (check out 'Preserving Your Super Fortune', later in the chapter).

✔ **Choose an appropriate income stream/pension.** You can use your super money to purchase different types of pensions and annuities from commercial pension providers, including those that pay you an income until the day you die, or until your spouse dies, or for a specified period (for example, until you reach your life expectancy age — life expectancy means how many years you're expected to live). If you intend to start a pension within your SMSF, however, then you have only two pension options. I explain your SMSF pension options in Chapter 21.

✔ **Understand what tax you pay.** If you choose to take your super as a lump sum, you may not have to pay tax, depending on the size of your payout and your age. Retirees who choose to take a pension in retirement also fare very well tax-wise. Most Australians pay no tax on super benefits from the age of 60, plus earnings on assets financing a retirement pension are exempt from tax. (I explain the ins and outs of taxation when you retire in the sections 'Retiring Early (Before 60) Means Tax — Usually' and 'Retiring On or After 60 Means No Tax', later in this chapter, as well as in Chapter 13.)

✔ **Assess your eligibility for the Age Pension.** The Age Pension is supposedly a safety net for those who haven't saved for their retirement. Interestingly, however, around 80 per cent of all retirees over the Age Pension age receive a full or part Age Pension (see Chapter 20). Many retirees can structure their financial situation in a way that entitles them to the following:

• Superannuation income stream (pension)

• Full or part Age Pension, and perhaps even a public pension from overseas

• Small or non-existent tax bill

✔ **Consider any estate planning issues.** You may be able to choose to pay your spouse or dependent children a pension when you die (a superannuation income stream death benefit), or you can leave the balance of your super account to your family as a lump sum (a superannuation lump sum death benefit). See Chapter 24 for information on death benefits and estate planning.

Your prospective retirement is definitely the right time to call in the experts — because a tax-effective and financially sound retirement plan usually involves a delicate balance of superannuation, taxation and social security (Age Pension) laws. Anyone taking a pension from a SMSF (see Chapter 21), particularly an individual planning to make further super contributions while receiving a SMSF pension (see Chapter 22), ought to be discussing the SMSF and retirement rules with an expert. In Chapter 5, I chat about what to look for when hunting down an appropriate adviser.

A preliminary question you need to think about when embarking on your retirement journey is: How much money is enough for the lifestyle that you anticipate? I discuss this at length in Chapter 3, but briefly, the answer to the question depends on four main elements:

✔ Level of income that you hope to receive each year

✔ Your life expectancy; that is, how long you expect to live

✔ Level of investment earnings you can expect to receive on your pension account in retirement

✔ Whether you intend to continue working and/or contributing to your super fund in retirement — check out Chapter 22 for details about the implications of contributing while taking a SMSF pension

Retiring too early

The earlier you retire, the more money you're going to need to finance your lengthier retirement. Are you planning to retire too early?

You can retire and access your superannuation between the ages of 55 and 60 (see 'Preserving Your Super Fortune', later in the chapter) but, importantly, you can't receive the Age Pension until you reach the age of at least 65 and as late as age 70 (depending on your date of birth, and subject to legislation). The age when you can claim the Age Pension is called your Age Pension age. The Age Pension age is rising above age 65 from July 2017, until it reaches age 70 in 2035 (subject to legislation).

If you're retiring before Age Pension age, then you have to rely on your super and non-super savings until you reach your Age Pension age, assuming you're eligible to receive the Age Pension. I further explore the Age Pension rules, including the impact of your super pension on Age Pension eligibility, in Chapter 20.

Working, and contributing, after retiring

Statisticians and financial analysts are predicting that more Australians are set to continue working after they 'retire' from the workforce, either by choice or, more likely, due to financial need. This prediction may sound scary, but think about what your retirement age may be. If you're born before 1 July 1960, you can retire and cash in your super from the age of 55. Then, on average, at current life expectancies you have another 27 (male) to 31 (female) years in retirement.

The federal government recognises that not everyone ceases all work at the same age and that some people want to work well beyond Age Pension age. You don't have to retire when you reach your preservation age of 55 or older (see the next section). You don't even have to retire at the age of 65, or even 70. You can work for as long as you're alive if you want to, and you can continue contributing to super until you turn 75. I explain your superannuation contributions options post-retirement in Chapter 22, and contributions generally in Chapter 4.

Preserving Your Super Fortune

In most cases, your superannuation benefit is *preserved*; that is, you generally can't access your benefit until you reach a certain age and retire. The federal government places this restriction, known as *preservation*, on superannuation benefits to ensure you have money for when you eventually finish work rather than have you draw on your super before you retire like an everyday bank account. In return for locking your savings away, the government offers a swag of tax incentives (refer to Chapter 13), or disincentives, depending on your view, to make the long-term saving experience worthwhile.

The most compelling argument for keeping your money in the super system is that you receive your super benefits tax-free on or after the age of 60, provided you satisfy a condition of release. Even when you do retire before the age of 60 you may be surprised by the tax incentives available (see 'Retiring Early (Before 60) Means Tax — Usually', later in the chapter).

Your superannuation account can include three types of benefits, which determine when you can take your money out of the super system. In straightforward terms, your super can be made up of the following:

- ✔ *Preserved benefit* — you can't access this part of your super until you retire on or after you reach your preservation age (at least the age of 55, increasing to age 60 for anyone born after June 1964). Most superannuation benefits are preserved. Note that you may be able to access this benefit earlier in special circumstances. I explain preserved benefits in the next section, 'Gaining access to your super benefits'.

- ✔ *Restricted non-preserved benefit* — a benefit that's restricted until you leave your job. Your super may include this type of benefit if you were a super fund member before 1 July 1999. You can cash this benefit when you resign from the employer who's contributing to your super fund.

- ✔ *Unrestricted non-preserved benefit* — no restriction and no preservation means you can access this benefit at any time.

For easier reading throughout the rest of this chapter, I use a short form of the terms to emphasise their key meanings — preserved, restricted and unrestricted. I also use these terms interchangeably with their long-winded names — preserved, restricted non-preserved and unrestricted non-preserved.

The quickest way to work out what parts of your benefit are preserved, restricted or unrestricted is to check out your *member report*, also known as a *member statement*. When running your own super fund, you need to track these benefits yourself, although in most cases, your fund administrator (if you have one — refer to Chapter 10) uses a software program to produce member statements and financial reports.

Gaining access to your super benefits

In most cases, preserved benefits must be kept in the super system until you retire from the workforce on or after reaching your *preservation age*, which represents the age at which your preserved benefits can be paid out from your super fund. In some cases, you can access your preserved super without retiring — such as, when you reach the age of 65 — or if you start a transition-to-retirement pension (TRIP) (I show you how a TRIP works in Chapter 21), or if you satisfy another condition of release (see the next section).

As shown in Table 19-1, your preservation age is at least 55 years and can be up to 60 years, depending on your date of birth. The government has gradually raised the preservation age from age 55 to age 60 in an attempt to ensure that money contributed to superannuation funds is kept for retirement.

Table 19-1	Working Out Your Preservation Age
Your Date of Birth	*Your Preservation Age*
Before 1 July 1960	55
On or after 1 July 1960 but before 1 July 1961	56
On or after 1 July 1961 but before 1 July 1962	57
On or after 1 July 1962 but before 1 July 1963	58
On or after 1 July 1963 but before 1 July 1964	59
On or after 1 July 1964	60

Retiring is a must, in most cases

You can access your preserved superannuation benefits when you reach your preservation age *and* you genuinely retire.

Retirement is considered a *condition of release*; that is, you can take your super as cash. On retirement (and reaching your preservation age), your preserved benefit is released — becoming an unrestricted benefit. Also, you can take your preserved benefits if you satisfy a condition of release other than retirement, such as reaching the age of 65 or becoming permanently incapacitated, or starting a transition-to-retirement pension (TRIP; see Chapter 21).

Retiring before 60

If you're under the age of 60 (but you have reached your preservation age), being retired means an employment arrangement has come to an end and your super fund's trustee is satisfied that you don't intend working again for more than ten hours a week.

Retiring or resigning on or after 60

After reaching the age of 60, you can access your preserved benefit when you retire from the workforce, or, when you resign or are made redundant from a job. Ceasing an employment arrangement when you're 60 years or over is considered to be retiring under the preservation rules. This special rule for Australians aged 60 years and over acknowledges that many people who leave jobs at this age may be retiring or are less likely to find another job before they officially retire.

You can find more about the preservation rules in the ATO publication *Running a self-managed super fund* (NAT 11032). I also explain the preservation rules in more detail, including the 14 main conditions of release on my website, SuperGuide (www.superguide.com.au).

Leaving your money in super indefinitely

You don't have to withdraw your super money from your super account. You can leave your savings in the super structure indefinitely — or at least until you die (for information on what happens to your super after you die, see Chapter 24). If you choose, you can leave your super account in accumulation phase (that is, without drawing a pension from your account); you're not forced to take a lump sum or start a pension. By choosing such a strategy, however, your super account's fund earnings on assets in accumulation phase continue to be subject to up to 15 per cent earnings tax (refer to Chapters 13 and 18).

Taking a Lump Sum and/or Pension

Before you retire, you need to make a few key decisions. One important step in retirement planning is deciding which superannuation option you want, as shown in Table 19-2. Will you take your super as a lump sum, as a pension, or as a combination of both? You're facing one of the biggest financial decisions you have to make for your life in retirement.

Table 19-2	Superannuation Options for Retirement
Superannuation Decision	*Issues to Consider*
Lump sum only	Do you have any other sources of income? Have you considered the tax implications if you're retiring before 60?
Pension only	Do you need cash to clear major commitments? Can you structure your circumstances to minimise tax (if you're under the age of 60, or a long-term public servant receiving a taxable pension)?

(continued)

Table 19-2 *(continued)*

Superannuation Decision	Issues to Consider
Lump sum and pension	Can you structure your circumstances to minimise tax (if you're under the age of 60, or a long-term public servant receiving taxable super benefits)?

Retirement (and Lifestyle) Questions	Issues to Consider
Do you want to keep working?	Consider all the issues listed above. Consider a transition-to-retirement pension (see Chapter 21) Can you make super contributions (refer to Chapters 4 and 22)?
Do you want to continue contributing to super?	If you're over the age of 65 you must satisfy a work test before contributing (refer to Chapters 4 and 22)
What happens to your super account or pension when you die?	See Chapter 24

Taking your superannuation as a lump sum means your savings leave the tax-friendly superannuation environment, whereas taking a pension means your savings continue to receive the tax concessions associated with super benefits. Tax concessions include tax-exempt earnings for assets financing a superannuation pension, and tax-free benefits when paid to individuals aged 60 or over (except for some public servants, who may pay tax on retirement benefits from certain public sector funds — I explain the tax treatment of the super benefits paid from older public sector funds on my SuperGuide website, www.superguide.com.au).

In Chapter 21, I explain the two types of pensions that you can run from your SMSF, and the steps involved in setting up a SMSF pension.

Retiring Early (Before 60) Means Tax — Usually

If you retire before the age of 60, your super benefits are likely to be subject to tax — but not always. With the right structure, and usually with expert advice, many Australians retiring early can end up paying no tax.

The federal government has set up the superannuation tax system so that retirees aged 60 or over can receive super benefits tax-free. Retirees under the age of 60 with substantial assets (more than $185,000 in super for the 2014–15 year), are likely to pay tax, however; when they take their super as a pension, they have access to a tax offset on pension income.

Super benefits can be made up of two components — 'tax-free' and 'taxable'. When you retire before the age of 60, the *tax-free component* is, as you'd expect, tax-free, while the *taxable component* is usually subject to tax (I explain these components in detail in Chapter 21). How much tax you pay on your super benefit when you cash your super before the age of 60 depends on:

- **The size of your super lump sum benefit:** The first $185,000 (for the 2014–15 year) of your taxable component is tax-free, except for certain benefits paid to some public servants. The tax-free limit of $185,000 is known as the *low-rate cap*.

- **Whether your lump sum benefit includes a tax-free component, which you receive tax-free:** The tax-free component represents your non-concessional (after-tax) contributions and, if you were a member of a fund before July 2007, several other elements of your super benefit (see Chapter 21 for information on pre-July 2007 benefits). The tax-free component is always tax-free.

- **Whether you take a pension:** A superannuation lump sum is taxed differently from a benefit that you convert into a superannuation pension. If you retire before the age of 60, you may receive a tax-free amount as part of your pension, and also be eligible for a 15 per cent pension offset on the taxable component of your benefit. The pension offset reduces your tax bill, potentially to zero. (I talk about the types of pensions on offer in a SMSF in Chapter 21.)

- **Whether you receive a benefit from a taxed source or an untaxed source:** All super benefits from a SMSF are considered to be from a taxed source, unless you or your beneficiary receive an insurance payout, which may be treated as coming from an untaxed source if the fund has claimed a tax deduction for premiums. You pay more tax when you receive a benefit from an untaxed source — a life insurance payout from a SMSF may be treated as a benefit from an untaxed source. Apart from insurance payments, untaxed benefits are generally paid from older public sector super schemes (now closed to new members).

The $185,000 low-rate cap (for the 2014–15 year) for the taxable component of lump sums is in addition to any tax-free component making up your super benefit. A single $185,000 low-rate cap is a lifetime limit that applies to all benefits received after your preservation age, rather than a fresh limit applicable for each benefit payment. If you have withdrawn any super benefits in the past, you may have used up some or nearly all of your low-rate cap of

$185,000, which means you may have to pay tax on nearly all of, or the entire, taxable component when receiving a lump sum. But when you reach age 60, the low-rate cap is not important, because all lump sums are tax free except for some payments from some government super funds.

The rate that you need to withhold tax is detailed in the ATO document *Schedule 12 — Tax table for super lump sums*. Within 14 days of making a lump sum payment to a SMSF member under the age of 60, you must provide a *PAYG payment summary — superannuation lump sum* (NAT 70947) to the lump sum recipient.

Retiring On or After 60 Means No Tax

If you're aged 60 and retired, you can receive your superannuation benefits tax-free — as a lump sum or as a pension). It sounds incredible, but this tax-free option is certainly true. You can enjoy a tax-free income in retirement assuming you have sufficient super savings (refer to Chapter 3) to deliver you that regular income in retirement.

Tax-free super has always been a feature of Australia's retirement system but, before July 2007, you usually had to hire advisers, and get involved in financial gymnastics, to secure the tax-free income. And before July 2007, how much super you could receive at concessional rates was limited. Not any more.

The good news keeps on coming. Since 2007, you can earn non-super income in addition to your superannuation income and still pay little or no tax because your superannuation benefit isn't counted as income for income tax purposes and, also, isn't included in your tax return. For example, you can, say, receive $100,000 income from your super fund, and $20,542 (for the 2014–15 year) from part-time work and pay no tax. If you're aged 65 or over, you can earn even more non-super income and pay no tax — see my SuperGuide website (www.superguide.com.au) for information about the income tax deal for older Australians.

If you plan to leave your super to your adult children when you die, your death benefit may be hit with tax — even though you would have received that benefit tax-free while you were alive. In Chapter 24, I explain how your super benefits may be taxed after you die.

Accessing super: Turning 55, or even 60, isn't enough

Although your preservation age is the age that you can access your super benefits, such access doesn't happen automatically. You must have at least reached your preservation age *and* you must have retired from the workforce.

Your preservation age can be as young as 55 years and as old as 60 years, depending on your date of birth (refer to Table 19-1 for your preservation age). Retirement from the workforce, for the purposes of accessing super, generally involves the trustee of a super fund being reasonably satisfied that the person retiring intends never again to be gainfully employed, either on a full-time or a part-time basis. Note that 'part-time' is defined as working up to 30 hours a week and a minimum of 10 hours a week.

If a person intends to work fewer than 10 hours a week, then that person is considered 'retired' for the purposes of accessing super benefits, provided the person ceases his current employment arrangement. In nearly all cases, the super fund will request that the retiring individual sign a declaration stating that he or she never intends to be gainfully employed for more than 10 hours per week. In the case of a SMSF, it's a prudent measure for the member (you) to sign a retirement declaration and give it to the SMSF trustee (you).

If you don't want to retire, you can also access your super benefits when you reach your preservation age by starting a transition-to-retirement pension (TRIP) — a super pension that you can start when you reach your preservation age (I explain TRIPs in more detail in Chapter 21).

Merely turning 65 is also considered a condition of release when accessing super benefits, which means you can continue working and withdraw super benefits. You can also access your super benefits in other specific circumstances. I explain the 14 main conditions of release for accessing super benefits on my SuperGuide website (www.superguide.com.au).

Chapter 20

Your Super and the Age Pension

*F*or many Australians the Age Pension is the pot of gold at the end of the retirement rainbow — the reward for paying taxes and being law-abiding members of the community. With around 80 per cent of retired, older Australians on a full or part Age Pension, the rainbow theory seems to ring true. However, according to the federal government, the Age Pension is designed to provide a modest retirement for those people who are unable to fully support themselves. Do you notice a glaring gap in expectations? Life on the Age Pension probably sits somewhere between the popular pot-of-gold view and the government's 'safety net' policy position.

Can Australia afford to continue paying a full Age Pension of around $22,200 a year for a single person or about $33,500 for a couple (applicable to March 2015) to nearly half of the senior population, and a part Age Pension to another third of senior Australians when everyone is living longer and there are less taxpayers to foot the bill?

Apparently so. The federal government is anticipating that the number of Australians receiving a full Age Pension is set to eventually fall to about a third of the eligible population within the next 35 years, while Australians receiving a part Age Pension will increase to around half of the eligible population.

In this chapter, I highlight the main ways your superannuation and the Age Pension work together. I explain how the Age Pension operates, including when you're eligible for the Age Pension and what benefits you can expect.

If you're retiring within the next five to ten years, the Age Pension is probably going to look fairly similar to how it looks today, but don't bet your retirement savings on my prediction. If you're in your 30s or 40s now, you're likely to have accumulated a healthy super benefit by the time you retire. You can probably expect a part Pension or no Age Pension depending on how many assets you have when you retire, although if you were born after 1965, you can't claim the Age Pension until the age of 70 (subject to legislation).

Without sufficient planning, life can be harsh in retirement, although anyone with enough super savings to justify a SMSF can expect a not-so-harsh retirement lifestyle (for info on the cost of a modest or comfortable lifestyle, refer to Chapter 3). If you have a superannuation benefit, and expect to claim the Age Pension, then getting on top of the Age Pension and other social security rules (and tax rules) and seeking advice regarding the best scenario for you and your partner, is the only way to go. Do some research (for resources, see Appendix B at the end of the book), or seek advice (refer to Chapter 5) regarding the best scenario for you and, if applicable, your partner.

How Does Your Super Affect Age Pension Entitlements?

Depending on the amount of super that you have and other assets that you own, your super can affect how much Age Pension you receive in the following ways:

- ✔ **Your super has no effect:** If the value of your assets (including super) and the level of your income are under the minimum threshold for the Age Pension assets test and income test, your super has no effect on the amount of Age Pension that you receive — you're entitled to the full Age Pension. I explain what these tests are and how they work in the section 'Passing Your Age Pension Exams', later in this chapter.

- ✔ **Your super supplements the Age Pension:** Your superannuation may provide you with a small income in addition to you receiving a substantial part Age Pension or full Age Pension. Starting a super pension (for the details, see Chapter 21) with your super benefit rather than taking a lump sum may increase the possibility of you receiving a full Age Pension or a larger part Age Pension, depending on your other assets and income. I explain the effect of your super pension on your Age Pension entitlement later in this chapter, in 'Deeming Income from Super Pensions and Other Financial Investments'.

✔ **The Age Pension supplements your super benefit:** If you have substantial superannuation benefits (up to around $770,000 for a single person, and up to around $1.1 million for a home-owning couple), you may be able to access a part Pension or at least be entitled to a Pensioner Concession Card. A *Pensioner Concession Card* entitles Age Pensioners and other social security recipients to prescriptions at a lower cost, and discounts on public transport, rates and utility bills.

✔ **You receive no Age Pension because your super and other assets exceed the income and assets thresholds:** If you fall into this category, you're either financially comfortable or very unlucky. For some individuals, a lifestyle asset such as holiday home can knock them out of Age Pension eligibility because of the effects of the assets test (I explain the assets test in 'Passing Your Age Pension Exams' later in this chapter).

If you aren't eligible for the Age Pension, you may be entitled to the *Commonwealth Seniors Health Card* (CSHC). The CSHC is a special card that gives you cheaper prescriptions and medical services when your income is below a certain threshold: Under $51,500 a year for a single person and under $82,400 for a couple. The income thresholds are applicable until 19 September 2015, and then indexed annually, each September. I explain the rules applicable for the CSHC, and the thresholds for later years, on my consumer website, SuperGuide (www.superguide.com.au).

Claiming the Age Pension

The Age Pension is a fortnightly income payment potentially payable for life when you qualify, and you satisfy certain tests on an ongoing basis. Claiming the Age Pension is basically a four-stage process. You must

✔ **Meet residency requirements:** You must be an Australian resident for at least 10 years or be a refugee or former refugee. You must also be an Australian resident on the day you apply for the Age Pension, and be in Australia when you submit your application. If you were born overseas, and your country of birth has an International Social Security Agreement (ISSA) with Australia, you may have more chance of becoming eligible for the Australian Age Pension. You may also be eligible for a pension from your country of origin or the country where you worked, if you have worked overseas. For more information about overseas pensions, phone Centrelink's International Services Infoline on 13 16 73.

✔ **Reach Age Pension age:** Age Pension Age is between the age of 65 and 70 (subject to legislation), depending on your date of birth. I explain the age rules for the Age Pension in the next section.

✔ **Satisfy the assets test and the income test**: Anyone applying for the Age Pension is subject to means testing under an income test and an assets test. A means test is an assessment of any resources you may have available to support you (see the section 'Passing Your Age Pension Exams', later in this chapter).

✔ **Receive the lowest amount**: Your Age Pension entitlement is based on the means test calculation that gives you the lowest Age pension amount. For example, if the Age Pension payable according to the assets test is lower than the amount payable under the income test, your Age Pension entitlement is based on the calculation under the assets test.

Reaching Age Pension age

Your Age Pension age is the age that you become eligible to claim the Age Pension, subject to meeting the assets and income tests. Your Age Pension age depends on your date of birth and is gradually increasing from the age of 65 to age 70 (subject to legislation).

As shown in Table 20-1, you can claim the Age Pension when you reach the age of 65 if you were born before July 1952. If you were born after June 1952, then your Age Pension age is older than 65 years. For anyone born after December 1965, your Age Pension age is 70 years (subject to legislation). For anyone born before January 1966 and after June 1952, your Age Pension is older than 65 years, but younger than 70 years (subject to legislation).

At the time of writing, the gradual increase in Age Pension age to 70 years was not yet law. If the proposed increase does not become law, then the maximum Age Pension age will be 67 years for those born after December 1956. I explain the Age Pension age in more detail, including confirmation or otherwise of the proposed increase in Age Pension age to 70 years, on my consumer website, SuperGuide (www.superguide.com.au).

Table 20-1	Working Out Your Age Pension Age	
Date of Birth	*Age Pension Age (Years)*	*Effective From*
Before 1 July 1952	65	
From 1 July 1952 to 31 December 1953	65.5	1 July 2017
From 1 January 1954 to 30 June 1955	66	1 July 2019

Date of Birth	Age Pension Age (Years)	Effective From
From 1 July 1955 to 31 December 1956	66.5	1 July 2021
From 1 January 1957 to 30 June 1958	67	1 July 2023
From 1 July 1958 to 31 December 1959	67.5	1 July 2025
From 1 January 1960 to 30 June 1961	68	1 July 2027
From 1 July 1961 to 31 December 1962	68.5	1 July 2029
From 1 January 1963 to 30 June 1964	69	1 July 2031
From 1 July 1964 to 31 December 1965	69.5	1 July 2033
On or after 1 January 1966	70	1 July 2035

Source: Adapted from Social Security and Other Legislation Amendment (2014 Budget Measures No 2) Bill 2014. At the time of writing, increasing the Age Pension age to 70 years was not yet law. Used with permission from the Australian Government Department of Human Services. The information published in this table is correct as of November 2014. Please visit humanservices.gov.au *for the most up-to-date information.*

Receiving an indexed pension for life

The federal government pays a full or part Age Pension to around 80 per cent of retired Australians, but this income support isn't intended to provide a replacement income for all of those years of hard work. Instead, the Age Pension is available to give you a modest retirement, according to the federal government.

A 'basic retirement' is probably a more accurate term for living solely on the Age Pension, although some people manage to live happily on the Age Pension only. (In Chapter 3, I compare the cost of different lifestyles when I talk about working out how much super is enough.)

So, how much money do you need to live a 'basic' retirement? According to the government, you need 27.7 per cent of Male Total Average Weekly Earnings. Until June 2017, to ensure the Age Pension reflects this amount over time, the Age Pension is adjusted twice yearly in line with increases in the Consumer Price Index, or adjusted to reflect growth in the Pensioner and Beneficiary Living Cost Index, whichever of the two indices record the highest growth. The *Consumer Price Index (CPI)* measures quarterly changes in prices, while the *Pensioner and Beneficiary Living Cost Index (PBLCI)* is designed to reflect actual living cost changes, and is used to index base pension rates when the living cost index is higher than CPI. *Note:* If average wages grow at a faster rate than CPI or PBLCI, then the pension is indexed against the increase in average wages for males.

From July 2017, the Age Pension will be indexed in line with CPI only, taking effect from the September 2017 Age Pension rate adjustment (subject to legislation).

Table 20-2 lists the Age Pension amounts payable until 19 March 2015, which are then indexed again on 20 March 2015 and then September 2015 and so on.

If only one member of a couple is eligible for the Age Pension, don't expect to receive the single Age Pension rate. You receive half the couple rate (see the 'Couple (Each)' column in Table 20-2) and half the supplements. The one exception is when a couple is separated due to illness. You may then each be entitled to the single Age Pension rate, and subject to more generous means-testing when working out your entitlements. I explain the means-testing rules in 'Passing Your Age Pension Exams' later in this chapter.

Table 20-2	Age Pension Amounts per Fortnight for Singles and Couples (Until March 2015)		
	Single	*Couple (Each)*	*Couple (Combined)*
Base	$776.70	$585.50	$1171.00
Supplement	$63.50	$47.90	$95.80
Energy Supplement	$14.10	$10.60	$21.20
Total	**$854.30**	**$644.00**	**$1288.00**
Estimated Annual Age Pension Income			
Annualised	**$22,211.80**	**$16,744**	**$33,488**

Source: Compiled from information (as at 20 September 2014 and applicable until 19 March 2015) on the Centrelink section of the Department of Human Services website (www.humanservices.gov.au). Note: The Age Pension is indexed in March and September each year in line with increases in average wages or the cost of living or increases in CPI. Used with permission from the Australian Government Department of Human Services. The information published in this table is correct as of November 2014. Please visit humanservices.gov.au for the most up-to-date information.

Going to war over the DVA pension

The *Age Service Pension* is similar to the Age Pension but is payable to veterans five years earlier than the Age Pension by the Department of Veterans' Affairs (DVA). The earlier payment age recognises that the stresses of war may result in premature ageing. An invalidity Service Pension is also available for veterans.

If you're a veteran who served in Australian Defence Force operations and incurred danger from hostile forces, you may be able to claim an Age Service Pension provided you have reached Service Pension age. The current Service Pension age is 60, although this age is expected to increase in line with the increase in the general Age Pension age (refer to 'Reaching Age Pension age' earlier in this chapter).

The Age Service Pension can also be paid to eligible partners, widows and widowers, and is subject to income and assets tests in a similar way to the Age pension payable by Centrelink.

Note: You're entitled to a special health card if you receive a Service Pension, which may be a Gold, White or Orange DVA card. All of these cards entitle you to cheaper prescriptions, but the White (service-related conditions) and Gold (all conditions) cover your healthcare costs.

Passing Your Age Pension Exams

Make the most of your holiday home while you're working because you may have to sell your beach shack if you're intent on claiming the Age Pension. Anyone applying for the Age Pension is subject to *means testing*, which is an assessment of how wealthy you are and whether you already have enough money and resources to look after yourself.

You must satisfy both an income test and an assets test to become an Age Pensioner. Means testing can be mean if you want the full Age Pension, but not so bad when you're combining your existing assets or income with a top-up from the Age Pension treasure chest.

Many Australians who believe they own too many assets to be eligible for a part Age Pension could receive a pleasant surprise when they do the calculations. I explain the Age Pension assets test later in this section.

If you pass the assets test but fail the income test, or fail the assets test and pass the income test, you can't receive the Age Pension. If you satisfy both tests, then you rely on the test that gives the lower rate of Age Pension.

I focus on the Age Pension rules and how your SMSF pension interacts with the Age Pension in this chapter. For more information on the Age Pension and the latest rates beyond March 2015, check out the Centrelink section of the Department of Human Services website (www.humanservices.gov.au) or my free website, SuperGuide (www.superguide.com.au).

Taking the assets test

According to Centrelink, an *asset for the purposes of the Age Pension assets test* 'is any property or item of value you (or your partner) own or have an interest in, including those held outside Australia'.

Table 20-3 sets out the assets thresholds that you must stay within to receive a full or part Age Pension. Your home isn't counted when working out the value of your assets, but most other assets, such as your super pension, real estate, shares, term deposits, cars and home contents do count when determining if you're eligible for the Age Pension. Shares and term deposits are classified as financial assets and are assumed to earn a certain rate of income for the purposes of the income test. Since 1 January 2015, new super pensions (and existing super pensions of new Age Pensioners) are also considered financial assets, and a certain rate of income is assumed for super pensions when assessing your eligibility for the Age Pension (see the section, 'Deeming Income from Super Pensions and Other Financial Investments', later in the chapter).

If you own assets worth more than the amounts listed in the 'Full Age Pension' columns of Table 20-3, then your Age Pension entitlements (if any) are reduced by $1.50 per fortnight (or $39 a year) for every $1,000 of assets above the value listed under the 'Full Age Pension' columns.

The Age Pension assets test thresholds for the full Age Pension are indexed on 1 July of each year, while the assets test thresholds for a part Age Pension are adjusted in March, July and September of each year. The full Age Pension assets test thresholds listed in Table 20-3 apply until 30 June 2015, and the part Age Pension upper assets test thresholds in Table 20-3 apply until 19 March 2015. From 1 July 2017, the Age Pension assets test thresholds will be frozen for three years, subject to legislation.

Table 20-3	Size of Your Age Pension Depends on Assets (for 2014–15 Year)			
	Full Age Pension*		Part Age Pension**	
	Home Owner	Not Home Owner	Home Owner	Not Home Owner
Single	Up to $202,000	Up to $348,500	Up to $771,750	Up to $918,250
Couple (combined)	Up to $286,500	Up to $433,000	Up to $1,145,500	Up to $1,292,000
Illness-separated couple (combined)	Up to $286,500	Up to $433,000	Up to $1,426,000	Up to $1,572,500
One partner eligible (combined)	Up to $286,500	Up to $433,000	Up to $1,145,500	Up to $1,292,000

Source: Compiled from information about asset test thresholds for full Age Pension (for 2014–15 year, applicable until 30 June 2015) and part Age Pension (as at 20 September 2014 and applicable until 19 March 2015) on Centrelink section of Department of Human services website (www.humanservices.gov.au). Used with permission from the Australian Government Department of Human Services. The information published in this table is correct as of November 2014. Please visit humanservices.gov.au for the most up-to-date information.

* Asset test thresholds for full Age Pension are adjusted on 1 July each year.

** Assets test thresholds for part Age Pension adjusted in March, July and September.

From 1 July 2017, the thresholds for full and part Age Pension will be frozen for three years, subject to legislation.

Note: Assets over the amounts listed in the 'Full Age Pension' columns reduce the rate of pension you receive by $1.50 per fortnight for every $1,000 above the threshold.

Taking the income test

Your income is taken into account when working out whether you're entitled to the Age Pension. Table 20-4 sets out the income thresholds that you must stay within to receive a full or part Age Pension.

If you earn income worth more than the amounts listed in the 'Full Age Pension' columns of Table 20-4, then your Age Pension entitlements (if any) are reduced by $0.50 per fortnight for every $1.00 of assets above the value listed under the 'Full Age Pension' 'per fortnight' column. The full Age Pension income test thresholds listed in Table 20-4 apply until 30 June 2015, and the part Age Pension upper income test thresholds in Table 20-4 apply until 19 March 2015.

If you have financial investments, such as your super pension, shares or term deposits, you count your 'deemed income' for social security purposes rather than your actual income. To understand deemed income and how it works in practice, including the deeming rules, check out the next section 'Deeming Income from Super Pensions and Other Financial Investments'

Table 20-4	Size of Your Age Pension Depends on Income (for 2014–15 Year)			
	Full Age Pension*		Part Age Pension**	
	Per Fortnight	Annualised Income (Approx)	Per Fortnight	Annualised Income (Approx)
Single	Up to $160	Up to $4,160	Up to $1868.60	Up to $48,584
Couple (combined)	Up to $284	Up to $7,384	Up to $2,860.00	Up to $74,360
Illness-separated couple (combined)	Up to $284	Up to $7,384	Up to $3,701.20	Up to $96,231
One partner eligible (combined)	Up to $284	Up to $7,384	Up to $2,860.00	Up to $74,360

Source: Compiled from information about income test thresholds for full Age Pension (for 2014–15 year) and part Age Pension (as at 20 September 2014 until 19 March 2015) on Centrelink section of Department of Human Services website (www.humanservices.gov.au). Used with permission from the Australian Government Department of Human Services. The information published in this table is correct as of November 2014. Please visit humanservices.gov.au for the most up-to-date information.
* Income test thresholds for full Age Pension are adjusted on 1 July each year.
** Income test thresholds for part Age Pension are adjusted in March, July and September of each year. From 1 July 2017, the thresholds for full and part Age Pension will be frozen for three years, subject to legislation.
Note: If you have been receiving the Age Pension since before September 2009, you may be subject to slightly different Age Pension test thresholds. For more information, see the Centrelink section of the DHS website (www.humanservices.gov.au).

Deeming Income from Super Pensions and Other Financial Investments

Income from financial investments is assessed differently under the Age Pension income test, compared with income from other assets. If you have financial investments, such as your super pension (although not for all Age Pensioners), or personally held shares or personally held term deposits, you count your deemed income rather than your actual income. *Deemed income* is when you assume a rate of return even when that rate is not what you actually earn on your investment.

Financial investments for the purposes of the Age Pension income test include:

- ✔ Super pensions commenced on or after 1 January 2015 or existing super pensions, held by Age Pensioners who became eligible for the Age Pension on or after 1 January 2015 (I explain how this works later in this section)

- ✔ Cash, or accounts, held with banks, building societies or credit unions

- ✔ Term deposits

- ✔ Listed shares and other listed investments

- ✔ Bonds and debentures

- ✔ Shares in unlisted public companies

- ✔ Interests in managed funds, or similar investments

- ✔ Bullion, such as gold, silver and platinum bullion

The two deeming interest rates used to assess your financial investment income are reviewed periodically, while the income thresholds used to determine which deeming rate applies to your financial investments are adjusted annually, on 1 July. At the time of writing, you must use the following thresholds and deeming rates:

- ✔ 2 per cent for the first $48,000 of a single person's financial investments, and for the first $79,600 of a couple's financial investments (for the 2014–15 year).

- ✔ 3.5 per cent for the remaining balance of financial investments for a single person or a couple.

From September 2017, the federal government intends to reset the deeming thresholds, which will mean more of your financial assets are deemed to earn income at the higher rate of 3.5 per cent (or whatever deeming rate is applicable in September 2017). On 20 September 2017, the federal government will reset the deeming thresholds to $30,000 for a single person, and $50,000 for a couple (subject to legislation).

Since 1 January 2015, new SMSF pensions and other super pensions started on or after 1 January 2015 are subject to the deeming rules when working out what income counts towards the Age Pension income test. Existing super pensions, started before 1 January 2015, will also be subject to the deeming rules, but only when the individual is applying for the Age Pension on or after January 2015. If an individual was receiving the Age Pension before 1 January 2015, and was also receiving payments from a super pension before that date, then the deeming rules do not apply to the super pension asset; rather, the old income test rules apply.

Existing Age Pensioners as at 1 January 2015, who were receiving existing superannuation pensions as at 1 January 2015, are subject to the old rules for assessing super pensions against the Age Pension income test. If your super pension continues to be subject to the old income test rules, then your superannuation pensions are counted against the Age Pension income test by firstly calculating an amount that recognises the return of capital that forms part of every super pension payment. This special amount is deducted from your actual pension income to determine the amount of income to count towards the Age Pension income test. ***Note:*** The account balance of your SMSF pension is also counted against the assets test, unless you have one of the older-style pensions that are no longer available to new retirees (see Chapter 21 for more information on this special type of pension). I provide more details on the treatment of super pensions under the old and new rules applicable for the Age Pension income test on my website, SuperGuide (www.superguide.com.au). You can also get more information about the Age Pension generally from the Centrelink section of the DHS website (www.humanservices.gov.au).

Chapter 21

Running a DIY Super Pension

*R*unning a SMSF in retirement phase is often when the fun begins for SMSF trustees/members. You usually have more time to spend on running your fund (if that's your inclination), and you start reaping the rewards of your many years of saving and investing. Ideally, your super account should provide the income necessary to live the retirement lifestyle you choose.

The primary purpose of having a superannuation account is to finance your retirement lifestyle in a tax-effective way. If not for the tax concessions associated with super (refer to Chapter 13), Australians would simply save and invest outside the superannuation structure. The tax concessions attached to super can continue into your retirement, which is a major incentive for many Australians to take an income stream (pension) from their superannuation account.

In this chapter, I guide you through super pension land. I briefly explore the implications of leaving your SMSF when you retire rather than starting a SMSF pension, then I take you through the two phases of a SMSF, and the two types of SMSF pensions. I also explain the main steps involved when starting a SMSF pension, including the tricky aspects of calculating the taxable and tax-free components of the pension.

Facing the DIY Fork in the Road

As a prospective retiree, you have three main choices when you start drawing cash from your superannuation benefit. You can take

✔ A lump sum

✔ An income stream (that is, a pension — a series of regular payments over time)

✔ A combination of both lump sum and pension

I explain the implications of these three choices in Chapter 19.

If you retain your savings in the super system by starting a pension, then you must decide whether you plan to

✔ Run the pension from your SMSF

✔ Withdraw your super money from your SMSF and purchase a pension from another super fund or financial organisation

Retiring using your SMSF

Most individuals who choose to run a SMSF during their working life intend also to run the SMSF during retirement. For some individuals, however, running a SMSF pension may not turn out to be the best option. For example, if you're intending to spend lengthy periods overseas (for info about managing a SMSF while outside Australia, refer to Chapter 8), or if you or your partner have failing health, then running a pension within a SMSF may not be your most practical option.

For some Australians, using a SMSF structure can be helpful for the purposes of estate planning. I discuss estate planning and refer to the possibility of winding up your SMSF in Chapter 24.

Due to the size of many SMSF account balances, an individual who runs a SMSF is more likely than many other Australians to be a self-funded retiree. A *self-funded retiree* is an individual who doesn't receive any Age Pension payments. Even so, if you satisfy the eligibility tests for the Age Pension, you can receive an income stream from your SMSF and a part (or even full) Age Pension from the government. You can check out the Age Pension rules, and how the Age Pension interacts with your super benefits, in Chapter 20.

Cashing out and buying a commercial pension

If you cash out your SMSF account and purchase a pension from a financial organisation or large superannuation fund, you need to be aware that the sale of your SMSF assets can attract capital gains tax in the fund. If a SMSF member hasn't yet started a SMSF pension — that is, the member's account is still in accumulation phase — and the fund member chooses to transfer the account balance to another fund, then the capital gains on the sale of any assets are subject to earnings tax within the fund (refer to Chapters 13 and 18). I briefly explain your non-DIY pension options in 'Contemplating Your DIY Super Pension Options', later in the chapter.

If a SMSF member starts a SMSF pension, and *then* decides to transfer his account balance to a large super fund (refer to Chapter 2), or to a product offered by a financial organisation, no capital gains tax is payable on the profits from the sale of assets financing that SMSF pension while the account is in pension phase. Any earnings, including capital gains, on assets financing a pension are exempt from tax (refer to Chapters 13 and 18). You must, however, still meet the pension's payment rules for the year in which the transfer takes place (see the section 'Activating your account-based pension', later in the chapter).

Changing from Accumulation to Pension Phase

Your SMSF can have two phases — accumulation phase and pension phase — that can run concurrently or at different times.

When you make super contributions, and those contributions are recorded in your member account and then invested in assets, your member account is in accumulation phase. Your super account can be in accumulation phase even when you're not making super contributions. You can think of it as: When you're not taking a pension from a super account.

When you're drawing a pension from a member account then that account is in pension phase.

The key difference between accumulation phase and pension phase is the tax treatment of fund earnings. In pension phase, fund earnings on assets, including any capital gains that your fund receives on the sale of pension assets, are exempt from tax. In contrast, earnings on assets in accumulation phase are subject to 15 per cent earnings tax. If you choose not to draw a pension from your SMSF in retirement, then the 15 per cent earnings tax applies on your super account (see Chapters 13 and 18 for more detail on super earnings and tax).

Considering the many SMSF combinations

The simplest version of a SMSF is where one or more members are in accumulation phase and then, at a later date, all of the members retire at the same time, move into pension phase and start drawing pensions.

Your SMSF can, however, have fund members in both accumulation and pension phase concurrently. You may have one or more members in accumulation phase and one or more members in pension phase. You can even have every fund member in both phases. You can also have a fund member or fund members with multiple pension accounts (although a SMSF member can have just one SMSF accumulation account, unless she starts another SMSF). I explain the additional requirements when a SMSF is paying a pension and also accepting super contributions in Chapter 22.

Preparing your SMSF pension paperwork

Although starting a SMSF pension is a significant event for your fund and for the member involved (probably you), the paperwork necessary to convert an accumulation account to a pension account isn't too onerous. Recognising the change of interest from an accumulation account to a pension account usually requires an accounting and administration change (including preparing some documentation), rather than a change in assets.

You also must calculate the components of your SMSF pension when the pension commences. Super benefits can be made up of two components — 'tax-free' and 'taxable'. The tax-free component is always free of tax while the tax payable on the taxable component depends on the age of the SMSF member, and the size of the benefit (refer to Chapters 13 and 19 for the tax treatment of benefit payments from a super fund). I explain the calculation process in the section 'Calculating Your Pension Components', later in the chapter.

Changing from accumulation phase to pension phase can be a good time to review your SMSF's asset allocation (for more information on SMSF investment strategies, refer to Chapter 15): For example, a pension phase account may need a greater level of cash to cover pension payments each year. The SMSF trustees may even decide to invest in more income-producing assets, and sell other assets. *Note*: Fund earnings, including capital gains, in pension phase are exempt from tax, while earnings (including capital gains) in accumulation phase are taxed (refer to Chapters 13 and 18).

Contemplating Your DIY Super Pension Options

If you plan to start a pension within your SMSF, you can choose from only one of the following two types of pensions:

- ✔ **Account-based pension:** An *account-based pension* is a flexible income stream that gives you unlimited access to your capital but no guarantees on how long your income lasts. You must withdraw a minimum pension payment each year.

- ✔ **Transition-to-retirement pension (TRIP):** A TRIP is a superannuation pension that you start before you retire and before you reach age 65, subject to special conditions. A TRIP operates in a similar way to an account-based pension but with two extra features — the pension is non-commutable (that is, the preserved components of the pension can't be converted into a lump sum payment), and you can withdraw a maximum of 10 per cent of your account balance each year. You can take a TRIP from when you reach your preservation age (the age of 55 for those born before July 1960 — refer to Chapter 19), without retiring from the workforce.

I explain how these two types of pensions work later in this section. (If you started your SMSF pension before September 2007, then you may be receiving a different type of pension that's no longer available to new SMSF retirees — see the sidebar 'If you started your SMSF pension before 20 September 2007. . .' later in this chapter.)

Alternatively, if you opt to transfer your SMSF monies to a pension provider, such as a large superannuation fund or financial organisation, you can generally purchase one of the following types of income streams:

- ✔ *Account-based pension/income stream* — a financial organisations usually market account-based income streams using the name 'allocated pensions'. You can also start an account-based pension in a SMSF.

✔ *Lifetime pension/income stream* — a guaranteed income stream for your lifetime and, maybe, your spouse's lifetime too. This type of income stream may suit those who want the certainty of a fixed income because the amount is defined in advance.

✔ *Term-certain pension/income stream* — a guaranteed income stream for a set period of time; for example, your life expectancy (the statistically based average of the number of years that you're expected to live, determined from the date you purchase your income stream). You can choose to receive back part of your investment at the end of the period. This return of capital is known as your *residual capital value*.

✔ *Transition-to-retirement pension or income stream (TRIP)* — an income stream that's account-based, but it must not permit preserved components to be taken as a lump sum. You can also start one of these types of pensions in a SMSF.

Activating your account-based pension

An account-based pension is basically an investment account that you can access regularly. Your account balance increases (or decreases) in line with your account's investment earnings (or losses), and decreases as you draw down regular income payments, and lump sums when necessary.

An account-based pension, like other income streams, can give you the peace of mind of a regular income with full access to your super money whenever you need it. Your account-based pension lasts as long as you have money in your SMSF pension account.

The main restriction when operating an account-based pension is that you must withdraw a minimum amount from the pension each year; although, you're permitted to take out as much money as you like. The minimum amount each year is based on your age as at 1 July. You have total flexibility in when you receive this cash — weekly, fortnightly, monthly, quarterly, annually.

You work out the minimum pension amount on 1 July each year using a percentage linked to your age and your pension's account balance:

Minimum payment = account balance × percentage factor

Table 21-1 lists the minimum percentage factors for account-based pensions for each age group, using a $500,000 pension account balance as an example. If you retire at the age of 65 on 1 July, your minimum annual pension payment for the first year is 5 per cent of the account balance of your account-based pension as at 1 July. If you're 64 or under, your minimum payment is 4 per cent. For example, if you're 60 and your account balance is $500,000, your minimum withdrawal amount for the year is $20,000 (4 per cent of the account balance).

Table 21-1	Account-Based Pension Payment Rules	
	Minimum Percentage Factor	*Minimum Pension Payment for $500,000 Account Balance*
Age of Beneficiary	*% of Account Balance*	
Under 65	4	$20,000
65 to 74	5	$25,000
75 to 79	6	$30,000
80 to 84	7	$35,000
85 to 89	9	$45,000
90 to 94	11	$55,000
95+	14	$70,000

Source: Adapted from Schedule 7, Superannuation Industry (Supervision) Regulations 1994, although the example and minimum pension payment amounts are calculated by the author, Trish Power.

Special payment rules applied for the 2008–09, 2009–10, 2010–11, 2011–12 and 2012–13 years (see the sidebar 'Temporary payment cuts for tough times').

The minimum payment is rounded to the nearest $10. If you start an account-based pension part-way through the year, then the minimum pension payment is pro-rated from commencement day. And, if you start an account-based pension on or after 1 June, then no minimum pension payment is required for that first financial year ending 30 June.

Taking a TRIP

By starting a transition-to-retirement pension (TRIP) within your SMSF, you can access your superannuation benefit without retiring, and enjoy the tax advantages associated with income streams, such as:

- ✔ Tax-exempt earnings on SMSF assets financing the TRIP.

- ✔ A 15 per cent tax offset on the taxable component of your pension income if you're under the age of 60, or tax-free income from your pension payments if aged 60 years or over. (I discuss the tax treatment of retirement benefits in the section 'Calculating Your Pension Components', later in this chapter, and in Chapters 13 and 19.)

Temporary payment cuts for tough times

Due to the market upheaval experienced during 2008 and 2009, and the relatively flat (but volatile) markets of 2010 and 2011, the federal government gave retirees a pension payment break for a few years. For the 2008–09, 2009–10 and 2010–11 years, individuals receiving certain superannuation pensions were permitted to halve the minimum pension payments withdrawn from their pension accounts.

For example, John was 75 and had $500,000 in his SMSF pension account on 1 July 2010. If you're aged 75 to 79, the usual minimum percentage factor is 6 per cent. For the 2010–11 year (and for the 2008–09 and 2009–10 years), the minimum factor was halved to 3 per cent, which meant John had to withdraw only $15,000 as pension payments for that year, rather than $30,000.

For the 2011–12 and 2012–13 years, minimum pension payments were reduced by 25 per cent for all ages. If you were aged 65 to 74 during that year, ordinarily the minimum pension payment for an account-based pension is 5 per cent of your pension's account balance. For the 2011–12 and 2012–13 years, the minimum payment was 3.75 per cent of your account balance.

For example, Betty is 68 and has $500,000 in her SMSF pension account. Her minimum pension payment usually would be $25,000, but under the temporary relief for the 2012–13 year, her minimum payment was $18,750.

The government made these decisions because it recognised that the market downturn had a negative effect on the pension account balances of retirees. Due to the massive fall in the value of account balances, some retirees were forced to sell assets in a depressed market to fulfil the minimum pension payment requirements.

Minimum pension payment factors returned to normal from the 2013–14 year.

I often describe the TRIP as the 'having your cake and eating it too' pension option. Introduced by the federal government from July 2005 to help those who want to gradually transition out of the workforce via part-time work before eventually retiring, the popularity of TRIPs has really taken off since the new regime of tax-free super for over-60s began from 1 July 2007.

A TRIP works the following way: You can start a pension while you continue working, and work can be part-time, full-time or even casual work. Generally, you must be at least 55 years of age (and under 65); although the pension that you use as a TRIP can continue beyond the age of 65. A transition-to-retirement pension is 'transitional' because the rules associated with a TRIP last for a maximum of ten years (55 to 64 years). When you turn 65 (or retire at an earlier age), your super benefits are no longer preserved, which means the TRIP rules restricting commutation are generally no longer relevant. Once you confirm your retirement (or turning 65), your income stream then mirrors a regular income stream such as an account-based pension.

If you choose to start a TRIP within your SMSF, be mindful that you must meet at least three conditions:

- ✔ **You must have reached your preservation age. Anyone born before 1 July 1960 has a preservation age of 55.** I discuss the preservation rules, including working out your preservation age, in Chapter 19.

- ✔ **You can withdraw no more than 10 per cent of your account balance each year.** If your TRIP started before July 2007, then the maximum amount is roughly 10 per cent.

- ✔ **You can't convert your TRIP to a lump sum (that is, a TRIP is a non-commutable pension), until you satisfy a condition of release.** Your TRIP is an account-based pension, which means you can commute your TRIP into a lump sum when you retire, or turn 65, or satisfy some other condition of release (refer to Chapter 19 for the rules about accessing super benefits).

A popular strategy for a growing number of SMSF members is taking a TRIP from your SMSF, while also making concessional (before-tax) contributions. You may be able to reduce the amount of tax you pay while boosting your super benefit. One of the more popular TRIP strategies is to salary sacrifice personal income into your super fund, and replace that income with tax-free (if over 60) or concessionally taxed (if under 60) pension payments. For more information on the implications of making contributions while taking a pension from your SMSF, see Chapter 22.

Reminiscing about complying income streams

If you started a SMSF pension before 20 September 2007, you may have chosen to purchase a complying income stream. A *complying income stream* is a special type of pension or annuity that ordinarily takes the form of a lifetime or life expectancy income stream, or a term allocated pension (also known as a market-linked income stream). Generally, a complying income stream can't be converted into a lump sum payment at any stage, and you must receive income at least once a year. I explain the pre-September 2007 pension options for SMSFs in the sidebar 'If you retired before 20 September 2007. . .'.

If you retired before 20 September 2007 . . .

If you started your SMSF pension before 20 September 2007, you may be receiving one of the following pensions (which are no longer available to future retirees, apart from the transition-to-retirement pension) from your SMSF:

✔ **Allocated pension:** An *allocated pension* is similar to the account-based pension, except that with an allocated pension, you're also subject to a maximum annual payment. The allocated pension was the most popular choice for Australian retirees before the introduction of the account-based pension. If you're running an allocated pension, and you want to remove the upper cap on pension payments, you can move to the account-based pension by organising for your SMSF to formally adopt the payment rules of an account-based pension — if you haven't done so already.

✔ **Market-linked pension:** A *market-linked pension* (also called a *growth pension* or a *term-allocated pension*) is a flexible income stream with a fixed term based on your average life expectancy (or life expectancy as if you were five years younger), or a period of no greater than the number of years until you turn 100 years of age. This type of income stream was only available from 20 September 2004 until 19 September 2007, and also qualifies as a complying income stream. A complying income stream is a special type of pension or annuity that continues to provide recipients with greater social security benefits (refer to the section 'Reminiscing about complying income streams' in this chapter).

✔ **Defined benefit pension:** A *defined benefit pension* is a lifetime or life expectancy pension payable from a SMSF. This type of income stream also qualifies as a complying income stream (refer to 'Reminiscing about complying income streams' in this chapter). Since 1 January 2006, new defined benefit pensions have not been permitted in SMSFs.

✔ **Transition-to-retirement pension or income stream (TRIP):** An income stream that can be any of the income streams previously listed, but has limits on converting preserved components to lump sums. An allocated pension TRIP, however, can be commuted when a condition of release occurs. Since 20 September 2007, a new TRIP started in a SMSF can only be an account-based pension.

You can't convert an existing SMSF complying income stream (such as a term-allocated pension or a non-commutable lifetime pension) into an account-based pension.

What's the big deal about complying income streams? Well, if you chose a complying income stream, the following may apply:

✔ **100 per cent assets-test exempt:** You have access, or greater access, to the Age Pension; complying income streams purchased before 20 September 2004 are 100 per cent exempt from the Age Pension assets test.

✔ **50 per cent assets-test exempt:** Any complying income stream purchased on or after 20 September 2004, but before 20 September 2007, is 50 per cent Age Pension assets-test exempt.

You can find out more about the Age Pension assets test in Chapter 20. For more info about the Age Pension implications when receiving an Age Pension assets-test exempt income stream from your SMSF, check out the 'income streams' page of the Centrelink section of the Department of Human Services website.

Starting Your SMSF Pension — One Step at a Time

When starting an account-based pension (or an account-based TRIP) within your SMSF, like any major financial decision relating to your SMSF, you must complete some important procedures.

Assuming the SMSF member is legally permitted to withdraw SMSF super benefits (for these rules, refer to Chapter 19), the main steps involved in starting a SMSF pension are as follows:

1. **Check your fund's trust deed to ensure the deed permits an account-based pension or account-based TRIP.**

   If not, the fund's deed may need to be updated (refer to Chapter 7). Updating your trust deed is a good idea anyway if you've been running your SMSF for a long time, and you haven't updated your fund's deed since the introduction of account-based pensions and tax-free super in July 2007.

2. **Ensure the SMSF member (you or another member) requests in writing that she would like to begin drawing an account-based pension.**

   The member must also specify what level of her benefits she wants to use for the pension; for example, 100 per cent of the benefits held within the accumulation account.

3. **The trustees of the SMSF acknowledge in writing the request by the members and request that the members specify what size pension payment they require.**

4. **Hold a trustee meeting to acknowledge and consider the request, and prepare minutes.**

   The trustee meeting minutes should outline the member's eligibility for the pension, along with relevant details, including start date, level of benefits and timing of pension payments.

5. **Conduct a valuation of the fund/account balance up until the date of commencement of the account-based pension.**

   This calculation also helps determine the pension's annual minimum payment.

6. **Calculate the proportion of tax-free and taxable component immediately prior to the commencement of a pension.**

   I explain this step in the next section, 'Calculating Your Pension Components'.

7. **Hold a trustee meeting to acknowledge the implementation of the account-based pension and produce minutes as a record of this decision.**

8. **Produce a pension agreement between member and trustees, which includes an account-based pension calculation sheet.**

   The pension calculation sheet forms part of the agreement and outlines the level of benefit allowed for the fund member, and the timing of any payments.

9. **Consider reviewing reversionary beneficiaries, binding death benefit nominations or equivalent, and life insurance requirements.**

   I explain these concepts in Chapter 24.

10. **Review the fund's investment strategy to ensure it remains suitable for an account in pension phase.**

    The benefits of holding greater levels of cash to ensure cashflow and protect capital often become of greater importance when a SMSF member is in pension phase. For info on reviewing your SMSF's investment strategy, refer to Chapter 15.

11. **Issue a Product Disclosure Statement that explains the pension to the member.**

    For the details required in a Product Disclosure Statement, refer to Chapter 7.

12. **Ensure your SMSF's software (if doing your own administration) reflects the commencement of the pension and tax-exempt earnings.**

    I cover managing your fund's administration in Chapter 10.

13. **Register the fund for Pay-As-You-Go (PAYG) withholding tax, if the member receiving the pension is under the age of 60.**

    The rate of tax that you need to withhold is contained in the ATO document *Schedule 13 — Tax table for superannuation income streams*.

14. **Issue the fund member with the ATO form** *PAYG payment summary — superannuation income stream* **(NAT 70897) and send a copy to the ATO.**

    This form must be issued to the fund member by 14 July following the end of the financial year in which the pension payments were made, if you have withheld tax from a pension payment. You must also send the 'ATO copy' to the ATO by 14 August following the end of the financial year.

Calculating Your Pension Components

You must calculate the components of any super benefit before paying out the benefit. The tax-free component is always free of tax, while the tax payable on the taxable component depends on the age of the SMSF member, and the size of the benefit (refer to Chapters 13 and 19 for specific tax rules).

The tax-free and taxable components of a SMSF lump sum payment are calculated just before a lump sum is paid, while the components of a SMSF pension are calculated at the time the income stream is created, and apply for the duration of the SMSF pension.

The timing of the calculation for pensions means that a higher tax-free component delivers a higher tax-free income from a SMSF pension in the following circumstances:

✔ **Fund member is under the age of 60:** A pension with no taxable component, paid to a member under the age of 60, means the total value of pension payments from such a pension are tax-free for the life of the pension, regardless of the growth in assets from fund earnings. For example, if you start a pension immediately after making 100 per cent non-concessional contributions (refer to Chapter 4) and your account contains only those contributions, the pension is made up of a 100 per cent tax-free component, and no taxable component.

✔ **When a member dies and leaves super benefits to non-dependants:** For example, if your super benefit has a 100 per cent tax-free component, and no taxable component, and the benefit is then paid to a non-dependant (under the tax laws) on your death, the original proportion — 100 per cent tax-free component — would also apply to the death benefit. (I explain death benefits in Chapter 24.)

Calculating the tax-free component

If you make non-concessional (after-tax) contributions to your super fund (refer to Chapter 4), you can expect to receive a tax-free component as part of your super benefit. The tax-free component is the total value of two segments:

✔ **Contributions segment:** A *contributions segment* ordinarily includes non-concessional contributions made from 1 July 2007, which also include spouse contributions and co-contributions. Any earnings on these contributions, however, form part of your taxable component.

✔ **Crystallised segment:** If you were a member of a superannuation fund on 30 June 2007, the fund was required to calculate a *crystallised segment* as at 30 June 2007. The calculation consolidated up to five pre-July 2007 benefit components. Most Australians have a crystallised segment that is made up only of pre-July 2007 after-tax contributions; although, if you have had super for a long time, then your crystallised segment also includes a pre-July 1983 component. The *pre-July 1983 component* represents your employment period before July 1983 when an employer provided super, even when that superannuation was provided long after you started with that employer.

You can find more information on pre-July 2007 benefit components by visiting the ATO website (`www.ato.gov.au`).

Calculating the taxable component

The taxable component of a SMSF benefit is calculated by subtracting the tax-free component from the total value of the super benefit. The annual earnings on your member account form part of your benefit's taxable component. Any concessional (before-tax) contributions (refer to Chapter 4) also form part of your benefit's taxable component.

If you were a member of a super fund before July 2007, what was previously known as the post-June 1983 component forms part of your taxable component. The *post-30 June 1983 component* represented your benefit for the period post-30 June 1983, but excluded your after-tax contributions.

Sliding along the proportioning rule

When an individual receives a super benefit payment (lump sum or pension), the benefit reflects the tax-free and taxable components in the same proportion as the components that make up the total account. Applying the components in this way is known as the *proportioning rule*. For example, if the super benefit is made up of a taxable component representing 75 per cent of the benefit, and a tax-free component representing 25 per cent of the benefit, then the pension payment is to be paid out reflecting the relevant proportions. This is important if your pension is taxable or a superannuation death benefit is paid to a non-dependant for taxation purposes. In Chapter 22, I explain what happens to your benefit components if you decide to stop your pension for a while, and then start a new super pension.

Chapter 22

Making Contributions while Taking a Pension

....

In This Chapter

▶ Grasping the contribution opportunities in retirement

▶ Running a SMSF in two phases

▶ Consolidating accounts means restarting pensions

▶ Taking a TRIP and salary sacrificing can mean more super and less tax

....

*T*he idea of working full-time one day, and retiring from the workforce the following day, is a popular concept but reflects a historic trend rather than the current reality. Although virtually all Australians do eventually retire fully from the workforce, the growing trend is for Australians to continue working in some form for the first five to ten years of their retirement.

The event or process known as 'retirement' takes many forms — the lines have become blurred between the younger retired and the older workforce, with many Australians choosing to downshift and work fewer hours as they transition into retirement. Other Australians exit the workforce permanently but then return to employment in a part-time capacity, or on an ad hoc basis to supplement their retirement savings or simply for the stimulation that paid work can offer.

Some retired Australians even choose to return to full-time work — a trend that has taken hold in recent years due to the poor-performing sharemarkets of 2008 and 2009 carving a large chunk out of the life savings of retirees. During those horror years, the collapses of some high-yield investment products, such as property trusts and mortgage funds (as outlined in Chapter 17), have also led some of our retired Aussies back to the world of the working.

In this chapter, I explain the superannuation rules that enable you to continue contributing post-retirement. I take you through the main issues you need to consider when running a SMSF pension while also contributing to your SMSF. I also explain the implications of stopping your SMSF pension and then restarting a SMSF pension, if you choose to consolidate your contributions and existing pension account into a new SMSF pension account. And for those looking for an outstanding tax break while enjoying the benefits from a SMSF pension without having to retire, I explain the popular strategy of taking a transition-to-retirement pension (TRIP) from your SMSF, while also making concessional (before-tax) contributions.

Retiree-Friendly Contribution Rules

Retiring early is a dream for many Australians but the word 'early' can mean different things for different people. The most common meaning of retiring early is stopping work before the age of 65. If you retire before the age of 65, you don't have access to the Age Pension, which means you must rely on your private savings, including superannuation benefits. *Note:* Anyone born after June 1952 has an Age Pension age older than 65 and, anyone born on or after 1 January 1966 has an Age Pension age of 70 (subject to legislation). Refer to Chapter 20 for more information on the Age Pension rules.

You can access your super benefits as young as the age of 55 (if you were born before June 1960 — refer to Chapter 19), provided you retire or start a transition-to-retirement pension (TRIP) or satisfy another condition of release. You can access your super savings even earlier if you satisfy certain conditions of release, such as becoming permanently incapacitated. The earlier you retire, of course, the bigger your nest egg needs to be to finance a longer life in retirement (for help estimating the length of your retirement, refer to Chapter 3).

Continuing to contribute to super during retirement may be triggered by necessity, to ensure your super and non-super savings last your lifetime and beyond, while for others who are more financially robust, the opportunity to make super contributions during retirement may simply be the most tax-effective way to accumulate wealth and to pass on this wealth to the next generation. (To find out what happens to your super upon your death, see Chapter 24).

I explain the contribution rules in detail in Chapter 4 but, briefly, your superannuation contribution options post-retirement are as follows:

- ✔ If you're under the age of 65, you can continue contributing to super whether you're working or not.

- ✔ If you're aged 65 or over, provided you're gainfully employed for at least 40 hours within 30 consecutive days during a financial year, you can make a super contribution during that financial year. You can do this each year up to 28 days after the month in which you turn age 75, assuming the contribution is received and recorded by your fund within this timeframe.

✔ You may be able to claim a tax deduction or salary sacrifice your super contributions until the age of 74.

✔ For as long as you continue to work — for example, even beyond the age of 100 — and you're an eligible employee, you're entitled to the compulsory 9.5 per cent Superannuation Guarantee (SG) contributions from your employer.

If your fund runs a reserve account, amounts paid from such an account may be paid to a member's account without the need to satisfy a work test, although these amounts are likely to be treated as concessional contributions. A SMSF *reserve account* is ordinarily created for a specific purpose, such as an investment reserve account to smooth fund earnings. I also briefly discuss the role of reserve accounts in Chapter 24, although any SMSF trustee considering the use of reserves should be making an appointment with a SMSF expert.

If you're planning to claim a tax deduction for any super contributions, you must have assessable income against which to claim that deduction. Income from the SMSF pension is tax-free for over-60s, and concessionally taxed for under-60s, which means that retired individuals seeking to claim tax deductions for super contributions must be earning non-super income. Concessional (before-tax) contributions aren't tax effective if you pay more tax on your super contributions than you do on your personal income. I explain super and taxes in more detail in Chapter 13.

Running Two Phases Involves Extra Expertise

Your SMSF is in pension phase when you're drawing a pension from a member account. Your SMSF can also be in accumulation phase — when one or more of your SMSF members is not drawing a pension from a super account. Although you can run your SMSF in both accumulation phase and pension phase, your SMSF pension account cannot receive super contributions. For example, if a SMSF member is currently in pension phase only within a SMSF, and he or she plans to make super contributions, then the fund member must open a new accumulation account within the SMSF, rather than attempt to record contributions against a pension account.

Mixing it up equals actuarial certificate

If you plan to start a pension in your SMSF, and you also want to retain some of your super savings in an accumulation account, then, as trustee, you must decide whether to segregate (that is, separate) the assets financing the SMSF pension from the assets representing your SMSF accumulation account. You must make a similar decision when one fund member starts a pension, while one or more SMSF members remain in accumulation phase.

If you choose not to separate SMSF pension assets from your other fund assets, then your fund must obtain an actuarial certificate for each year. As mentioned in Chapter 5, the actuarial certificate is produced by an actuary and identifies the percentage of earnings that relate to tax-exempt income financing the SMSF pension. Earnings from assets that are financing a SMSF pension — officially known as exempt current pension income (ECPI) — are exempt from tax. The requirement to obtain an actuarial certificate indicates the ATO wants to ensure that only those assets financing such a pension (rather than other fund assets) receive tax-exempt status. For more information on ECPI, refer to Chapter 18.

A SMSF with members in both pension and accumulation phase doesn't need an actuarial certificate when the SMSF ensures the assets financing the pension are segregated from the assets representing the accumulation accounts. For example, shares are fairly easy to identify and account for separately. If a property is involved, however, segregating assets is more difficult unless your SMSF has a substantial amount of money and the property can be segregated as a pension asset or linked to an accumulation account or accounts. *Note:* Segregating assets can be difficult to administer and can mean higher administration costs for the fund.

If your fund is taking the 'segregated asset' approach, a prudent measure is to run two bank accounts for investing fund assets, or at least segregate pension income and assets using a sub-account. According to the ATO, segregation can involve either a sub-account separately identified by the bank involved, or a single bank account for both pension and accumulation phases, but the SMSF segregates the amounts for the different phases using an internal sub-account. One bank account is used when investing monies from the account or accounts in accumulation phase, and the other bank account, or sub-account, is used to hold and invest monies for the accounts in pension phase. Taking such a measure ensures the money and investments representing pension accounts are segregated.

If you start a SMSF pension part-way through a financial year, your fund must obtain an actuarial certificate for that year, unless the assets financing the pension are segregated from the first day of pension phase.

Note: Even when your fund takes the segregated asset approach from part-way through the year, your fund's assets must be valued immediately before the commencement of pension phase. I explain the implications of making super contributions and then starting a pension using those contributions in the same year in the next section.

If you run one of the older style pensions within your SMSF, such as a defined benefit pension or term allocated pension (refer to Chapter 21), then chat to the ATO or your adviser about your fund's actuarial certificate obligations.

Contributing and starting a pension in same year

Ordinarily, you can make super contributions and start a SMSF pension in the same financial year.

If you start the SMSF pension after you make the super contribution, then the entire amount, including the latest contribution, can be converted to pension phase without maintaining separate accounts. If you decide to make further contributions at a later date, and you don't segregate the assets representing the accumulation phase and those representing the pension phase, then your fund must obtain an actuarial certificate each year stating the percentage of earnings that relate to tax-exempt income financing the pension (that is, exempt current pension income).

If you don't want to incur the cost of an annual actuarial certificate, ensure you maintain separate investments representing the pension phase and the accumulation phase.

If you're planning to start a SMSF pension in the same year that you make concessional (before-tax) super contributions, and those concessional contributions are going to form part of your SMSF pension assets, then you need to ensure that you follow certain steps. More specifically, if you're claiming a tax deduction for your super contributions in a financial year, and those tax-deductible contributions are forming part of your SMSF pension commencing in the same financial year, then you must complete and lodge a *Notice of intent to claim or vary a deduction for personal super contributions* (NAT 71121), and give it to your fund before you start the income stream. I explain the process involved in claiming a tax deduction for super contributions in Chapter 4.

Restarting Pensions Means New Components

A popular question asked by individuals planning to make super contributions while receiving payments from a SMSF pension is: Can I consolidate my accumulation account representing my super contributions with my pension account at the end of each financial year?

The answer is yes; restarting a super pension at the end of each financial year and incorporating the contributions made during the year is possible. Such a strategy doesn't involve making super contributions to a pension account: rather the SMSF pension is stopped and a new pension is started using the balance of the old pension account and the accumulation account.

If you're claiming the Age Pension (refer to Chapter 20) or hold a Commonwealth Seniors Health Card (CSHC), then stopping a SMSF pension and starting a new pension can potentially have serious implications for the amount of Age Pension you can receive, or the level of income that's tested for your eligibility for the CSHC. As I explain in Chapter 20, the CSHC is available to retirees who aren't eligible for the Age Pension, and who earn income below a certain threshold. For more information on the CSHC, see my website, SuperGuide (www.superguide.com.au).

Recalculating your benefit components

The implications of restarting a SMSF pension, by combining the account balance of an accumulation account with a pension account, is that the tax-free and taxable components of the new SMSF pension are then re-calculated at the time the new SMSF pension is started (refer to Chapter 21). The taxable component is calculated by subtracting the tax-free component from the total value of the super benefit. Any benefits paid from pensions must reflect the relevant proportions of tax-free and taxable components that make up the total value of the superannuation interest at the time the pension is started.

For example, say you start a pension immediately after making non-concessional contributions (refer to Chapter 4) and assume that 90 per cent of your pension account represents those non-concessional contributions, and the balance of the pension account forms your pension account's taxable component. The SMSF pension will be made up of 90 per cent tax-free component, and 10 per cent taxable component. A major advantage of a pension with a small taxable component is that when you retire before the age of 60, the pension payments from such a pension are 90 per cent tax-free for the life of the pension, regardless of the growth in assets from fund earnings. If you're aged 60 or over and receiving a SMSF pension, then the size of your tax-free component is not relevant because you receive 100 per cent of your pension free of tax anyway.

The tax-free component remains important beyond the age of 60, if you receive a benefit from certain public sector funds (for info on these, refer to Chapter 2) or you leave your super to non-dependants (under the tax laws). If the balance of your pension account, outlined in the example in the previous paragraph, is then paid to a non-dependant (under the tax laws) on your death, the original proportion — 90 per cent tax-free component — would also apply to the death benefit. I explain death benefits in Chapter 24.

Running, or stopping, more than one SMSF pension

In theory, a SMSF member is able to run many SMSF pensions within the one fund by maintaining the original SMSF pension, and also starting a separate new pension at the beginning of each year with the previous year's super contributions. Be aware, though, that such an approach is cumbersome and can be expensive to administer.

You must pay a minimum pension payment at least annually when you run an account-based pension, which means when you stop a SMSF pension, you must pay a pro-rata minimum amount (which represents the period in pension phase) before the pension is commuted. The minimum withdrawal amounts are based on the percentages listed in Chapter 21.

Taking a TRIP Saves Tax

A tax-saving strategy that's triggering a super boom among over-60s, and for many over-55s, involves taking a transition-to-retirement pension (TRIP) while salary sacrificing contributions (or making tax-deductible contributions) into a super fund.

I detail how TRIPs operate in Chapter 21, but briefly, a TRIP is a pension that you can start before you retire, but the pension can't be converted to a lump sum (unless you retire or satisfy another condition of release).

Salary sacrificing involves making super contributions from before-tax salary as negotiated with your employer. Tax on concessional (before-tax) contributions is a maximum of 15 cents in the dollar (or 30 per cent if you earn more than $300,000 — refer to Chapters 4 and 13) rather than whatever marginal tax rate you normally pay on your salary, which can be up to 49 per cent (including Medicare levy of 2 per cent).

If you're not an employee, you can also receive similar tax benefits by making tax-deductible super contributions (refer to Chapter 4).

The main benefit of taking a TRIP and salary sacrificing (or making tax-deductible contributions) for those aged 60 and over is that you can accumulate additional super benefits while paying no tax on the SMSF pension payments derived from the TRIP. *Note:* You can enjoy the same tax benefits by making super contributions while receiving a regular account-based SMSF pension, but starting such a pension requires you to have retired from the workforce; while you can start a TRIP and continue working at your same job.

A typical TRIP strategy is to salary-sacrifice up to your annual concessional contributions cap, and then receive pension income from a TRIP. The contributions cap applicable to anyone aged 55 years or over is $35,000 (for the 2014–15 year, refer to Chapter 4). The TRIP and concessional contributions strategy can offer the following advantages:

✔ Salary sacrificing reduces a person's taxable income while the sacrificed contributions are now invested within a concessionally taxed environment: the fund earnings on the contributions that are invested by the fund, are subject to up to 15 per cent tax compared to a person's marginal rate of tax on income outside the fund.

✔ Earnings on pension assets are exempt from tax within the fund.

✔ If you're under the age of 60, the taxable component of the pension payments remain part of your assessable income, although you're eligible for a 15 per cent pension offset/rebate.

✔ If you're aged 60 or over, the pension payments from a TRIP are tax-free, which means tax is payable only on the reduced taxable income from your salary.

If you choose to take advantage of the TRIP and concessional contributions strategy within your SMSF (or make super contributions while running a SMSF account-based pension), you must either segregate your fund's pension assets from those assets representing the accumulation phase, or obtain an annual actuarial certificate (refer to the section 'Mixing it up equals actuarial certificate', earlier in the chapter).

Chapter 23

Divorce and Your SMSF

. . . .

In This Chapter

▶ Choosing between three super options when divorcing

▶ Splitting super interests on relationship breakdown

▶ Looking after your SMSF, or moving to another fund, beyond the divorce

. . . .

*I*f your marriage or de facto relationship breaks down, you have to decide who gets the house and other assets. You also have to negotiate what happens to another significant family asset — your superannuation, and what then happens to your self-managed super fund (SMSF).

Taking control of your super, and protecting your financial future, is important at any time, but it becomes even more important when a relationship breaks down. When working out your property settlement, your super and your spouse's super is treated like any other property in the marriage or de facto relationship.

When you run a SMSF and your relationship breaks down, you have to consider two important issues:

▶ How will your super benefits, and your spouse's super benefits, be split, if at all?

▶ Who gets to keep the SMSF, and what happens to your spouse's benefits if you maintain control of the SMSF?

In this chapter, I discuss how superannuation can be divided after a relationship break-up. I briefly cover some of the issues you may face when splitting super benefits held in a SMSF, including what happens to your SMSF after you and your spouse have parted ways.

This book isn't about family law or divorce or separation, although I briefly touch on these issues in this chapter. For further information on family law matters, and in particular, superannuation and relationship breakdown, I suggest you check out the federal government's family law section on

'Divorce won't happen to me'

I'm certain that many people hold the view that divorce happens to other couples, and I hope that turns out to be true for those with that point of view. You may, however, be one of the thousands of Australians who are currently enduring the divorce process, or have family, friends or work colleagues who've divorced or are divorcing. In many ways, divorce can have a similar effect as a death in that it touches so many lives and relationships. Three facts about Australian marriages make this chapter a must-read:

✔ Around one-third of marriages break down, resulting in divorce. For some couples the marriage may last 12 months or less, whereas other couples can be together for 30 years or more before they divorce. The positive side to this dreary statistic is that around two-thirds of marriages don't end up in divorce.

✔ After the family home, superannuation is often a family's biggest asset. Superannuation account balances are growing each year — an increasing number of Australian workers can expect to have hundreds of thousands of dollars' worth of super by the time they retire. Eventually, super may become the most significant asset within a relationship, particularly if both parties have superannuation accounts.

✔ Around 50,000 married couples each year go through the ordeal of divorce. At the same time, around 123,000 couples are getting married. In other words, for every two or three marriages during the year, you can expect another couple, somewhere in the country, is getting divorced.

the Attorney-General's Department website and visit the 'superannuation splitting' page (www.ag.gov.au/FamiliesAndMarriage/Families/ SuperSplitting/Pages/default.aspx), or talk to your lawyer.

Dissecting Your Super in Three Ways

If your relationship breaks down, you don't have to be a married couple to divvy up your super benefits in a property settlement. If you're a member of a heterosexual, or same-sex, de facto couple, you can also split your super benefits if your relationship breaks down. The only exception is in Western Australia where for de facto relationships, superannuation is treated as a 'resource' of a relationship, not as an item of property. A *resource* is an asset of the relationship that's not able to be split, but can be taken into account when working out the division of assets between the two parties.

In all Australian states (apart from the treatment of de facto couples in Western Australia), you generally have three options when deciding what to do with your super when your relationship breaks down. Generally, you can opt for one of the following outcomes:

- ✔ **Split your super interest**: The most popular option is splitting the super interest and severing financial ties with the ex. If your super account is still in accumulation phase (that is, not paying a pension), then the super benefit is subject to an *interest split*, which means it cannot be paid out until a condition of release (refer to Chapter 19) is satisfied. If your super account is in pension phase, then your super benefit is subject to a *payment split* and can be paid out to your ex-partner. I explain the splitting process in the next section, 'Doing the Super Splits'.

- ✔ **Flag the super benefit:** You can decide to defer the decision until a later date. This arrangement is known as *flagging*. For example, if you or your ex-spouse are close to retirement, you may want to wait until you or your ex-spouse retire before making any decisions regarding super, because you then know the precise value of any super benefit. Alternatively, you may be awaiting the valuation of a property held within your fund that's taking some time to resolve. Your super fund mustn't deal with your super account until the 'flag' is lifted via another agreement made by you and your ex-spouse.

- ✔ **Take super into account, but leave benefit intact:** With this arrangement you divvy up the other property of the marriage, rather than super benefits, to represent each person's contribution to the marriage.

Love can be blind, but you don't have to suffer from that affliction when separating or divorcing. Get advice and do the numbers before signing anything. Your lawyer needs to work hand-in-hand with your accountant (assuming he also knows about the super laws), because splitting a super benefit has financial and tax implications, especially for the spouse receiving a new super benefit or interest.

Splitting benefits is different from super contributions splitting. A married or de facto can split concessional (before-tax) contributions and redirect those contributions to their spouse's super account throughout their relationship, subject to meeting certain conditions. I briefly explain this opportunity in Chapter 4 and on my SuperGuide website (www.superguide.com.au). In comparison, a super benefit can only be split when a marriage or de facto relationship ends.

Doing the Super Splits

If you both agree with how your super is to be split, you can seek a *consent order* from the Family Court confirming your decision, or you can choose to use a superannuation agreement.

A *superannuation agreement*, which generally details how your super interest — or your spouse's super interest — is to be split, must be in writing and signed by both parties to be considered valid. Your agreement must also state that you each received independent legal advice and your lawyers must provide a certificate stating they provided you with this advice. You and your spouse then each receive a copy of the agreement. If you don't get legal advice about how to treat your superannuation, your agreement is considered non-binding on your super fund's trustee, and the Family Court may make an order dealing with the super benefits that may not reflect your intentions.

If you can't agree on how you both want your superannuation interests to be dealt with in a property settlement, the Family Court decides for you by making a 'splitting order' or a 'flagging order', or leaving your super intact. A *splitting order* is where the Family Court decides how super benefits will be dived up between a couple, while a *flagging order* involves the Family Court deferring the splitting decision until a later date.

Understanding the splitting process

Typically, the main steps in the super splitting process are:

1. **Find out about your spouse's super benefits.**

   As a SMSF trustee this should be straightforward, and each trustee needs to remember they're forbidden by law to exclude another trustee from decision-making, including withholding information about fund members. If you also have super held in a large super fund, the process is more formal when seeking information.

2. **Value the super benefit to be split.**

   The trustee of the super fund (you) must provide you and your spouse with all the information that you both need to value the superannuation benefit. I discuss the different valuation methods that super funds use in the following section, 'Splitting more than straws'.

3. **Reach an agreement or apply for a court order.**

   You and your spouse have the opportunity to agree on how or whether you split your super. You can decide to use a superannuation agreement or to have a consent order registered through the court. If you don't agree, you can apply to the Family Court, which can issue a splitting or flagging order (as described in the preceding section).

4. **Give a copy of the splitting agreement or draft consent order to the fund's trustee.**

   Your agreement sets out how you want your benefit to be treated. Some super funds can't retain split interests: If you're a non-member spouse of a SMSF, then your benefit will be transferred into another super fund. I discuss who gets to keep the SMSF in the section 'What Happens to Your SMSF After Divorce' later in this chapter.

5. **Split the benefit.**

   If a benefit split results in a new superannuation interest, the new interest is treated like any other super interest. Any superannuation rules that apply to the original super benefit apply to the newly created interest. For example, if the original benefit is preserved, the split benefit is also preserved unless the new member satisfies a condition of release (refer to Chapter 19). If you're retired, and you're separating from your spouse, you can split a super pension that you receive from a superannuation fund. If you do split a pension, a second pension may be created, and all the rules that relate to income stream payments apply. Alternatively, and more likely in a divorce involving a SMSF, the split can be taken as a lump sum by the ex-spouse receiving the interest, subject to the rules of the super fund.

Splitting more than straws

A superannuation agreement or consent order must state how you want your superannuation interest to be split. You can choose, generally, between two valuation methods:

- ✔ **Base amount:** Your agreement or consent order can state a fixed dollar amount known as the *base amount*. For example, the agreement or order may specify that the spouse who isn't a member of the fund will receive $200,000 from a $400,000 total super benefit. You receive the amount specified, as well as any earnings related to that amount while it remains in the fund.

- ✔ **Percentage approach:** Your agreement or consent order can state that you each receive a percentage of each splittable payment from a superannuation interest. The percentage approach is suitable when a benefit is payable, either as a lump sum or pension, instead of when your super interest is growing in the fund and can't be cashed for several years.

What Happens to Your SMSF After Divorce?

Dealing with the impact of divorce on your SMSF requires you to consider nearly every aspect of your SMSF. This includes deciding on how you plan to transfer your benefits, or your spouse's benefits, from the SMSF, and whether you keep the SMSF or your spouse takes the SMSF.

If both spouses have super interests in the SMSF, then generally one member needs to transfer his or her super benefits from the SMSF to another SMSF, or to a large fund.

If you or your spouse start another SMSF, then you can transfer assets in specie, and take advantage of a capital gain tax exemption applicable to the transfer of super assets from a family law split. What this means is that when transferring super assets from one SMSF to another SMSF under a superannuation agreement or consent or court order, capital gains won't be triggered upon transfer.

However, if you or your spouse opt to transfer your super interest to larger super fund, you'll need to sell assets to enable a transfer in cash to a larger super fund. Selling assets in this way is not considered a CGT-exempt event, which means the SMSF will have to pay tax on any capital gains upon sale of the assets. A prudent measure is to estimate the tax payable on such a sale before finalising a superannuation agreement.

If a new SMSF needs to be set up to accept the new super interest (I explain the set-up process in Chapter 7), then you need to ensure that the new SMSF is created before the superannuation agreement is delivered to the trustees (you) of the original SMSF.

If your ex-spouse is a trustee of your SMSF, then you need to ensure that the trust deed is able to remove your spouse as trustee, and enable you to take steps to ensure that you still meet the definition of a SMSF. If removing your spouse as a trustee means that you become a single member SMSF, you either need to appoint another person as a trustee of your SMSF, or replace individual trustees with a corporate trustee director, with you as a single trustee director (for the special trustee rules applicable to a single member SMSF, refer to Chapter 8).

If you're a SMSF trustee facing or considering a relationship break-up, get specific advice. Seek legal and financial advice on your personal circumstances and the consequences of a relationship breakdown on the SMSF.

Chapter 24

Looking After Your Family

'*H*ope for the best but plan for the worst' is a saying that my great-aunt Noreen often used. Noreen left this world at the grand old age of 87, but she outlived her five siblings, who had mixed fortunes in the 'long life' stakes. Planning for unpleasant contingencies can be confronting, but applying my great-aunt's practical advice allows anyone to safely ask the 'What if' questions about their superannuation (or anything else) without feeling ghoulish or morose. Questions such as 'What if I get sick or die?' or 'What if my spouse dies?' extend beyond superannuation but, on the financial side of life, super can often be the biggest asset after the family home.

In this chapter, I take you through some of the essential financial housekeeping matters that many individuals find disconcerting, such as considering your life insurance needs, keeping your will up to date and deciding who you want to get your super benefits if you die. I explain how the super and tax laws deal with what happens to your superannuation benefits after you die, and how the taxman treats your dependants differently from your non-dependants. I also briefly explore what happens to your self-managed super fund (SMSF) when you leave this world.

Note: This chapter provides an overview of the super and tax rules that affect your super benefits after you die. I explore these rules in greater detail, including more information on what to do if you decide to wind up your SMSF, on my free website, SuperGuide (www.superguide.com.au).

Protecting Your Health, Wealth and Family

Are you going to live long enough to enjoy your retirement? Do you plan to have a long retirement? Scary questions with a reasonably upbeat answer: Australians are living longer, but not everyone lives a long life. You can expect some people to leave this world earlier than expected.

The possibility of early death can have greater implications if you have heavy financial commitments or you have dependants such as young children.

Life expectancy statistics provide helpful guidance on how many years you're expected to live, on average. For example, a 50-year-old male can expect to live, on average, for another 31.5 years, while a 50-year-old female can expect to live, on average, for another 35 years. Around one-half of these 50-year-olds are likely to live longer than 31.5 years (male) and 35 years (female), and the other half are likely to die before they reach 81.5 years (for a male) and 85 years (for a female). I talk about life expectancy in more detail in Chapter 3. The positive aspect to these statistics is that most Australians live long and mainly healthy lives. A possible long life, however, is an unconvincing argument for failing to plan for the unexpected, and the inevitable.

When planning for your retirement, and running your SMSF, make sure you consider the following matters:

- ✔ Your insurance needs, and whether those needs can be catered for within your SMSF.

- ✔ Your estate planning needs, and whether you have an up-to-date will. (Your *estate* is typically the non-superannuation assets that you own.)

- ✔ The list of people you wish to receive your super benefits after you die, and ensuring that this list of 'nominated beneficiaries' remains current.

- ✔ The tax implications of your death in terms of your super benefit and your SMSF (see 'Tracking the Taxman from Beyond', later in the chapter).

Introducing life insurance and protecting income

As a SMSF trustee, you're required by law to consider your fund members' insurance needs when drafting and implementing your fund's investment strategy (for more information on your fund's investment strategy obligations, refer to Chapter 15).

Three types of insurance are usually available within a super fund:

- ✔ **Life insurance**: If you die, and you have *life insurance* (also known as *death cover*) through your SMSF, or another super fund, your family receives your superannuation benefit account balance, plus an insurance benefit. Depending on your insurance policy, your family can receive these benefits as a pension (if they're your spouse, or your child under the age of 18, or your financially dependent child if aged 18 or over but under the age of 25, or your child of any age and the child has a disability) or as a lump sum. Life insurance premiums inside a super fund are tax-deductible, although the rules applicable to such tax deductions can be complex, which means seeking tax advice on this matter is a good idea.

- ✔ **Total and permanent disability insurance**: If you have *total and permanent disability (TPD) insurance*, you receive a payment if your insurer deems you to be totally and permanently disabled. You usually receive a lump sum payment plus your superannuation account balance. Tax deductibility with this type of insurance depends on the insurer's definition of TPD.

- ✔ **Income protection insurance**: If you become too sick or disabled to work and you have *income protection insurance*, the insurance company usually replaces your income with a monthly income benefit of 75 per cent or 85 per cent of your salary. The benefit ceases when you recover or, usually, after two years. A 2007 tax ruling means that some super funds may offer income protection insurance beyond two years. Depending on your marginal tax rate, it may be more tax effective to have income protection insurance outside of your SMSF.

Buying insurance within a SMSF is usually more expensive than equivalent cover under a 'group' arrangement offered via a large super fund. Under a group arrangement, your employer is, or becomes, an employer sponsor of the fund. A SMSF member seeking individual cover is usually required to undergo a medical test before receiving insurance cover. Some insurance broking networks, and online insurance groups, now offer discounted group-style cover for SMSFs.

A life insurance policy held by a member (or relative of a member) is specifically prevented from being acquired by the member's superannuation fund under section 66(2A) of the *Superannuation Industry (Supervision) Act 1993* (SIS Act). A life insurance company may, however, agree to cancel the policy and reissue the policy in the name of the SMSF trustees without losing any of the benefits of the original policy.

TIP

Retaining existing super insurance

Depending on your health and age, you may have difficulty obtaining insurance cover, especially if you have pre-existing health problems. Instead of applying for new life insurance cover within your SMSF, another option is to retain existing insurance cover within your previous super fund, or continue a policy you may hold outside the super environment.

An alternative, shorter-term strategy is to take advantage of an insurance grace period — if offered by your previous fund.

The grace period is known as a *continuation option* that covers you while you apply for new insurance cover. What this approach means is that your old fund, if it offers this option, continues to provide insurance cover for 60 or 90 days (depending on the terms and conditions of the option).

Before you close your super account with a large fund, check your insurance coverage and compare the cover with what you could obtain if you applied for individual death cover or TPD cover as a SMSF member. In some instances, retaining your existing cover with a large fund may be the cost-effective option.

Using your will

A *will* is a document that states how you want your assets distributed after you die, and making a will is a major component of any estate plan. Taking care of your family if you die can be an important consideration when drafting a will, particularly if you have a young family. If you don't make a will, the law (the specifics vary in each state or territory) makes assumptions about who gets your money and other assets, which may not reflect how you want your assets to be distributed.

REMEMBER

Making a will means your non-superannuation assets are likely to end up in the hands of those you expect, but a will doesn't necessarily guarantee your super ends up where you want it to. You can control where your super ends up in two instances:

✔ **Binding nomination**: With a 'binding death benefit nomination' in place (for details about binding nominations, see the next section), you direct your fund's trustee to pay your death benefit to your estate. However, you need to be careful about the tax implications of this decision if you plan for non-dependants to receive your death benefit (for an explanation of the important difference between dependants and non-dependants, see the section 'Tracking the Taxman from Beyond', later in the chapter).

✔ **No dependants**: If you have no dependants, the SMSF trustee — your legal personal representative in role of SMSF trustee — usually pays your death benefit to your estate. (But if you don't have a will in place, your trustee may decide to pay the benefit to your next of kin or another person with a close relationship to you.)

If you have a child going through difficulties, a binding nomination and an up-to-date will may be the best way to manage your super benefit after you're gone. For example, you may have a child suffering a drug addiction or who may be bankrupt or in the midst of a marriage breakdown. You can include terms in your will that authorise the executor of your estate to establish a testamentary trust. A *testamentary trust* can control who gets your super and other assets, while protecting your estate from business creditors and wayward children, or as a means to look after children who can't look after themselves. You can give the trustee of this trust, who is often the same person administering your will, total discretion about how to pay out your estate, or you may specify strict payment conditions that the testamentary trust trustee must follow to the letter. Testamentary trusts can be useful also for tax-planning purposes because you can distribute income in a flexible way. Anyone considering this option needs to chat to a lawyer and a tax expert, typically an accountant.

Nominating beneficiaries

When joining a large super fund (like those I discuss in Chapter 2), the fund ordinarily gives a new fund member a form that allows the member to nominate the people he wants to receive his super in the event of his death. The people that the member nominates on this form are called his *nominated beneficiaries*. Anyone a fund member nominates as a beneficiary must be a dependant under the super laws (see the section 'Depending on You — Your Dependants' later in this chapter), or the member's legal personal representative.

Even when a fund member does complete the nominated beneficiary form, the trustee of a large fund may not be bound by the member's nomination. Many nominations made by fund members of large super funds are 'non-binding'. A *non-binding nomination* means that your trustee can ignore your nominated beneficiary wishes if the trustee determines other people are entitled to receive your death benefit. In most cases, however, your non-binding nomination helps the trustee to decide who's eligible for your death benefit, especially when a lot of people may claim to be financially dependent on you.

The alternative to making a non-binding nomination — when conducting the same nomination process for your SMSF — is choosing to make a 'binding nomination' or a 'non-lapsing binding nomination'. A *binding nomination* (also known as a *binding death benefit nomination*) means that your legal personal representative acting as SMSF trustee must follow your instructions relating to what happens to your super benefit after you die. A *non-lapsing*

binding nomination ensures it remain in place indefinitely, unless you change or cancel the nomination.

Many binding nominations used by large funds have a lifespan of only three years (although an increasing number of funds are now offering non-lapsing versions). Your SMSF can offer non-lapsing binding nominations too, subject to your fund's trust deed permitting such binding nominations. Remember that the non-lapsing binding nomination remains in place until you change or cancel it.

A binding nomination gives you a lot more certainty about who receives your super benefit when you die. For a nomination to be binding, you must nominate that your death benefit is to be paid to one or more of your dependants (and the percentage allocation for each dependant), or is to be paid to your estate. If you make a binding nomination instructing your fund's trustee to pay your death benefit to your estate, the *executor* of your estate (the person appointed by your will to administer your estate) then pays out your super according to the terms of your will.

A binding nomination is valid when two witnesses (aged over 18 years) sign the nomination document confirming that the contents of the document reflect your wishes. You can't use witnesses who may benefit from your nomination. For more information about SMSFs and non-lapsing binding nominations, check out the ATO's SMSF Determination SMSFD 2008/3 on its website (www.ato.gov.au).

If you divorce, remarry or have children, make sure you update your nominated beneficiaries to reflect your new circumstances. If you're planning to direct your super benefit to your estate, then ensure your will is current. For example, if you remarry, you may not wish to leave your superannuation benefit to your ex-husband or ex-wife. I explain the implications of divorce for your SMSF in Chapter 23.

Where Does Your Super Go When You Go?

Your superannuation benefit lives on after you die — taking the form of a *superannuation death benefit*. A death benefit can also be a direct lump sum payment from your employer, which is called a *death benefit termination payment*.

A superannuation death benefit ('death benefit') is a fund member's super entitlement from his super fund at the time of his death. If you have life insurance (also known as death cover) within your fund, your death benefit usually includes your insurance payment. If you don't have life insurance, your death benefit is the same figure as your account balance.

The following is a summary of who gets your super benefit when you die and how your benefit is treated:

- ✔ **Paying a lump sum or pension**: A lump sum death benefit is more precisely described as a *superannuation lump sum death benefit*. A death benefit payable as an income stream/pension is called a *superannuation income stream death benefit*. The legal personal representative of the deceased member acts as SMSF trustee until the death benefits are paid (as a lump sum) or begin to be paid (as a pension). I explain how the two types of death benefits are treated in the following section and in 'Tracking the Taxman from Beyond', later in the chapter.

- ✔ **Inheriting tax-free payments**: Death benefits from superannuation funds are tax-free when paid to individuals considered dependants under the tax laws, but watch out. For tax purposes, the official term is *death benefits dependant*, although the term *tax dependant* may also be used, which has a slightly different usage than the term 'dependant' used for superannuation purposes. This difference means that your children may be entitled to receive a super benefit, but they can only receive that benefit free of tax if they're a 'death benefits dependant'. If the person is a non-dependant under the tax laws (as most adult children are) although a dependant under the super laws, then the benefit may be subject to tax. I demystify the tax implications of death benefits in the next point, and later in this chapter (see the section 'Tracking the Taxman from Beyond').

- ✔ **Leaving your super to dependants**: Your superannuation death benefit is directly payable to your dependants or, in some cases, to your estate. Your dependants under the super laws include your spouse or your children, or anyone who's financially dependent on you. A dependant can also potentially be a person who may have a close personal relationship with you, such as a sibling who shares a house with you. I explain dependants more fully in the following section.

Depending On You — Your Dependants

Ordinarily, your dependants, or your legal personal representative, are the only people who can receive a death benefit directly from your superannuation fund. Individuals who aren't your dependants under the superannuation laws may receive your death benefit but, usually, that can only happen when the death benefit is first paid to your estate. If you have no dependants, your death benefit is paid to your estate.

For the purposes of super benefit payments when you die, your *dependants* can be one or more of the following:

- ✔ **Spouse**: Your *spouse* can be your married or de facto partner of the opposite sex, or of the same sex. Before July 2008, your 'spouse' could only be a partner of the opposite sex.

- ✔ **Children**: All of your children, including adopted children and stepchildren, are considered dependants for receiving your super entitlements upon your death. *Note:* An important distinction exists for the tax treatment of benefits paid to children:

  - **Under age 18**: Only children under the age of 18 are automatically considered death benefits dependants. A death benefits dependant can receive the death benefit free of tax.

  - **Aged 18 or over:** Any of your children aged 18 or over may be considered a non-dependant for tax purposes, which means although they can receive your super benefits directly from your SMSF, tax may be payable on any death benefit that one or more of your adult children receives, unless they are considered to be financially dependent on you, or have an interdependency relationship with you (see next two bullets). For the tax treatment of death benefits, see the section 'Tracking the Taxman from Beyond', later in the chapter.

- ✔ **Anyone who has an interdependency relationship with you:** An *interdependency relationship* is a close personal relationship between two people who live together, where one or both provides for the financial and domestic support, and personal care of each other. This type of relationship can include sibling relationships and parent–child relationships that don't fall within other definitions of dependant appearing in this bullet list. A person with a disability living in an institution, or not living with the other person, may also be considered in an interdependency relationship.

- ✔ **Anyone whom the trustee of your fund considers to be financially dependent on you at the time you die**: For example, an adult child over the age of 18 may be considered financially dependent when he still lives at home and relies on you for living costs. A grandchild receiving financial support from you, may, depending on the facts, be considered to be financially dependent on you. The trustee of your fund decides whether a person was financially dependent on a fund member.

The complicating factor when paying out a death benefit is that a person may be a dependant under the superannuation laws but not a dependant under the tax laws — for example, a financially independent adult child of a fund member. What does that difference mean for a member of your family receiving some or all of your death benefit? An adult child living independently is a dependant under the super laws, which means the child is entitled to receive a death benefit from the deceased member's account. A financially independent adult child, however, is considered a non-dependant under the tax laws; that is, they're not a death benefits dependant (as explained in the preceding section), which means that although the child can receive the benefit, he must pay tax on the taxable component of the benefit. A death benefits dependant receives death benefits tax-free, while a non-dependant receives death benefits after tax is deducted. I explain the tax treatment of death benefits paid to non-dependants in the section 'Tracking the Taxman from Beyond', later in the chapter.

Your death benefit can be paid to your death benefits dependants as a lump sum (superannuation lump sum death benefit) or as a pension (superannuation income stream death benefit), although most adult children can't receive death benefits as a pension. Non-dependants under the tax laws and/or the super laws can only be paid death benefits as a lump sum.

Paying lump sum death benefits

Your super fund can pay a tax-free lump sum death benefit to your dependants under the tax laws (death benefits dependants) — namely, your spouse or your children (under the age of 18, or disabled), or a person (including your adult child) who has an interdependency relationship with you. Any other person (including your adult child) who is financially dependent on you can also receive a tax-free lump sum death benefit.

Non-dependants under the tax laws (for example, financially independent adult children) or non-dependants under the super laws (for example, extended family, friends or a charity) can only receive your death benefit as a lump sum rather than as a pension. Non-dependants under the super laws ordinarily receive a death benefit when your super fund pays your death benefit to your estate.

Paying income stream death benefits

Since July 2007, a SMSF (or any other type of super fund) is permitted to pay a death benefit pension only to certain death benefits dependants, such as the deceased's spouse or children under the age of 18, or financially dependent children under the age of 25. With the exclusion of adult children of the deceased, a death benefit pension can also be paid to an individual who had an interdependency relationship with the deceased, or who was financially dependent on the deceased at the time of death,

A child who is considered a dependant of a deceased fund member can receive a death benefit pension until the age of 24 (and longer if the child suffers a disability), depending on the rules of the SMSF. The balance in the fund must then be paid out as a tax-free lump sum.

A SMSF is not permitted to pay a death benefit pension to a non-dependant under the tax laws (such as an independent adult child). Individuals considered 'non-dependants' under the tax laws can only receive a death benefit as a lump sum. An existing SMSF pension also can't revert to a non-dependant on the death of a fund member. Such a pension, when reverted to a dependant, is known as a *reversionary pension*.

The ban on death benefit pensions to certain categories of dependants, and to non-dependants (under the tax laws), applies even when you nominated a beneficiary before July 2007. What this rule means is that even where you had a nomination in place before July 2007 (when this ban was introduced), an adult child, or non-dependant under the tax laws can't receive a death benefit pension from your fund upon your death. Only death benefit pensions commenced before July 2007 can continue to be payable to non-dependants after July 2007.

Tracking the Taxman from Beyond

In July 2007, the tax rules applying to superannuation benefits changed dramatically. Most Australians aged 60 or over can now receive their super benefits free of tax; benefits which previously had been subject to tax.

Superannuation death benefits paid from a SMSF to individuals treated as death benefits dependants (dependants under the tax laws), rather than non-dependants, are also tax-free, subject to one exception — relating to death benefit pensions paid to dependants under the age of 60.

Unfortunately, death benefits paid to non-dependants under both the super and tax laws may still be subject to tax. The difference in tax bills can be substantial when you consider, in most cases, dependants under the tax laws (death benefits dependants) receive tax-free death benefits, while non-dependants can pay up to 17 per cent tax (including 2 per cent Medicare levy), and in some cases 32 per cent tax (including Medicare levy).

No tax for dependants

Lump sum death benefits from a SMSF paid to death benefits dependants are tax-free.

Tax-free cash is good news for anyone aiming to leave a lump sum to a spouse or other death benefits dependants. And your SMSF may also be able to secure a refund of contributions tax that has been paid in the past on the super account of a deceased member (including you). Is your SMSF in a position to claim a refund of all contributions tax paid on the account that is about to be paid out as a lump sum death benefit? I explain how a SMSF can take advantage of this rule in the sidebar 'Refunds, reserves and contributions tax'.

Ordinarily, income tax isn't payable on a death benefits pension paid to dependants from a SMSF, except if the deceased fund member was under the age of 60 at death and the dependant receiving the death benefit pension/income stream is also under the age of 60. In such circumstances, any pension payment forms part of the dependant's assessable income, and is subject to income tax, although the dependant is entitled to a 15 per cent tax offset on the taxable component of the pension payments.

Non-dependants pay tax

A SMSF superannuation death benefit may consist of a:

- ✔ **Tax-free component**: This component is always tax-free, even when paid to a non-dependant under the tax laws.

- ✔ **Taxable component**: This component is subject to tax when paid to a non-dependant. The taxable component can include:

  - An element taxed in the fund.

  - An element untaxed in the fund. For SMSF members, an untaxed taxable component can be the insured component of a benefit if paid to a non-dependant (under the tax laws), and the SMSF has claimed tax deductions for the insurance premiums.

When your lump sum death benefit is paid to someone other than your death benefits dependant — that is, the benefit is paid to a non-dependant under the tax laws — the taxable component of the lump sum payment is taxed at 15 per cent (plus 2 per cent Medicare levy) when paid from a SMSF.

Refunds, reserves and contributions tax

In 1988, when the federal government introduced a 15 per cent 'contributions' tax on before-tax contributions, the tax laws were changed to permit a refund of the contributions tax upon the death of a super fund member. This obscure and little-known rule can deliver a refund of all contributions tax paid during a deceased member's lifetime. A payment, known as an anti-detriment payment, can be made to the dependant/s (under the tax rules) of the deceased, and the super fund can claim a tax deduction for making this payment, provided the SMSF's trust deed allows for such a payment.

The rationale behind this refund is to ensure that the wife or husband or children or other dependants of the deceased aren't detrimentally affected by the imposition of the contributions tax. The rule only applies to lump sums, rather than death benefit pensions, paid to dependants. If a death benefit pension is in place, the dependant is already being compensated for the contributions (earnings) tax via a tax-free income stream, or a 15 per cent pension offset (if deceased and dependant are under the age of 60).

Here's how it works: The amount paid in contributions tax for the life of the deceased member is paid to that member's dependants and the SMSF claims that payment as a tax deduction. For the SMSF to claim a tax deduction, the fund needs assessable income, which generally means the SMSF requires other fund members to be in accumulation phase in the current and following financial years.

The trickiest aspect of this scenario is how the SMSF is going to find the cash to pay out the refund to the dependant/s. The ATO doesn't return cash to the SMSF; rather, the SMSF can use the tax deduction to reduce the SMSF's tax bill over a period of time.

In most cases, the answer to this cashflow issue is to use a reserve, although some SMSFs use life insurance payouts. Reserves are one of the more complex areas in super and I suggest you head straight to an adviser to assist you, if you're considering taking advantage of the anti-detriment rules. You may even need to arrange for your existing adviser to outsource this particular strategy to a SMSF reserving specialist such as a SMSF lawyer.

Example: If the taxable component of your super benefit is worth $500,000, your adult child receives $425,000 (less Medicare levy) of this amount and the tax office gets 15 per cent of the benefit — $75,000, plus Medicare levy — when you die.

Where the SMSF death benefit paid to a non-dependant includes an insurance payout, then the insurance payout can be taxed at 32 per cent (including 2 per cent Medicare levy).

If your death benefit is paid to your estate, and then paid to your death benefits dependants or non-dependants, your benefit is treated, tax-wise, the same way as if the benefit were paid directly to these individuals. No Medicare levy, however, is payable on a death benefit paid to your estate.

If you plan to leave your super to your adult children when you die, your death benefit may be 'hit' with tax, even though you were going to receive that benefit tax-free while you were alive. Here's a crazy idea: If you withdraw your SMSF money the day before you die and give it to your adult children or friends, you pay no tax on the money if you're 60 or over. If you die before you have the chance to cash your super and you then leave your super to non-dependants under the tax laws (such as your financially independent adult children), the taxable component of the benefit is 'hit' with 15 per cent tax (or 30 per cent tax, on life insurance payouts), plus Medicare levy.

If punting on when you're going to die isn't what you have in mind for your tax planning, you can consider other options, such as boosting the tax-free component of your super benefits while you're alive. I discuss this strategy on my website, SuperGuide (www.superguide.com.au), although if you're considering such an option, then a chat with a SMSF adviser is definitely in order.

SMSF Succession Planning

What are the succession plans for your SMSF, if your personal circumstances change? What happens if you

- Get tired of running your SMSF?
- Get sick?
- Want to live overseas?
- Die?

Typically, a SMSF has two members/trustees, namely a husband and wife. Ordinarily, one trustee does most of the work relating to the fund, while the other trustee gets involved when key decisions need to be made.

Such a SMSF can exist for as long as the two members live, although the fund may strike trouble if the trustee who does most of the day-to-day SMSF work dies first. A couple who plan ahead may invite their children to join the SMSF, lengthening the life of the fund and ensuring someone else is available to take over the main running of the fund if one or more of the parents get sick or die.

When a SMSF trustee/member dies, the legal representative of the deceased member can act as trustee of the SMSF until the death benefits are paid or begin to be paid. If the death benefit is paid as a SMSF pension, the recipient of the income stream must be a member and trustee (or become a member and trustee) of the fund.

A two-member fund may decide to continue on as a single member SMSF if one trustee dies (for info on how a single member SMSF operates, refer to Chapter 8). Eventually, winding up the SMSF may become the best option. The decision to wind up a SMSF structure doesn't have to be triggered by something as tragic as death. A SMSF trustee may suffer illness preventing him from devoting sufficient time to the SMSF trustee responsibilities. Or, SMSF trustees may decide to move overseas, precluding them from running a SMSF (refer to Chapter 8).

The harsh reality of running your own super fund is that at some stage the music stops; that is, a member dies, and your fund either continues with the remaining fund members or you wind up the fund. The ATO has produced a very helpful publication to assist SMSF trustees considering winding up a SMSF, called *Winding up a self-managed super fund* (NAT 8107). You can obtain a copy from the ATO website (www.ato.gov.au) or by phoning 13 10 20.

Part VI
The Part of Tens

Enjoy an additional (and free!) online Part of Tens chapter about DIY super. Visit www.dummies.com/extras/diysuperau.

In this part . . .

✔ Explore ten alluring and unique features of DIY super, including discovering some downright fascinating morsels of information.

✔ Work through ten very serious aspects of running a SMSF — what can be considered the ten commandments of DIY super.

Chapter 25

Ten Special Features of DIY Super

*I*f you're been reading through this book, you already know about the main advantages of superannuation, such as tax-free super for over-60s, concessional tax treatment of super fund earnings and the marvels of compound earnings.

Choosing a self-managed super fund (SMSF) — rather than opting for one of the larger super funds — probably means that one or more of the ten special features of DIY super, explained in this chapter, has grabbed your attention.

Becoming a Member of a Fast-Growing Club

Without doubt, the rise of DIY super is the biggest story in super after the introduction of tax-free super for over-60s in 2007 (refer to Chapter 13 and Part V) and the Global Financial Crisis of 2008 and 2009 (refer to Chapter 14).

More than 530,000 or so SMSFs run by more than 1 million Australians (that is, just over 4 per cent of the Australian population) control around one-third of all superannuation wealth in Australia — nearly one in every three super dollars is held in a SMSF!

Potentially, SMSF trustees can become the most influential citizens in Australia, having a greater say over government super policies, encouraging the creation of financial products targeting SMSFs, and controlling a substantial percentage of the money invested in the Australian sharemarket. That's what I call people power!

You can find the latest SMSF statistics on the ATO website (go to www.ato.gov.au and click on Super⇨Self-managed super funds⇨Statistics⇨Quarterly reports). For details on how you can become more involved in influencing superannuation policy, see my SuperGuide website: www.superguide.com.au.

Having No More than Four Members

A super fund must meet basic conditions to be considered a SMSF. Your SMSF must have four members or less, and all members must be trustees, and all trustees must be members. A member can't be an employee of another member unless they're relatives, and no trustee can receive payment for performing the role of trustee.

If a SMSF doesn't meet the basic requirements for a SMSF, it may be deemed to be a small APRA fund, which means it needs to have a professional trustee who holds an RSE licence. The ATO usually works with the trustees of the SMSF to help them meet the requirements of a SMSF. Alternatively, the ATO gives the trustees time to wind up the fund, or the opportunity to use a licensed trustee and move to become an APRA-regulated fund.

For the basics on the four-member/trustee rule, turn to Chapter 2. For info on the rules applying to SMSF trustees, refer to Chapters 8 and 9.

Appreciating that You're the Boss

Wanting to have total control over your super savings is a compelling reason for starting a SMSF — if you appreciate that running a SMSF is a lifetime commitment. And, unlike professional trustees, you're not permitted to receive payment for your task.

Think carefully about why you want to run your own super. Is it for the love of responsibility, and the honour of taking control of your super savings? Or, are you setting up, or have you set up, your SMSF for other reasons? I list some of the more popular reasons in the next section, 'Finding Flexibility'.

For the duration of your trusteeship, the *Superannuation Industry (Supervision) Act 1993* (the SIS Act) and trust law require you to

✔ Act honestly in all matters relating to your SMSF

✔ Exercise the same degree of care, skill and diligence as you'd expect from an ordinary prudent person

✔ Act in the best interests of all fund members

In case you forget, as trustee you must run your SMSF in compliance with the SIS Act, the tax laws and in accordance with your fund's trust deed (refer to Chapters 9 and 11).

Finding Flexibility

Control is often the number one reason cited for why SMSF trustees set up SMSFs (refer to Chapter 1). But seeking flexibility when saving for retirement, and when taking a pension, must come a close second. Arguably, having flexibility is one of the main reasons individuals want control over their retirement savings.

Some of the typical and valid reasons why individuals set up SMSFs include

✔ A greater choice in what you can invest in, including direct property and collectibles, such as works of art, coins or antiques. (I take you through your SMSF investment responsibilities and opportunities in Part IV.)

✔ The ability to take advantage of tax benefits linked with super (see 'Managing Tax for You, Not for Thousands', later in the chapter).

✔ Flexibility in when and how you fund your retirement, including making super contributions while taking a pension from the same SMSF, but not from the same SMSF account (refer to Part V).

✔ The prospect of purchasing business property, such as an office, within the SMSF, and to use the property in your business (refer to Chapter 17).

✔ Opportunities to make in specie contributions; that is, transfer assets into the DIY super fund rather than contribute money (refer to Chapter 4).

✔ The ability to provide for future generations in a flexible way. (I discuss death benefits in Chapter 24.)

Understanding It's a Super Structure

Contrary to popular opinion, your SMSF is an investor, not an investment. Many Australians, including journalists and commentators, confuse the underlying investments of a super fund, such as shares or property, with the investment vehicle, which is the super fund.

Commentators often observe that super is a 'good' or a 'bad' investment, which means they don't understand how super works. If you're purchasing shares directly (for example, through a stockbroker), you don't call yourself an investment — you're the investor. Likewise, when your super fund is purchasing shares directly on your behalf, your fund isn't the investment, even though it oversees an investment portfolio.

I take you into the world of SMSF investing in Part IV.

Managing Tax for You, Not for Thousands

One of the major advantages of running a SMSF is that your retirement plans can be integrated into your working life and personal life. Any adviser worth his or her salt, assessing the suitability of a SMSF for a client, takes into account business and family commitments, existing investments held within super and outside super, and the client's level of personal income and possible tax bill.

In relation to specific tax management within a SMSF, a major advantage of running such a fund is that you can actively manage your fund's tax bill. On the other hand, a large super fund, which is investing on behalf of thousands of members, often doesn't have the capacity to individually monitor the tax implications of each decision for each member — although some large funds do offer this flexibility. (For more information on how large super funds work, refer to Chapter 2.)

Some investors may prefer holding their super investments within a wrap, rather than a SMSF. For such investors, they may seek to secure some tax management flexibility without taking on trustee responsibilities (refer to Chapters 8 and 9).

Purchasing Australian shares that pay dividends can give your SMSF a nice surprise at tax time. I cover the benefits that your SMSF can derive from franked dividends in the section 'Frankly, My Dear, I Love Franked Dividends', later in this chapter.

Running Two Phases, on Your Terms

Your SMSF can have two distinct phases — accumulation phase and pension phase — that can run concurrently or at separate times. The key difference between the accumulation phase and the pension phase is the tax treatment of fund earnings. In pension phase, fund earnings on assets, including any capital gains that your fund receives on the sale of pension assets, are exempt from tax. In contrast, earnings on assets in accumulation phase are subject to 15 per cent earnings tax.

The tax treatment of the two phases is the same whether you're in a large fund or a SMSF. When you run a SMSF, however, you have considerable flexibility in how you allocate your assets when your SMSF moves from accumulation phase only, into running the fund with both accumulation and pension phases. Having this flexibility is very important because you can claim fund expenses as tax deductions in accumulation phase, which isn't possible if your account is in pension phase. The flipside of this scenario is that you pay tax on earnings derived from savings held in your accumulation account.

As a SMSF member, you also have a lot more flexibility when considering stopping and restarting pensions and even returning an account to accumulation phase (refer to Chapter 22), compared with a larger fund. The SMSF trustees are also the fund members, which means transactions can be conducted in a short time frame. In large funds, such transactions generally take much longer due to the sheer number of fund members and transactions that large funds must deal with.

'Frankly, My Dear, I Love Franked Dividends'

Purchasing Australian shares that pay dividends may give your SMSF access to franked dividends — company share dividends that represent income on which the company has already paid 30 per cent tax. The pre-paid tax is known as franking credits. Subject to legislation, the company tax rate may be reduced to 28.5 per cent, which will slightly reduce the tax benefits of franked dividends.

In accumulation phase, your SMSF can offset the tax payable on fund earnings (refer to Chapter 18) and concessional contributions (refer to Chapter 4) by taking advantage of franking credits. If no tax is payable by your SMSF or the amount of the franking credits plus any PAYG tax paid by the fund is greater than its tax bill, your fund can receive a tax refund when your SMSF is entitled to franking credits.

In pension phase, franking credits are very tax-friendly for SMSFs because a SMSF receiving tax-exempt fund earnings pays no tax. What this means is that a SMSF in pension phase is in a zero-tax environment, and franking credits are repaid to the fund as a tax refund. Lovely!

Creating Family Wealth

Most SMSFs are two-member funds run by couples — which is one of the major attractions of the SMSF structure. A couple can save for retirement together, including deciding on the most tax-effective way to structure their pensions. An increasing number of SMSFs are also admitting their children as members, particularly as a couple get older, creating continuity for the SMSF and the potential to utilise reserves to access a refund of contributions tax (see the next section).

For many SMSF members, the power to direct what happens to super benefits after a fund member dies is one of the compelling reasons for using the SMSF structure. For example, a SMSF member may decide to leave his super benefits to his financially dependent children — considered 'dependants' under the tax laws — who receive death benefits tax-free, and leave his non-super assets to his independent adult children, who are considered 'non-dependants' under the tax laws. The taxable component of superannuation death benefits paid to your non-dependants (under the tax laws, such as financially independent adult children) is hit with tax. I discuss death benefits in Chapter 24.

Considering a Refund of Contributions Tax

Upon the death of a super fund member, and under certain circumstances, the tax laws permit a refund of all contributions tax paid during a deceased member's lifetime. A payment, known as an anti-detriment payment can be made to the dependant/s (under the tax laws) of the deceased and the super fund can claim a tax deduction for making this payment, provided the SMSF's trust deed allows for such a payment.

Most large funds don't offer this opportunity, and many SMSF trust deeds don't allow for such payments, or don't allow for fund reserves, which can be used to finance such payments. If your fund plans to access this opportunity, the death benefit must be paid as a lump sum, and you must have fund members in accumulation phase to be able to claim the tax deduction. I explain this scenario at the end of Chapter 24.

Chapter 26

Ten Commandments of DIY Super

*W*hen becoming a SMSF trustee, you must sign a SMSF trustee declaration stating that you're responsible for ensuring your super fund complies with the super laws. If you became a SMSF trustee before July 2007, you don't have to sign a trustee declaration, but you must comply with the same super rules as the newer trustees. Doing your job as SMSF trustee is all about steering your fund's super CART — that is, looking after your fund's **C**ompliance, **A**dministration, **R**eporting and **T**ax management responsibilities.

For the past decade, when presenting to forums on DIY super, I often use the term 'ten commandments' as a tool to help the audience grasp the major rules that apply to SMSFs. Following the ten commandments in this chapter is a handy way to help steer your super fund's CART in the right direction. Respecting the promises you make when signing your SMSF trustee declaration can also keep your fund on the right side of the super laws.

You Shall . . . Always Remember You're in Control

Your role as a SMSF trustee isn't a dress rehearsal: You must take it seriously from day one. If you put in the time to understand the rules, and seek advice when you need it (see the section '. . . Seek Professional Advice,

When Necessary', later in the chapter), the prospect of complying with the superannuation laws shouldn't deter you from running a SMSF.

If you do find the compliance side too overwhelming, you can delegate some of the tasks, but not the responsibility, to service providers (refer to Chapter 10), or in extreme cases, you can wind up your SMSF (refer to Chapter 24).

My checklist, which I call the 'DIY Super 6C Challenge', can help you decide whether a DIY super fund is the 'right fit' for you, and for your retirement planning needs. You can find the checklist in Chapter 1.

Outsourcing your obligations doesn't remove your ultimate responsibility as trustee of your own fund. You may choose to hire a company to look after your administration and compliance, or to use a wrap account that looks after your investment administration; but, in the end, you're responsible for what happens in your fund.

For lots more info on outsourcing your fund's administration, turn to Chapter 10. For details on using wraps for investment administration, check out Chapter 14.

... *Comply with the Sole Purpose Test*

In the SMSF trustee declaration that new trustees must sign (refer to Chapter 9), the trustee declares that he or she understands '. . . it is my responsibility to ensure the fund is only maintained for the purpose of providing benefits to the members upon their retirement (or attainment of a certain age), or their beneficiaries if a member dies'.

If you enjoy a direct or indirect benefit before retirement from your SMSF's investment — that is, more than an incidental or insignificant benefit — your fund is probably breaching the sole purpose test. I also explain the meaning of the test in Chapter 9, and provide more information on how the sole purpose test plays out in practical terms in Chapter 11.

... *Follow Your Fund's Trust Deed*

Your SMSF is a trust, evidenced by your fund's trust deed, which means your fund is subject to trust law. Every SMSF trustee is subject to general trustee duties, which are listed in the SMSF trustee declaration that new trustees must sign.

The trust deed is your SMSF's rule book. As a SMSF trustee, you must act in accordance with your trustee responsibilities as set out in your fund's trust deed. If that document isn't enough incentive, the *Superannuation Industry (Supervision) Act 1993* (the SIS Act), the main legislation governing super, also imposes minimum requirements on trustees, which are general trustee duties under law, and penalties for non-compliance apply if you don't. I discuss trust deeds in Chapter 7, and the cost of trust deeds in Chapter 6.

. . . *Comply with the SIS Act*

The superannuation laws are set out in the SIS Act, and the *Superannuation Industry (Supervision) Regulations 1994*. A SMSF, as with all super funds, must comply with the SIS Act and regulations, including the following rules:

- ✔ **Contribution rules:** You must satisfy the contribution rules. For example, if a member is aged 65 or over they must satisfy a work test before contributing (refer to Chapters 4 and 22).

- ✔ **Investment rules:** You must satisfy special investment rules. See the following commandments '. . . Formulate an Investment Strategy' and '. . . Not Break Any Investment Rules'.

- ✔ **Benefit payment rules:** You must not breach the payment rules when paying a lump sum or pension; for example, a SMSF member must satisfy a condition of release to access preserved super benefits (refer to Chapter 19).

- ✔ **Administrative obligations:** Your fund must meet its administrative obligations such as preparing minutes of trustee meetings and decisions, and keeping accounting records (Chapter 12) — including recording all contributions (Chapter 4), expenses (Chapter 12), tax paid (Chapters 13 and 18), investment transactions (Chapter 15) and other transactions throughout the year.

. . . *Formulate an Investment Strategy*

The super laws demand that trustees formulate, implement and regularly review a super fund's investment strategy. The SIS Act states that when formulating your strategy you need to take into account:

- ✔ Likely risk and return of any investment

- ✔ The fund's investment objectives

- ✔ Diversification — investing across a broad range of assets, and any risks from investing in a small number of assets, or a single asset

- ✔ Liquidity — the ability of the fund to pay taxes, expenses and members' benefits

- ✔ Insurance — the insurance needs of the fund members, although the SMSF trustees are not compelled to purchase insurance cover for fund members

If you ignore the requirement to formulate, implement and regularly review your fund's investment strategy, you can be fined up to $17,000. Any investment decisions you make must be made in accordance with your fund's strategy. I discuss your fund's investment strategy in more detail in Chapter 15.

. . . Not Break Any Investment Rules

Besides the requirement to create an investment strategy for your SMSF, you must also ensure your SMSF doesn't breach any of super's special investment rules. I explain these rules in Chapter 15.

The SMSF trustee declaration clearly lists these rules as follows:

- ✔ Ensure your SMSF meets the sole purpose test (refer to the section '. . . Comply with the Sole Purpose Test' earlier in this chapter).

- ✔ Ensure the members of your SMSF can only access super benefits if they satisfy a legitimate condition of release.

- ✔ Keep personal money separate from SMSF assets (see '. . . Keep Your Fund Separate from Your Personal Finances', later in the chapter).

- ✔ Protect the ownership of fund assets.

- ✔ Don't lend money or provide other forms of financial assistance to fund members or relatives of fund members.

- ✔ Don't purchase assets from fund members, unless those assets are listed securities, business real property or managed funds.

- ✔ Don't borrow money on behalf of your SMSF, unless it falls within one of the exceptions.

- ✔ Don't have more than 5 per cent of the fund's total assets as in-house assets. An in-house asset is a loan to, or investment in, related parties of the fund, or a lease arrangement with related parties.

- ✔ Ensure any fund investment is made on an arm's-length basis.

- ✔ Refrain from getting involved in transactions that circumvent restrictions on the payment of benefits.

. . . *Arrange for Your SMSF to Be Audited*

The SIS Act states that trustees of a SMSF must appoint an 'approved SMSF auditor' in each income year to audit the fund's operations of the fund, and that the auditor must provide the trustees with an audit report in the approved form. You can appoint only a registered approved SMSF auditor to conduct these audits. Every SMSF auditor must be registered by ASIC, and each registered SMSF auditor has a unique SMSF auditor number (SAN).

Any appointment of an approved SMSF auditor must be via a letter of engagement signed by the auditor and the fund's trustees.

Your approved SMSF auditor must give you an audit report stating that your fund has been audited. If the auditor is of the view that your fund breaches the superannuation laws, she must notify you immediately. In certain cases, your fund's auditor is compelled to report the breach also to the ATO. For more info on the role of an approved SMSF auditor, refer to Chapter 12.

. . . *Lodge Tax and Compliance Returns*

Your SMSF must lodge a return each year with the ATO on or before the due lodgement date. Don't get the ATO offside by lodging returns late or not at all. Incomplete returns also give the ATO reason to hit you with financial penalties, or put your fund on the ATO 'hit list'. I explain your fund's tax return lodgement requirements in Chapter 12.

When lodging your fund's return, you also must pay the annual supervisory levy of $259.

The annual return is designed to report income tax (refer to Chapter 13), report member contributions (refer to Chapter 4) and provide the ATO with key information about your compliance with the super and tax laws, and covers areas such as:

- ✔ Whether your SMSF meets the definition of 'Australian superannuation fund' and remains eligible for tax concessions (refer to Chapter 8).

- ✔ Whether your SMSF paid out any benefits during the year, in particular pension payments, to check that the benefit payment standards (Chapter 19) and minimum pension payment rules (Chapter 21) have been met.

... Keep Your Fund Separate from Your Personal Finances

You wear a very distinctive cap when you take on the role of SMSF trustee — you act on behalf of fund members, including yourself. Legally, your role as a SMSF trustee is different from your role as fund member, which means you must manage your SMSF separately from your personal and business affairs.

The ATO is very clear: You must keep your fund's assets, including bank accounts and supporting financial records, separate from your personal and business assets.

A simple way to help you comply with this rule is to maintain accurate financial and non-financial records for your SMSF. These records must be maintained separately to your personal records. As trustee of your SMSF, you must keep accurate accounting records for each year of income. Your recording obligations include

- Keeping accurate accounting records that are easy to read and explain the transactions and financial position of your fund. You must keep these records for at least five years.

- Preparing two annual statements — one showing the transactions, expenses and earnings for the year (operating statement), and one showing your fund's financial position. You must keep these records for at least five years.

- Keeping copies of lodged annual returns for at least five years.

- Keeping copies of all reports given to members for at least ten years.

- Keeping minutes of trustee meetings and decisions for at least ten years.

... Seek Professional Advice When Necessary

You shall seek professional advice before you set up your SMSF, and seek advice on an ongoing basis, when necessary:

✔ Even if you choose to do everything yourself (refer to Chapter 10); advice at the outset and regular chats to a chosen adviser are essential.

✔ Even if you choose to use that adviser as a coach or mentor, instead of getting him or her involved in the nuts and bolts of your fund.

Trust is important but not in the form of blind trust. A strong adviser–client relationship is one in which you can ask any questions and even challenge the recommendation you're being given. After all, you're the one who has to take the rap if your SMSF goes pear-shaped. I explain the different types of advisers that your SMSF can use in Chapter 5.

Part VII
Appendixes

Check out www.dummies.com/extras/diysuperau for free bonus content online relating to DIY super.

In this part...

- Refer to a comprehensive compliance and administration checklist, which includes chapter references where you can find more information about a particular task.

- Discover the details of websites and organisations that supply free and independent super information, and access a list of all ATO publications mentioned in this book.

Appendix A

SMSF Compliance and Administration Checklist

You can use the checklist in this Appendix (Table A-1) as a handy reference for running your SMSF, or as a benchmark when selecting a SMSF service provider. I explain what to look for when selecting a SMSF administrator or adviser in Chapters 5, 6, 7 and 10.

TIP

If you like checklists, you're going to love the convenience of the Record-Keeping Checklist in Chapter 12 as well, which lists all of the important SMSF documents you need to have, and states how long you need to store these documents.

Table A-1	SMSF Compliance and Administration Checklist	
Stage	*Task*	*Chapter Reference*
Setting Up Your SMSF		
Fund set-up	Set-up steps and other matters	6, 7, 8
	Sign SMSF trustee declaration	9
Running Your SMSF		
Accept contributions	Check member(s) entitled to make super contributions	4
	Check have member(s') TFN	4
	Ensure SMSF is an 'Australian superannuation fund'	8
	Accept only permitted contributions	4
	Obtain deduction notice(s) for concessional contributions	4
	Ensure in specie (non-cash) contributions are within rules	4, 15

(continued)

Table A-1 *(continued)*

Stage	Task	Chapter Reference
	Ensure assets held in name of fund	15
Pay benefits	Benefits (lump sums or pensions) paid in accordance with SIS Act, SIS regulations, and trust deed	19, 21, 22, 24
	Member satisfies condition of release before benefit paid	19
	Calculate and track benefit components	19, 21, 22, 24
	Register for PAYG withholding (if member under 60 receiving benefit payments, or paying death benefit from life insurance proceeds)	19, 21, 22, 24
	Issue payment summary (if tax withheld)	19, 21, 22, 24
	Obtain actuarial certificate when necessary	22
	Value assets at market value before pension starts	15, 21
Draft investment strategy	Draft strategy considering risk, return, cash flow, diversification and insurance needs of fund members	14, 15, 24
	Decide strategy at trustee meeting and minute the strategy	12, 15
	Ensure investments in strategy comply with super laws	9, 11, 15
	Review strategy regularly	15
Make investments	Separate bank account for SMSF	7, 11, 15, 21, 22
	Invest your super money	Part IV
	Comply with sole purpose test	9, 11, 15
	Protect ownership of SMSF assets	9, 15, 17
	Don't mix SMSF money with personal money	9, 11, 15

Stage	Task	Chapter Reference
	Don't provide financial assistance to members or relatives of members	15
	Don't have more than 5% of fund's assets in in-house assets	11, 15
	Don't use fund assets for personal use	9, 11, 15
	Purchase from members permitted assets only	15
	Ensure transactions are conducted at an arm's-length basis	15
	Ensure purchase or sale of assets are at market value	15
	Don't borrow money unless within an exception	16
	Record transactions	12
	Keep minutes of investment decisions and reasons for decisions	12
Reporting	Prepare fund's annual financial statements	12
	Appoint an approved SMSF auditor	12
	Lodge fund's annual return and report contributions by due date	12
	Pay ATO supervisory levy	12
	Lodge a Business Activity Statement (if registered for GST) — quarterly or annually	7, 17
Keep records	Ensure trustees understand record-keeping responsibilities	12
	Review trust deed and update when necessary	6, 7
	Hold copies of: consent to act as trustee, signed trustee declaration, fund's trust deed and fund's investment strategy	8, 9, 12, 15

(continued)

Table A-1 *(continued)*

Stage	Task	Chapter Reference
	Keep annual financial statements	12
	Keep copies of returns and member statements	12
	Keep contribution deduction notices	4, 22
	Keep other key documentation	12
Tax management	Claim deductions for fund's administrative and operating expenses	13, 18
	Track and report capital gains/ losses when buying and selling fund assets	12, 18
	Obtain tax file numbers of members	4, 13, 21, 22
	Track and record contributions tax	4, 13
	Track and claim franking credits	13, 18
	Pay tax and supervisory levy when due	12, 13
	Withhold PAYG (if applicable)	19, 21, 22, 24
	Claim deductions for insurance premiums providing death cover for members (if applicable)	24

Source: Adapted from a compilation of checklists contained in the following ATO documents: 'Role and responsibilities of trustees' (NAT 11032) (no longer in print), 'Setting up a self-managed super fund' (NAT 71923), and 'Running a self-managed super fund' (NAT 11032).

Appendix B

Handy Super Resources and ATO Publications

· ·

*Y*ou're never alone when you run your own super fund, because plenty of resources are available to help you understand the super laws, and you can even connect with other SMSF trustees and investors.

This appendix gives you the details of the only independent superannuation website for consumers in Australia — SuperGuide — and the contact details of some excellent not-for-profit organisations that can provide you with useful free (and in some cases, not free) information about different aspects of super, including DIY super. Also for your easy reference, I include a complete list of all ATO SMSF publications mentioned throughout this book, and the publication numbers of those documents.

SuperGuide — Did You Say Independent, and Free?

Have you heard of the mugrump? My mother uses the term to describe a fence-sitter — a person who has his mug (face) on one side of the fence and his rump (behind) on the other side of the fence.

One of the benefits of being a mugrump is that you can see over both sides of the fence — you're not biased or influenced by what's happening on a particular side of the fence. Providing independent information is very similar to fence-sitting and, in the finance industry, independence is a rare commodity.

I passionately believe that Australians are entitled to independent information about something as important as financial security, retirement and DIY super. For this reason, in 2009 I established the first, and at the time of writing, the only, independent website on superannuation solely for consumers in Australia — SuperGuide (www.superguide.com.au). And I intend to keep SuperGuide a free information site for all Australians.

Many organisations and individuals charge for providing information as if it is 'advice'. Advice is important and can help you create wealth over the long term, but educating yourself about super and other financial matters can protect you from bad or insufficient advice. Finding a reliable independent source of superannuation information can save you a lot of money, and help protect you from dodgy financial operators.

SuperGuide is a superannuation website for consumers, including SMSF trustees. Throughout *DIY Super For Dummies,* 3rd Australian Edition, references to SuperGuide point to a supporting resource — delving into further detail on a particular topic or providing updated rates and thresholds, or covering super and retirement topics that there isn't room to discuss in this book.

The website explains superannuation in simple, easy-to-understand language, and ensures the book you currently hold in your hand remains an up-to-date reference for a longer period of time. Also, visitors can subscribe to the SuperGuide free monthly newsletter.

As trustee, you must run your SMSF in compliance with the SIS Act, the tax laws and in accordance with your fund's trust deed. Although the SuperGuide website and ATO publications (see the section 'Helpful ATO Publications', later in this appendix) can save you time and money, when you're directing your own super fund, nothing can be a substitute for quality advice tailored to your personal circumstances. Good advice at key stages in your super fund's life, and in your own life, normally pays for itself. You need to ensure, however, that you rely on an adviser (or advisers) who understands SMSFs, who is a qualified tax expert and is also a dab hand at retirement planning. (I explain the types of advisers that can help your SMSF in Chapter 5.)

Not-For-Profit Information Services

Here you find the contact details for consumer-related organisations that may come in handy when you're seeking useful information about superannuation, retirement, investing or finding the right adviser.

Government-funded consumer services

The federal government funds four organisations that are handy sources of free financial information. The main source of free information for SMSF trustees is the ATO website, which I cover in 'Helpful ATO Publications' at the end of this appendix. Three other government-funded information sources are set out in this section.

Financial Information Service (FIS)

FIS is a not-for-profit financial education and information service that is available to anyone. FIS is government-funded under Centrelink's budget, but many of FIS customers aren't in receipt of Centrelink payments or services. You can be a self-funded retiree, or planning to be a self-funded retiree, and still attend a FIS seminar, or talk to FIS representatives over the telephone or face-to-face. You can also obtain booklets and fact sheets, or download these documents and videos from the FIS page on the Department of Human Services website.

I have attended two FIS seminars in the past, as part of my research in road-testing public information services for previous books. FIS brings in experts from the industry to take you through some of the issues you may face when investing generally or when planning for your retirement. In the free seminars that I attended the content was easy to follow and practical (and I also received a cuppa and some sandwiches). The great feature of the FIS seminars is that they're not trying to sell anything and they're free. You can contact FIS by

- ✔ **Phone:** 13 23 00 (Centrelink number), to make an appointment or request booklets or fact sheets
- ✔ **Financial Information National Seminar Booking Service:** Phone 13 63 57
- ✔ **Email (for making seminar bookings):** fis.seminar.bookings@ centrelink.gov.au
- ✔ **Website:** www.humanservices.gov.au

National Information Centre on Retirement Investments (NICRI)

NICRI is a free service funded by the federal government. It provides information on planning, saving for retirement and post-retirement investing. NICRI aims to improve the level and quality of investment information available for people with modest savings.

Anyone can use NICRI. The service can even give you guidance on finding a suitable financial planner, taking you through the different steps when seeking and using a financial planner. Because NICRI is purely an information service, you don't receive any investment advice. You can access this service by:

✓ **Phone:** 1800 020 110

✓ **Email:** nicri@nicri.org.au

✓ **Website:** www.nicri.org.au

✓ **Postal address:** PO Box 1339, Fyshwick, ACT, 2609

MoneySmart

ASIC is the consumer protection regulator for financial services, and runs a fantastic consumer website called MoneySmart. On this site, you can find out about the latest investment scams, helpful information about the different types of investments, warnings on dodgy investment products, and a selection of very useful financial calculators. You can also access information about licensed advisers and approved SMSF auditors.

✓ **ASIC InfoLine:** 1300 300 600

✓ **Online (via website):** www.moneysmart.gov.au/contact-us

✓ **Website:** www.moneysmart.gov.au

✓ **Postal address:** ASIC, PO Box 4000, Gippsland Mail Centre, VIC, 3841

Privately funded consumer organisations

The following organisations are independent, not-for-profit and funded by the individuals who join the organisations.

Australian Investors' Association (AIA)

AIA is an independent and non-profit association for individual investors, including SMSF trustees. AIA encourages networking between members and holds regular conferences and workshops on investing. Many AIA members run their own super funds, and the AIA hosts regular seminars for SMSF trustees. You can contact the AIA in the following ways:

✓ **Phone:** 1300 555 061

✓ **Email:** aia@investors.asn.au

✓ **Website:** www.investors.asn.au

✓ **Postal address:** PO Box 7439, Gold Coast, MC, QLD, 9726

Australian Shareholders' Association (ASA)

The ASA is for shareholders of Australian companies. Most SMSF trustees invest a significant chunk of their SMSF money in Australian shares (at the time of writing representing about 15 per cent of the Australian sharemarket), which means the ASA and SMSF trustees are likely to have similar interests — protecting shareholder value. Check out ASA by

- **Phone:** 1300 368 448
- **Email:** share@asa.asn.au
- **Website:** australianshareholders.com.au
- **Postal address:** GPO Box 359, Sydney, NSW, 2001

COTA Australia

COTA Australia, formerly called COTA Over 50s, is an independent consumer organisation run by (and for) older Australians. COTA stands for Council of the Ageing. COTA Australia pursues policy issues facing retirees and prospective retirees, and represents this demographic when dealing with the federal government. The COTA website is an excellent resource for those seeking more information on the current issues facing older people.

- **Phone:** 08 8232 0422
- **Email:** cota@cota.org.au
- **Website:** www.cota.org.au
- **Postal address:** GPO Box 1583, Adelaide, SA, 5001

National Seniors Australia

National Seniors Australia is an older Australian consumer lobby group with 200,000 members. National Seniors Australia makes submissions to government, publishes a monthly magazine and offers discounted services to its members.

- **Phone:** 1300 765 050
- **Email:** general@nationalseniors.com.au
- **Website:** www.nationalseniors.com.au
- **Postal address:** GPO Box 1450, Brisbane, QLD, 4001

Helpful ATO Publications

The ATO website is the key source of authoritative information for any SMSF trustee. You can visit the website, download publications, seek assistance or even watch educational videos on SMSF and super topics.

Throughout this book, I refer to publications and forms the ATO produces and has available on its website that can help you run your super fund, or that you must use when operating your SMSF. For example, when a SMSF member claims a tax deduction for super contributions (refer to Chapter 4) you must use a special form. You can find most of these documents mentioned alongside the Form Guide icon throughout this book, or occasionally alongside the Check the Net icon.

For convenience, Table B-1 details the complete list of ATO publications (including forms and fact sheets) that I mention in this book. *Note:* This list doesn't represent all the forms that your fund can access from the ATO; for example, the SMSF annual return form changes each year.

You can access these ATO publications in the following ways:

✔ Visit the ATO website (www.ato.gov.au), search the site for the publication that you want and then download the forms. Searching this way is the best option if you're trying to find an ATO ruling or determination.

✔ Order the forms or publications online (https://individuals .iorder.com.au/ilogin.aspx), and they're sent to your email inbox. You have to register for this service, and you have to generally know what you want, because this webpage doesn't provide a list of ATO publications, and when searching for a topic the search facility doesn't capture all publications under the topic.

✔ Access the ATO's publication ordering service by phoning 1300 720 092, assuming you know the number (or title) of the publication you're seeking (see Table B-1).

The ATO runs a SMSF newsletter, *SMSF News*, specifically for SMSF trustees (and SMSF advisers), which you can subscribe to via the ATO superannuation website (visit www.ato.gov.au and click on Super⇨Self-Managed Super Funds⇨News⇨SMSF News). You can arrange for the newsletter to be sent to you via email, or you can simply access it from the ATO website.

Table B-1	Helpful ATO Publications	
Publication Name	**ATO Publication Number**	**Chapter Reference**
Standard choice form	NAT 13080	4, 7
Notice of intent to claim a tax deduction for super contributions or vary a previous notice	NAT 71121	4, 22
Capital gains tax cap election	NAT 71161	4, 13
Contributions for personal injury	NAT 71162	4
Setting up a self-managed super fund	NAT 71923	7, 8, 12
Application for ABN registration for superannuation entities	NAT 2944	7
Running a self-managed super fund	NAT 11032	7, 11, 19
How your self-managed super fund is regulated	NAT 71454	7
Thinking about self-managed super	NAT 72579	1, 2
Winding up a self-managed super fund	NAT 8107	7, 24
Rollover initiation request to transfer whole balance of superannuation benefits to your self-managed super fund	NAT 74662	7
SMSF trustee declaration	NAT 71089	9, 11, 15
Self-managed super funds — key messages for trustees	NAT 71128	9
Self-managed superannuation funds: the application of the sole purpose test in Section 62 of the *Superannuation Industry (Supervision) Act 1993* to the provision of benefits other than retirement, employment termination or death benefits	SMSFR 2008/2	11
Self-managed superannuation fund annual return instructions	NAT 71606	12
Self-managed superannuation fund independent auditor's report	NAT 11466	12
Auditor/actuary contravention report	NAT 11239	12

(continued)

Table B-1 *(continued)*

Publication Name	ATO Publication Number	Chapter Reference
Self-managed superannuation funds: the meaning of 'borrow money' or 'maintain an existing borrowing of money', for the purposes of section 67 of the *Superannuation Industry (Supervision) Act 1993*	SMSFR 2009/2	16
Self-managed superannuation funds: business real property for the purposes of the *Superannuation Industry (Supervision) Act 1993*	SMSFR 2009/1	17
Limited recourse borrowing arrangements by self-managed superannuation funds — questions and answers	NAT 70793	17
Self-managed superannuation funds: limited recourse borrowing arrangements — application of key concepts	SMSFR 2012/1	17
Schedule 12 — Tax table for superannuation lump sums	Schedule 12	19, 24
PAYG payment summary — superannuation lump sum	NAT 70947	19, 24
Schedule 13 — Tax rate for superannuation income streams	Schedule 13	21, 24
PAYG payment summary — superannuation income stream	NAT 70897	21, 24
Self-managed superannuation funds: is there any restriction in the Superannuation Industry (Supervision) legislation on a self-managed superannuation fund trustee accepting from a member a binding nomination of the recipients of any benefits payable in the event of the member's death?	SMSFD 2008/3	24

Index

Notes

Notes

About the Author

Trish Power is an author and journalist, and co-founder of independent information websites SuperGuide (www.superguide.com.au) and LearnerInvestor (www.learnerinvestor.com.au).

Most of her time is now dedicated to the two websites, although she writes a regular column for the Fairfax publication *Smart Investor*, and an occasional article for *The Australian Financial Review*. Trish has also written 13 books (including two as co-author) in a 12-year period.

She has spent more than 25 years working in, or writing about the superannuation, SMSF and financial industries. Trish began her working life as a superannuation specialist, before embarking on a full-time writing career. She describes much of her financial writing as educative journalism. Trish is passionately committed to raising the level of financial literacy in Australia and empowering individuals to improve their financial circumstances.

She started her career working as a superannuation expert, including being responsible for public education at the Insurance and Superannuation Commission (predecessor to APRA), working on financial policy in the Office of the Chairman at ASIC, and was Technical Manager for CPA Australia's Superannuation Centre of Excellence in the 1990s, before moving into journalism and book writing. Trish has also worked on member communication campaigns for some of the largest superannuation funds in Australia.

Trish has both a law degree and an economics/commerce degree from the University of Melbourne, and holds a professional writing and editing diploma from RMIT University.

Trish is the author of the following *For Dummies* books: *DIY Super For Dummies* (three editions), *Superannuation For Dummies* (two editions), *Superannuation: Planning Your Retirement For Dummies*, *Superannuation: Choosing a Fund For Dummies*, and co-author of *Investing For Australians All-in-One For Dummies*.

Trish is also the author of the following books: *Super Freedom: A woman's guide to superannuation*; *How to make $300,000 without trying! (30 ways to save your super)*; *DEAR TRISH... DIY SUPER: 101 Q and As*; *DEAR Trish... SUPER – Tax-free superannuation dollars for you*; and co-author of *You Don't Have to be Rich to Become Wealthy: The Baby Boomers Investment Bible*.

Trish lives in Melbourne with her partner.

Dedication

My nephew passed away during the writing of the first edition of this book. I dedicate *DIY Super For Dummies*, 3rd Australian Edition, to Dale Power and to all of my nephews and nieces. On the 'Power' side, in order of youngest to eldest: Matthew, Alice, Grace, Gabrielle, Bridgette, Justin, Greg, Tanya and John. And to the nieces and nephews on my Irish side: Aidan, Kate, Ewan, Aaron, Flynn, Matthew, Tom, Brooke, Eamon, Tara and Erin.

Author's Acknowledgements

I have worked on eight *For Dummies* editions, including three editions of *DIY Super For Dummies*. None of these books would be possible without the Wiley team, and although it is difficult to select individuals from such a helpful team, I do want to personally thank Kerry Laundon, Dani Karvess and my copy editor, Maryanne Phillips. Maryanne grasped the super concepts effortlessly and was a pleasure to work with.

I am fortunate to work with Rob Barnes, fellow founder of my SuperGuide website and newsletter, and also co-founder of our beginner investor website, LearnerInvestor. Rob gets the importance of quality writing and providing independent information on super to Australians. Thanks, Rob, for your support, and many thanks to my SuperGuide readers who have supported our website for the past six years, and my books for the past decade or so.

A special thanks to Graeme Colley from the SMSF Professionals' Association of Australia (SPAA) for technically reviewing the final manuscript of *DIY Super For Dummies*, 3rd Australian Edition.

I first met Graeme Colley, SPAA's Director of Technical & Professional Standards, more than 20 years ago when we both worked at the Insurance & Superannuation Commission. I respect his intellect, technical knowledge and his considered opinions.

Thank you, Graeme, for making the time to review my book.

I also wish to acknowledge my technical reviewers from the first edition of *DIY Super For Dummies*, CPA Australia's Michael Davison and the director of chartered accounting firm 3 Dimensions, Peter Power (who also happens to be my brother). Thank you, Michael, for your professionalism and good humour. Thank you, Peter, for your practical suggestions on how the DIY super rules sometimes play out in the real world.

This book is a product of my 25-plus years of experience in superannuation and journalism, and everything I have done in the past has led to the writing and updating of this book. A long list of people have helped me, or encouraged me, in my career, originally as a super specialist and now as an author, journalist and commentator. Impossible as it is to name everyone, I also want to thank Lesley Williams (Beaumont), Janine Mace, Michaela Anderson, Kirsty Elliot, Judy Womersley, Brett Hoffmann, Peter Tratt, George Alba, Gary Edney, Murray Wyatt, Amanda Roach, Melda Donnelly, Kristen Hammond, Robi van Nooten, Andrea Coote, Tom Buchan, Alan Oakley, Rick Yamine, Liz Heath, Jackie Blondell, Ian Murdoch, Jamie Nemtsas, Kevin Kelly, Hilary Spear, Alan Kohler, James Kirby, Louise du Pre-Alba, Michael Wilkinson, Helen Cooper, Jamie Harrison, Susan Cameron, Kate McKinna, Silvanna Eccles, Janene Murdoch, Peter Power, Paul Lam, Stephen Pender, Sharon Shelley and Sally Haines.

I am fortunate to have a large and loving family — thanks to all of you for taking an interest. And thank you, Siobhan, for your ongoing support.

Publisher's Acknowledgements

We're proud of this book; please send us your comments through our online registration form located at dummies.custhelp.com.

Some of the people who helped bring this book to market include the following:

Acquisitions, Editorial and Media Development

Acquisitions Editor: Kerry Laundon

Editorial Manager: Dani Karvess

Production

Graphics: diacriTech

Technical Reviewer: Graeme Colley

Proofreader: Jenny Scepanovic

Indexer: Don Jordan, Antipodes Indexing

The author and publisher would like to thank the following copyright holders, organisations and individuals for their permission to reproduce copyright material in this book:

- **Cover image:** © iStock.com/TimAbramowitz

- **'Doing a number on SMSF trustees' sidebar, p. 13, 'Defending decent SMSF trustees' sidebar, p. 135, and 'SMSF investment: Three most popular asset classes' sidebar, p. 191:** Reprinted with permission Trish Power and SuperGuide.

- **'Life expectancy — living beyond an average life' sidebar and table, p. 54:** © Commonwealth of Australia, Australian Government Actuary, 2014

- **Table 8-1, p. 123-124, Figure 19-1, p. 136-137, Table 12-1, p. 161-162, Table 13-1, p. 172-173, Table A-1, p. 331-334:** Material from Australian Taxation Office © Australian Taxation Office for the Commonwealth of Australia.

- **Table 15-1, p. 202–203:** © Trish Power, Jamie Nemtsas and Ian Murdoch.

Every effort has been made to trace the ownership of copyright material. Information that enables the publisher to rectify any error or omission in subsequent editions is welcome. In such cases, please contact the Legal Services section of John Wiley & Sons Australia, Ltd.

Business & Investing

978-1-118-22280-5
$39.95

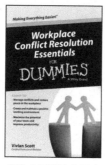

978-0-73031-945-0
$19.95

978-0-73031-951-1
$19.95

978-0-73031-065-5
$19.95

978-0-73030-584-2
$24.95

978-1-11864-126-2
$19.95

978-0-73031-949-8
$19.95

978-0-73031-954-2
$19.95

978-0-730-31069-3
$39.95

978-1-118-57255-9
$34.95

978-1-742-16998-9
$45.00

978-1-118-64122-4
$39.95

Order today!

e **Available in print and e-book formats.**

Business

Bookkeeping For Dummies,
2nd Australian & New Zealand Edition
978-0-73031-069-3

Businesst Planning Essentials For Dummies
978-1-11864-126-2

Communication Essentials For Dummies
978-0-7303-1951-1

Creating a Business Plan For Dummies
978-1-118-64122-4

Bookkeeping Essentials For Dummies, 2nd Australian Edition
978-0-73031-065-5

Getting Started in Small Business For Dummies, 2nd Australian & New Zealand Edition
978-1-11822-284-3

HR for Small Business For Dummies, Australian Edition,
978-1-11864-030-2

Leadership For Dummies, Australian & New Zealand Edition
978-0-7314-0787-3

Making Money on eBay For Dummies
978-1-74216-977-4

Mindfulness at Work Essentials For Dummies
978-0-7303-1949-8

MYOB Software For Dummies, 7th Australian Edition
978-1-74216-998-9

Project Management Essentials For Dummies
978-0-7303-1954-2

QuickBooks For Dummies, 2nd Australian Edition
978-1-74246-896-9

Small Business For Dummies, 4th Australian & New Zealand Edition
978-1-118-22280-5

Success as a Real Estate Agent For Dummies, Australian & New Zealand Edition
978-0-73030-911-6

Successful Job Interviews For Dummies, Australian & New Zealand Edition
978-0-730-30805-8

Successful Online Start-Ups For Dummies, Australian & New Zealand Edition
978-1-118-30270-5

Workplace Conflict Resolution Essentials For Dummies
978-0-7303-1945-0

Writing Resumes and Cover Letters For Dummies, 2nd Australian & New Zealand Edition
978-0-730-30780-8

Xero For Dummies
978-1-118-57255-9

Finance & Investing

Buying Property For Dummies, 2nd Australian Edition
978-0-7303-7556-2

CFDs For Dummies, Australian Edition
978-1-74216-939-2

Charting For Dummies, Australian Edition
978-0-7314-0710-1

DIY Super For Dummies, 3rd Australian Edition
978-0-7303-1534-6

Exchange-Traded Funds For Dummies, Australian & New Zealand Edition
978-0-7303-7695-8

Getting Started in Property Investing For Dummies, Australian Edition
978-1-183-9674-2

Getting Started in Shares For Dummies, 2nd Australian Edition
978-1-74246-885-3

Investing For Dummies, 2nd Australian Edition
978-1-74216-851-7

Making the Most of Retirement For Dummies
978-0-7314-0939-6

Managed Funds For Dummies, Australian Edition
978-1-74216-942-2

Online Share Investing For Dummies, Australian Edition
978-0-7314-0940-2

Property Investing For Dummies, 2nd Australian Edition
978-1-1183-9670-4

Share Investing For Dummies, 3rd Australian Edition
978-1-74246-889-1

Sorting Out Your Finances For Dummies, Australian Edition
978-0-7314-0746-0

Tax for Australians For Dummies, 2013–14 Edition
978-0-730-30584-2

Order today!

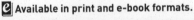 **Available in print and e-book formats.**

FOR DUMMIES
A Wiley Brand